D0786441

SAVING THE BEST OF TEXAS

NUMBER TWENTY-NINE
The Corrie Herring Hooks Series

SAVING THE BEST OF TEXAS

A Partnership Approach to Conservation

RICHARD C. BARTLETT

Photographs by LEROY WILLIAMSON

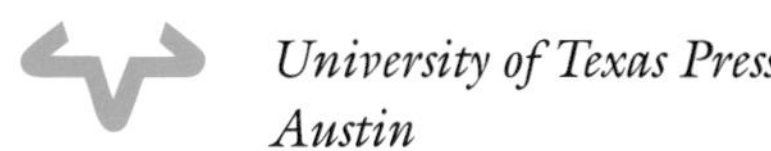

University of Texas Press
Austin

Printed in Hong Kong
First edition, 1995

Requests for permission to reproduce material
from this work should be sent to
Permissions
University of Texas Press
Box 7819
Austin, TX 78713-7819.

∞The paper used in this publication meets the minimum requirements of American National Standard for Information Sciences—Permanence of Paper for Printed Library Materials, ANSI Z39.48-1984.

LIBRARY OF CONGRESS CATALOGING-IN-PUBLICATION DATA

Bartlett, Dick, 1935–
Saving the best of Texas : a partnership approach to conservation / Richard C. Bartlett ; photographs by Leroy Williamson. — 1st ed.
p. cm.
Includes index.
ISBN 0-292-70834-3 (cloth). — ISBN 0-292-70835-1 (paper)
1. Nature conservation—Texas. 2. Environmental protection—Texas. 3. Natural history—Texas. 4. Texas Nature Conservancy.
I. Title.
QH76.5.T4B385 1995
333.7'2'09764—dc20 94-43734

FRONTISPIECE
A best of Texas already saved is this rugged canyon sequestered within the remote Big Bend Ranch State Natural Area. The canyon wends down to the second highest waterfall in the state, Madrid Falls.

PAGE VI
Sunset, Davis Mountains State Park.

Dedicated to JOANNE KRIEGER
and her partnership approach to love

CONTENTS

FOREWORD

As a native Texan I understand as well as most that special feeling that Texans have for their state, and for the land itself. We tend to find, for example, the South Texas brush country actually beautiful, just because it has character, and some of us prefer the Hill Country to the Rockies, native prairies to Palm Springs. We even have cowboys that write songs about these kinds of things.

And yet for too long, our appreciation of the land has been derivative in part of what we have been able to take from it—how well it harvested or what we could build on it, as opposed to what made it special and what species it would support. Timber, oil, cotton, condominiums—the land yielded product and progress for a long, long time.

But time is running out, and now more suddenly than seems possible, we run the risk of losing that very diversity and uniqueness that have made the landscape special. Where there were once twelve million acres of virgin blackland prairie, there are but five thousand left untouched today. Where there was once an isolated mountain range with bighorn sheep and aspen, now mobile homes stalk the summit. Today, there is Sabine River bottomland that supports wood ducks and two-hundred-year-old trees; today there is also a politician's blueprint for a recreation lake that will tomorrow quietly replace it. Over the last fifty years, we've lost tidal flats and wetlands, animals and plants; and as habitat gives way to urbanization, species drift into extinction. It's that simple.

However, with Texas fighting hard to rebuild its economy and create additional jobs, many think that conservation initiatives are not that important—certainly not that urgent. But that's shortsighted and dead wrong. Economic cycles swing up and down, but habitat preservation in Texas is at a critical stage, and the fight to save it will be won or lost over the next few years. Whether we like it or not, the time is now, and we are the ones that will have to make a difference.

OPPOSITE PAGE
Springs feed the Colorado River just below spectacular Gorman Falls, which are now a best of Texas saved within Colorado Bend State Park.

Dick Bartlett understands these things and has honed an approach to conservation that is both balanced and effective. Part businessman, part sportsman, part environmentalist, Bartlett weaves the discipline and enthusiasm of each into a credible perspective for effective conservation, one anchored by the concept of partnerships. Although he grew up in Florida and spent his early years there, his energy in conservation over the last ten years has been channeled almost exclusively to Texas.

As a businessman, Bartlett is vice chairman of Mary Kay Cosmetics, a highly profitable, $800 million U.S. Fortune 500 company, with a 350,000-person independent sales organization. Bartlett guided the marketing strategies of his company since 1973, and as its president, from 1986 to 1992, directed its operations at a 15 percent annual growth rate.

Along the way he served as chairman of the U.S. Direct Selling Education Foundation and was named Outstanding Marketer of the Year in 1991 by the Southwestern Marketing Association. Also, through Bartlett's direction, Mary Kay Corporation itself began to become more focused on the added value of adopting a more proactive approach both to conservation and to environmentally sound practices. Consequently, in 1990 the company received the first annual Earth Friendly Award for environmental excellence, in 1992 the Environmental Protection Agency presented Mary Kay with its regional Environmental Excellence Award, and in 1993 it won the Keep Texas Beautiful Award and the first United Nations Environmental Programme's Fashion and the Environment Award. In 1994 Mary Kay Cosmetics received the first Financial Times Television Award for Corporate Environmental Action and the Governor's Award for Environmental Excellence. This recognition would not have been possible without the commitment to a conservation ethic directed by Bartlett—one that says that good business and good conservation are not mutually exclusive, and that a sound environmental program can be good for business as well. From product packaging to cleaner indoor air at facilities to new green partnerships to recycling—all of these moves benefited the company in significant ways.

As an outdoorsman, Bartlett is an enthusiastic and accomplished fisherman and hunter and understands full well that habitat preservation is as important to the hunter as it is to the bird watcher. His credentials as a sportsman are impeccable: he is coauthor of the definitive hunting book *The Sportsman's Guide to Texas,* which advocates a conservation ethic, responsible hunting, and wildlife management. He is a life member of the Gulf Coast Conservation Association, which is credited with saving the redfish and trout in the Texas gulf when they were threatened significantly by commercial fishermen in the late seventies and early eighties, as well as a member of Ducks Unlimited, which has been responsible for the preservation and restoration of critical habitat for waterfowl from the breeding grounds of Canada to the potholes of the Midwest,

The Ochiltree County Springs, which create the clear flow of Wolf Creek, have sustained human life for more than 10,000 years, including Indians and early European explorers such as Coronado. At nearby Lake Fryer, a buried Pueblo Indian city has been discovered.

from the bottomlands along migration routes to the wintering marshes of the Gulf Coast.

Finally, as a conservationist and landowner, Bartlett extends the environment into his private life. As a member of the Texas Land Stewards Society he is working to protect an endangered species, the Golden-cheeked Warbler, on his own ranch in the Hill Country of Texas. He is both a member of the board of the Dallas Museum of Natural History and a founding member of Bat Conservation International. His real love, however, is The Nature Conservancy, because he sees embodied in the mission of that organization a welding of the principles of the environmentalist, businessman, landowner, and sportsman.

As chairman of The Nature Conservancy of Texas, Bartlett sees the Conservancy as a leader in carving out the middle ground to preserve important habitat, yet with a businessman's touch. Its approach to conservation has a different spin: it doesn't picket, boycott, or stake out any advocacy position. It simply preserves land the old-fashioned way—it identifies what's ecologically important, it buys it when it becomes available, and then it takes care of it. Even when special land is not available for sale, the Conservancy works with landowners to nurture ownership pride and to build good stewardship.

Although the Conservancy has been criticized by other conservation groups for its low-key, businesslike approach, it nevertheless gets the job done. Over the last few years, it has been able to preserve more than 300,000 acres of ecologically important land in thirty-two counties in Texas, more than 100,000 of which are wetlands up and down the Texas coast so critical to migratory waterfowl. In similar programs nationwide, the Conservancy has saved 6 million acres, and in so doing, it has become the largest private sanctuary in the world. Bartlett dedicates this book to The Nature Conservancy of Texas and to the participation of the private sector working in partnership with government agencies, community groups, hunters, bird watchers, and landowners to "save the best of Texas." He feels that there can be no better legacy than to conserve an important piece of the original Texas, so that our great-grandchildren can walk in a meadow in Hunt County that will have remained unchanged from the time of the buffalo and Comanche, or can hear the trumpeting of a Whooping Crane that would have been extinct but for the preserved Matagorda marshes. And he believes strongly that we as citizens can then take real pride that despite all that will have inevitably changed by then, we will have bequeathed some special, original land with its special, original species still on it—just the way it was when our great great-grandfathers settled Texas and the land became a republic.

Bartlett's book includes a composite of these special places, the focal point of *Saving the Best of Texas,* and is required reading for all Texans who have a special feeling for the land.

R. L. THORNTON III
Vice Chairman, Texas Commerce Bank–Dallas
Member, Board of Trustees
The Nature Conservancy of Texas

PREFACE

Saving the best of Texas has not been, nor will it ever be, easy. Texas is among the last of the fifty states in public ownership of land for parks, recreation, and wildlife conservation in comparison to total landmass. Each dollar for land acquisition and stewardship comes hard, whether it be funding for a national wildlife refuge, a state park or wildlife management area, or a private preserve. In fact, in the mid-eighties, the Texas Parks and Wildlife Department actually had to cut back on field personnel, and several state parks were threatened with closing. Partnerships are the *only* possible answers to conservation of our state's natural heritage.

There is no lack of rhetoric about protecting the environment in Texas. There are literally hundreds of nongovernment organizations (NGOs) exhorting us to take some sort of action, usually to contribute to some fund that will produce yet more rhetoric in the form of anti-this and anti-that literature and the ubiquitous lawsuits. Some of the best NGOs contribute unbiased, factual information and help us to reach responsible conclusions. They include NGOs such as Sportsmen Conservationists of Texas, Ducks Unlimited, and the Gulf Coast Conservation Association.

But there is only one major state NGO with a mission to conserve and protect land, and that is The Nature Conservancy (TNC) of Texas. Through 25,000 members, TNC has helped to protect more than fifty cooperative projects encompassing 260,000 acres of the best natural heritage of Texas in partnership with private organizations and state and federal agencies. Staff members work through the Texas Land Stewards Society to provide conservation know-how to private landowners on another 290,000 acres. The Nature Conservancy of Texas also directly manages more than thirty preserves totaling more than 50,000 acres.

The mission of The Nature Conservancy of Texas is straightforward. We *identify* plants, animals, and natural communities at risk. We *protect* these special places through direct purchase from willing sellers or by

American White Pelicans flock to the Texas Gulf Coast in the winter. Despite a wingspan to 9 1/2 feet, they are sometimes confused in flight with Snow Geese.

securing conservation easements and management agreements. We also develop relationships with private landowners who voluntarily protect rare species on their land. Finally, using good science, we *manage* these lands as part of the largest private nature sanctuary system in the world.

The Nature Conservancy of Texas seeks to build mutually beneficial alliances with a broad array of partners—business, government agencies, private landowners, and other groups. Often we are the catalyst, bringing diverse parties together to serve nature in practical, tangible ways. As you will see in this book, our programs and projects are as diverse as the lands and species they protect.

The real heroes saving the best of Texas are private and corporate landowners with a conservation ethic. Without them as generous, far-sighted partners, The Nature Conservancy, Texas Parks and Wildlife, the Forest Service, the U.S. Fish and Wildlife Service, and the National Park Service would not be able to conserve more of our best. There are many state groups doing a fine job of land conservation, and special credit is given to the Audubon Society, Ducks Unlimited, and the Parks and Wildlife Foundation of Texas for their land acquisition efforts. Many of these partners are recognized in this book, many more not, for space does not permit. But all are greatly appreciated.

The Nature Conservancy pioneered the idea of partnerships for land conservation more than two decades ago with its state natural heritage programs, database inventories of biodiversity. Pioneered in Georgia and South Carolina in 1973, the program came to life in 1974 as the Mississippi Heritage Program, part of an effort to save the best of an ecological treasure—the vast Pascagoula swamp. This successful effort proved the worth of a scientific approach to land conservation, a way to look around the corner and value ecosystems on a multispecies basis, factoring in economic issues. The Nature Conservancy has now installed this program in every state in a classic example of private-public partnership.

This book, then, is written with a threefold purpose:

1. To provide you, the reader, with a guide to some of the best that has already been saved in Texas, along with just enough naturalist grist to pique your interest and propel you outdoors.

2. To help you, both through Leroy Williamson's spectacular photography and your own hands-on experiences, to explore and perhaps even develop or strengthen your own conservation ethic.

3. To enlist your support in any way you see fit of efforts to conserve more of the best of Texas. Buy a nongame stamp or a federal duck stamp, join Audubon, Ducks Unlimited, or The Nature Conservancy, or better yet contribute by managing your 50,000-acre ranch as a wildlife preserve.

In addition to direct cash contributions, there are many ways of giving. TNC's trade-lands program utilizes gifts of surplus real estate, which when sold generate proceeds used to support ongoing conservation efforts. Trade-lands gifts usually earn donors tax credits. Many have included The Nature Conservancy in their wills, through various planned giving options, including bequests. Scores of corporations and individuals have contributed their conservation expertise. Every year thousands of volunteer hours are contributed to restoration efforts, plant surveys, trash removal, erosion control, maintenance, and even tree planting.

I like to say that The Nature Conservancy is as good a steward of your dollar as it is of the land. The value we place on your donation is reflected in the careful, responsible way it is used. For every dollar of funding, approximately ninety cents goes directly to land protection and stewardship programs. The sole beneficiaries of all donations are the rare and special lands of Texas and the rare and special plants and creatures that live upon them.

When you purchased this book, you helped. Every cent of my royalties will be split between the Texas Parks and Wildlife nongame program and The Nature Conservancy of Texas. I've already received my reward for doing this book by exploring and reveling in the areas profiled and many more that didn't make the editor's cut. Someone who had as much fun as I did stumbling through 100,000 miles of Texas backroads has already been amply rewarded.

On March 30, 1994, I had the rare privilege of being with Governor Ann Richards when she released a rehabilitated Golden Eagle from Big Hill on the Presidio highway northwest of Lajitas, opposite the Big Bend

Ranch State Natural Area. The release was to have symbolized a two-nation agreement to enable the states of Texas, Coahuila, and Chihuahua to work together on various conservation projects. Although the agreement signing was delayed, Governor Richards went ahead with the release; that eagle had waited long enough for her moment of freedom. Unhooded and unfettered, the majestic raptor perched on Ann's arm for what seemed an eternity, the epitome of the unleashed energy of wildness, inches from the governor's face. The two eyed each other closely, seeming to commune. Finally, the raptor sailed low into the surrounding spectators, nipping a fellow TNC trustee en route to freedom. (For the record, the eagle flew into the state natural area.)

Later, Governor Richards spoke of the spiritual quality of the moment and of her feeling of oneness with nature as the eagle soared. Although I believe Ann Richards already had a strong conservation ethic, based on her track record in office, at that very moment she may have truly comprehended her link with the natural world. Albeit in less spectacular fashion than releasing an eagle to the wild, this book has been written to help you seek understanding of your links.

The prime acknowledgment for this book goes to Leroy Williamson, retired dean of *Texas Parks and Wildlife* photographers. It was around a campfire at Dolan Falls that Leroy advanced the idea of such a book, and I unhesitatingly agreed to be his writer-partner.

The text is in itself an acknowledgment of a few of the many people who are dedicated to saving the best of Texas. I must apologize to those not recognized, for they are by far the majority.

A handful of knowledgeable Texas conservationists went well beyond the call of duty to help minimize the errors in this work. Any remaining errors, save those created by the ever-changing force of nature herself, are mine alone.

David Braun, James King, and Jeff Weigel, of The Nature Conservancy of Texas, spent hours in interview sessions with me. David Baxter, editor of *Texas Parks and Wildlife* magazine, Jim Teer, director of the Welder Wildlife Foundation, and Terri Bronoco of TNC were among the skilled readers of this work, each contributing much.

I want also to acknowledge copyeditor Lorraine Atherton, whose fine eye helped avoid some really embarrassing gaffes and who often added thoughtful insights of her own.

All the contributors cited in this book went out of their way to ensure both accuracy and completeness—displaying their personal ethic for sharing the message of our shared passion: Saving the Best of Texas.

There is a very special woman without whom the book could not have been—my partner, Joanne Krieger, who survived an earlier literary odyssey as coauthor of *The Sportsman's Guide to Texas* and who made an immeasurable difference to this undertaking.

INTRODUCTION

In the summer of 1994, along with three of my colleagues from Texas Parks and Wildlife, I had the privileged experience of viewing the last free-ranging herd of bison in the United States. They are in Texas and in danger of disappearing altogether, as the few remaining of our once-numerous vast ranches are themselves an endangered species.

It is because of this remarkable heritage of private land stewardship and a historic partnership with game wardens and biologists of state government that Texas today harbors the most prolific wildlife diversity in the United States. Thanks to enlightened management by private landowners, financing from hunters and anglers, and one of the nation's strongest state conservation programs, Texas has the largest population of white-tailed deer in the country, harvests more wild turkey than existed in the state before World War II, and is the number-one destination for bird-watching in the world.

Ironically, even as we reap the benefits of generations of public-private cooperation, the foundation for our cornucopia of natural diversity is threatened as never before. On one hand, as Texas families continue to migrate away from ancestral holdings, leaving more and more tracts of prime native country to subdivision and conversion, our most productive and diverse wildlife habitat is slowly and relentlessly evolving out of existence. Yet on the other hand, private landowners are more anxious about the role of government in their lives than ever before, and this very anxiety is today as great a threat to the future of natural diversity in Texas as an economic factor.

Such threats to Texas' natural treasures could not come at a more inopportune time. Nature tourism is the fastest-growing sector of the global travel industry, and rural Texas communities in desperate need of economic opportunity offer the best outdoor experiences money can buy. In this decade, for example, the Big Bend region has surpassed the

Alamo as our number-one destination for out-of-state visitors. As such resources become more scarce and inaccessible, we lose the promise of new and much-needed wealth to other states with more commitment than Texas to investment in outdoor infrastructure. On a per capita basis Texas, in fact, ranks thirty-first among the states in the acreage of parkland we have managed to preserve, and we are near the bottom in our investment in the outdoors.

Beyond economics—and much more alarming, as Richard Bartlett and Leroy Williamson so eloquently convey on these pages—key components of our Texas natural heritage are already close to extinction, including remarkably diverse bottomland hardwood forests in eastern Texas and critically needed aquifer recharge lands in the Hill Country. Tragically, in a land that was once almost entirely grasslands, only tiny remnants of Texas' native meadows remain today.

Against this sobering backdrop, the most promising possibilities arise from a resurgence of the spirit of partnership, which delivered this great legacy to our time. Today, private organizations like The Nature Conservancy of Texas and the Trust for Public Lands are teaming up with landowners and government in defense of nature. Additionally, many of Texas' largest corporations have become significant and frequent contributors to conservation. The most recent entrant is the Parks and Wildlife Foundation of Texas, which in a matter of months has helped protect two of Texas' most critically threatened river-bottom hardwood forests.

As I read *Saving the Best of Texas,* I thought of those last magnificent buffalo and wondered whether they and the habitat that sustains them will be there for my grandchildren. The only thing I know for sure is that they will not be unless we work together as partners to save them.

ANDREW SANSOM
Executive Director
Texas Parks and Wildlife Department

SAVING THE BEST OF TEXAS

YOUR CONSERVATION ETHIC

CHAPTER 1

The first peace, which is the most important, is that which comes within the souls of people when they realize their relationship, their oneness, with the universe and all its powers, and when they realize that at the center of the universe dwells the Great Spirit, and that this center is really everywhere, it is within each of us.

BLACK ELK

The Sacred Pipe: Black Elk's Account of the Seven Rites of the Oglala Sioux, 1953

When The Nature Conservancy president John Sawhill speaks of the organization's mission, he stresses that the goal is to preserve biodiversity by protecting ecosystems. As you will read later, species extinction continues rampant, linked tightly to the spiraling rate of habitat destruction. So, the Conservancy quietly goes about its mission the old-fashioned way, by buying the land that our scientists identify as critical for the protection of threatened species of animals and plants. To maintain this science-based focus requires great discipline, because The Nature Conservancy (TNC) is pulled in many directions by environmental groups, government agencies, business organizations, and even our generous members.

As daunting as this mission may be, Sawhill believes the Conservancy must also help nurture and promote a new conservation ethic in the American public. To me, our conservation ethic is not new at all and is one and the same with Black Elk's "first peace." Says Sawhill, "The conservation ethic I'm talking about cannot be measured in opinion polls. Already, three-quarters of Americans consider themselves to be 'environmentalists.' I am more interested in increasing the depth of the public's appreciation and understanding of conservation issues. We must

OPPOSITE PAGE
A silken web of death and life is found upon a Padre Island marsh, a lovely yet delicate reminder of the interrelationships of nature.

make explicit the connections between human well-being and ecological systems. We must communicate the message that protecting these systems is compatible, even essential, to economic growth."

Sources from the radical left and right uniformly and deliberately cast the Conservancy's efforts as tainted by the money we solicit from energy and chemical companies and other free enterprise corporations, or they imply we restrict the private property rights of individuals. The best response I've heard to the "tainted money" remark was made by a former TNC president, Pat Noonan, in answer to someone from a radical environmental group. Noonan replied, "Well, it might be tainted, but it taint near enough!" The claim of the so-called wise-use movement that the Conservancy is the enemy of private landowners is pure fiction, because the Conservancy itself, and much of its membership, rely on these same rights for their private transactions and in the *private* land acquisitions that are the hallmark of the organization.

Black Elk would be stunned by the hate that spews from some of today's activists, whether they be Earth First monkey wrenchers, Greenpeace guerrillas, or Wise Use lawyers. Ron Arnold speaks for both sides, activist environmentalists and the extremists of his Wise Use organization, when he emblazons a chapter in his book *Defeating Environmentalism* with the heading "Sue the Bastards." Both extremes are suing. America is awash in lawsuits involving the environment. Almost all Greenpeace and Sierra Club dues go to either legal funds or lobbying, as do those of Wise Use and various legal foundations. I wonder where "sue the bastards" is covered in Black Elk's seven rites?

I believe the vast majority of Americans are tired of this spiteful rhetoric. Most of us have the common sense to realize we have indeed imposed great burdens on our biosphere, on our land, air, and water, and are willing to do something positive about it. Sawhill puts it nicely, "In the past, Earth's bounty appeared limitless; nothing people could do, it seemed, would ever deplete that bounty. Today, of course, we know that we cannot systematically exploit our natural resources without adverse consequences. We know that we cannot pollute our rivers, fill in our wetlands, and indiscriminately dump toxins without affecting public health. Clearly, the long-term health of people depends on the health of our global life-support system—the environment."

Luckily, the biosphere retains the toughness to sustain life. But it does take personal and community attention to make things really happen. Many thanks and kudos go to so many: because of Rachel Carson we still have birds; Jacques Cousteau helps keep fish in the sea; the U.S. Congress, the U.S. Fish and Wildlife Service, and Texas Parks and Wildlife Department help ensure that some beasts remain in the little that is left of our wilderness; ranchers save our grasslands; industry and science are finding solutions and investing billions in the technologies to protect the environment while sustaining our economy. I think we have time, scientific knowledge, and the technical resources to conserve this earth for future generations. But, do we have the will? Do we have the soul?

Some do. In 1994, 800,000 individuals and corporate members of The Nature Conservancy gave more than $120 million of their hard-earned dollars to quietly conserve the last great places on earth. More than a million acres were protected in that year, and the Conservancy continued its tradition of making substantial contributions to state and federal bodies and conservation agencies. The value of land sold and contributed averages more than $100 million annually, an effort that results in an annual net loss to the Conservancy in the millions. A common myth expressed by wise-users is that the Conservancy profits from sales to governments.

The Conservancy is the largest private owner of preserves on earth, with assets of more than $1.1 billion in 1994 and more than $500 million equity in land holdings, mainly in the United States. Significantly, TNC spent more than $50 million on biological information and management, protection, stewardship, and conservation science in 1994. Only 5.4 percent of total revenues was spent on fund-raising, making the Conservancy one of the most efficient philanthropic organizations on earth. *Financial World* ranked the Conservancy as one of the best philanthropic organizations in America in 1993.

Most of us live in a world from which nature has been expelled. Dr. Larry Gilbert of the University of Texas calls us the "urban many." We have no earthly idea of what Black Elk is talking about because Western civilization tends to define "soul" in religious terms. But I can imagine that our souls have linkages beyond our comprehension, expressed in concepts such as love, intimacy, and a world beyond the self, which Native Americans called the "Great Spirit." As we reach the end of the twentieth century, we seem to have lost our native wisdom about matters of the soul, and about those of nature, which I believe are essentially the same thing. We have forgotten that we are utterly dependent upon nature for our fundamental needs.

All the "isms" that beset us are, if anything, wearisome and counterproductive to care of the soul. They are mere intellectual exercises operating at a level of supposed reason or rationality above that of the soul. The next argument often sways us to another position, and we find ourselves hugging trees or running amok with all-terrain vehicles, passionately defending our right to do so. Focused on our navels, we build elaborate mechanisms to rationalize our selfish position, that is, more energy, more development, more consumer goods, more, more, more, or rights for trees, rocks, and animals, including rats. Don't get me wrong. Provided you are prepared to accept responsibility, you are entitled to defend whatever right that turns you on, and I personally defend quite a few of my own.

Don't confuse these rights with care of your soul, from whence I believe a conservation ethic emerges. This is not an environmental ethic or even Aldo Leopold's land ethic, which presupposed, in Leopold's own words, "the existence of some mental image of land as a biotic mechanism."

I agree with Leopold that "we can be ethical only in relation to something we can see, feel, understand, love or otherwise have faith in." Sadly, most of us are far removed from the land itself and have little or no concept of its biotic mechanisms or of the "land pyramid" Leopold so eloquently described. In the research for this book, I have spent considerable time with people who possess a land ethic. These people are very concerned about their ability to pass it on. These are ranchers and farmers who, by virtue of a lifetime lived on the land, know its rhythms, its dependencies, its "biotic mechanisms" (I doubt, however, that you'll find that phrase in a rancher's or farmer's vocabulary). These ranchers feel implicit ethical obligations to the land but don't necessarily and automatically extend this ethical structure to embrace a conservation ethic. Productive land, as defined by units of livestock or bushels of grain per acre, takes precedence over land set aside for publicly owned parks and wilderness areas. To lose land for such purposes is an anathema to many landowners, and they often truly feel threatened. Many ranchers have come to use the word "environmentalist" as a pejorative. Name-calling is also popular with ecoradicals, who so despise ranchers that at least one group has lobbied to remove the word "ranch" from the name of Texas Parks and Wildlife's largest natural area, the Big Bend Ranch State Natural Area.

Over the years, I have taken scores of city children to backwoods habitats, and each year I am always amazed by their decreasing affinity for the land and its creatures. It is said some kids have no concept of whence milk comes. Sorrowfully, I find that despite a quasiwilderness upbringing, I, too, have lost some of the skills that enabled me to be closer to nature when I was young. Of course, I can't hear, see, or smell as well, and my life in a city has numbed many senses, profoundly altering my relationship with nature. I suspect I am not alone. But I can personally conserve more and consume less, be ethical, and contribute to well-directed efforts at land conservation on a broad scale.

Aristotle believed there were three components to the human soul, two linked specifically to the conservation of nature. The "nutritive soul" was shared with the plant kingdom; the "sensitive soul" was shared with the animal kingdom; the "intellectual soul" was the rational link to humans. Plato, Pliny the Elder, and Aristotle all believed, as did Black Elk, in the links between our souls and nature.

These Mexican free-tailed bats silhouetted against the evening sky are fearsome creatures of Halloween myth and superstition to many. Before daylight, this species of bat alone will have consumed more than one million pounds of insects in Texas, a major conservation achievement repeated nightly.

If you have made it this far, I presume you have at least a rudimentary conservation ethic, and perhaps you even have an interest in finding out why it may be important to protect some of Texas' remaining biological diversity. It might come as a surprise to you that Texas has more unprotected, endangered, and threatened species than any of the other continental states.

It might also come as a surprise that 80 percent of respondents to a random telephone poll of 400 Texans (conducted in 1994 by Bannon Research, of Washington, D.C.) agreed that there is a "moral obligation to future generations to protect the diversity of wildlife from pollution and extinction." In the same poll, 60 percent agreed that the state should set aside more public land for recreation and to protect endangered species and water quality.

Some of the endangered and threatened wildlife in Texas include black bears, Bald Eagles, Peregrine Falcons, Black-capped Vireos, Golden-cheeked Warblers, jaguarundis, ocelots, Attwater's Greater Prairie-Chickens, Kemp's ridley sea turtles, Whooping Cranes, Brown Pelicans, black-footed ferrets, Red-cockaded Woodpeckers, Concho water snakes, Houston toads, even horny toads, and scores more. There are many plants to add to this partial list.

You have to go back to whatever killed off the dinosaurs to find a period in the world's natural history in which individual species were being eliminated at today's rate. Some ecologists estimate 20 percent of all species of plants and animals will become extinct by the year 2020. Although extinction is irreversible, why should we worry? Aren't a lot of these extinctions just bugs and creepy, crawly things hidden away in West Texas springs or Hill Country caves? Who needs 'em—especially if they get in the way of new development or an industrial park, or impede the extraction of our natural wealth?

Edward O. Wilson, writing in *The Diversity of Life* (1992), puts it into perspective for us: "Biodiversity is our most valuable but least appreciated resource." Wilson estimates we lose 27,000 species per year, 74 a day, 3 every hour. He talks about how we have escalated our destructiveness to unprecedented levels, with the human population explosion creating a huge, aching hunger for agricultural land and grazing pastures. He says we are now wiping out entire ecosystems.

There are practical, short-term economic benefits to be gained from being loyal to the earth. Most environmentalists and their confrontational organizations rely on dire, long-term forecasts that predict nothing short of extinction. But just recently, in the rain forests of Western Samoa, Dr. Paul Cox found and saved trees containing a compound that protects cells against the AIDS virus, at least in a test tube. It will be years before it can be tested on humans, but National Cancer Institute research results are promising. Dr. Cox is an ethnobotanist and tropical rain forest biologist. The trees containing the potential miracle drug were saved from bulldozers when Dr. Cox purchased the forest by putting up his house as collateral. In the Pacific Northwest, the bark of the yew tree has been found to be effective in treatment of ovarian cancer. The rosy periwinkle, found on the island of Madagascar, contains alkaloids that are efficacious in treating leukemia, particularly in children.

Corn, an ancient symbol of life and fertility, is a major crop in Texas, so the story of the maize species *Zea diploperennis* is appropriate. This species is a wild relative of corn, discovered in the seventies in the Mexican state of Jalisco. When the rare maize was found, its territory had been whittled down to less than twenty-five acres, and machete-wielding workers were still whacking away. *Zea's* genes give it both disease resistance and the capacity for perennial growth. Botanists hope to clone these genes into domestic corn, with great benefit to humankind.

Another important Texas crop is wheat. Researchers at the International Maize and Wheat Improvement Center in El Batan, Mexico, have announced a cure for leaf rust, a blight that destroys much of our crop each year. The disease-resistant strain was crossbred from an old Brazilian-grown wheat. Texas farmers will one day be able to grow wheat along our Gulf Coast using the new strain.

Major U.S. pharmaceutical companies, such as Merck and Eli Lilly, are investing heavily in a search for plants that will be useful for treating infections. Roughly half of the drugs we use today are of a natural origin. Dr. Michael J. Balick, director of the New York Botanical Garden Institute for Economic Botany, refers to rain forests and other rich sources of biodiversity as "major pharmaceutical factories." Dr. Steven King, vice president of ethnobotany and conservation for Shaman Pharmaceutical, makes his living working with indigenous people in Central American rain forests, seeking new drugs to sell to Merck. This "treasure house," to use Wilson's description, is huge and just barely studied by pharmacologists, botanists, and other environmental scientists. The riches of these unclassified, unexplored species cannot be known if they become extinct.

These success stories should motivate us to protect biodiversity. The message from writers such as Paul and Anne Ehrlich, in their book *Extinction* (1981), is typical of many doomsayers: "As nature is progressively impoverished, its ability to provide a moderate climate, cleanse air and water, recycle wastes, protect crops from pests, replenish soils, and so on will be increasingly degraded. Rising death rates and a falling quality of life will lead to a crumbling of post industrial civilization. The end may come so gradually that the hour of its arrival may not be recognizable, but the familiar world of today *will disappear within the life span of many people now alive*." The emphasis is mine, and this thought echoes hundreds like it, particularly when a given organization is bent on confrontation and conservation by tort.

Nature Conservancy trustee Carol E. Dinkins, attorney with the firm of Vinson and Elkins, alerts us to what I call the warts of the Endangered Species Act, which has been a major tool of environmentalists. Even Oregon senator Mark Hatfield, one of the creators of the ESA, has said, "It is being applied far beyond the scope of what any of us who helped adopt it intended." The *Wall Street Journal* has called the ESA the "Emotional Species Act." There is no question about the ESA's effectiveness in protecting species that are at risk, and frankly its existence has been very beneficial to good conservation work throughout the United States.

Dinkins points out the flip side of the ESA, which will be debated for the balance of this century: "It is undisputed that the basic principles and underlying purposes of the ESA are laudatory. However, the administration and application of the act over the twenty years of its existence demonstrate that it does carry the potential to adversely affect private property rights and those who would propose private development projects. . . . The costs involved in complying with the ESA may prove prohibitive for many private property owners, particularly if the project is located in an area designated as a critical habitat for a species." Section 9, which regulates private action, is also questionable. This section provides that no one may harm an endangered species, and courts have

Coreopsis, known to early Texans as tick seed, is found over most of the state. This field blooms each year near Leroy Williamson's home on the Blackland Prairie, conserved by a thoughtful landowner.

interpreted harm to include destruction of habitat on private lands. To me, this is obviously unfair to the very landowners who have protected endangered species; because they have been good stewards, their land values have declined. In my opinion, this law should be reviewed as to its scientific applicability as well as its impact on private landowners. What is good can be made better.

The Nature Conservancy recognizes that the preservation of biological diversity in the United States cannot take place without the support and participation of the private landowner. About 60 percent of all endangered species in the United States are found on nonfederal land. There are a number of TNC strategies to achieve win-win solutions with private landowners. These include purchase of private lands from willing sellers; purchase of private lands from willing sellers through a cooperative agreement with state or federal agencies; registry programs, such as the Texas Land Stewards Society, for private landowners who voluntarily work to preserve endangered species on their land; habitat conservation plans that function under requirements of the Endangered Species Act; and innovative, large landscape conservation projects, including TNC bioreserves.

The Nature Conservancy has developed a strong set of principles to govern work with private landowners:

• The Conservancy respects the rights of private property owners and encourages private landowners to accept the responsibility of preserving biological diversity by managing their own lands wisely.

• The Conservancy believes that public policy should seek to make the presence of endangered species an asset to a landowner instead of a liability by providing incentives that make it easier and economically advantageous for private property owners to manage or convey their lands for conservation purposes. (Traditionally, the Conservancy has avoided involvement in promoting public policies that would infringe on private property rights, including involvement in legislative actions, administrative actions, and especially litigation. But the Conservancy does believe it can promote positive incentives that reward private landowners for properly managing their property for biodiversity.)

• The Conservancy promotes a policy of willing buyer–willing seller in its dealings with landowners.

• As a landowner itself, the Conservancy supports the rights of landowners to protect their communities from irresponsible neighbors and incompatible uses.

• The Conservancy has no powers of condemnation and has a policy against the recommendation of condemnation of private land.

• The Conservancy staff and affiliates will abide by all trespass laws in the collection of biological data.

The black-helmeted Peregrine Falcon is found on all continents except Antarctica, entitling this raptor to status as a global symbol for conservation. The U.S. Peregrine population is expected to be fully recovered by 2000.

Yes, we do have serious environmental problems in Texas, but fortunately we have awakened to many of them, and there are positive steps we can take while maintaining our quality of life and full employment.

We know that Texas has lost approximately 600,000 acres of its coastal wetlands, 54 percent. When our first settlers were crossing the river, Texas probably had 16 million acres of bottomland hardwoods. We've lost well over 60 percent and perhaps have only just over 5 million acres today. Nationally, we're losing an acre of wetlands every minute. Look out your window and try to imagine a full acre, slightly larger than a football field. If you're an urbanite, that's a lot of space. Sixty seconds from now, it's history.

Are wetlands good for anything? Don't they just produce mosquitoes and mud? Wetlands are the most productive ecosystems found in nature, and the most vulnerable. If you are a seafood fancier, not a bird watcher, you still have a major stake in wetlands conservation. Virtually every Texan has benefited from the water supply and recreational largess of our reservoirs, but those benefits have had a double negative effect on wetlands. The loss of bottomland hardwoods must be obvious to any reservoir angler; less obvious is the loss of fresh water into our coastal wetlands, which has been very damaging to wildlife in our bays and marshes.

What this book is designed to do is present a few of the Texas environmental facts that are generally accepted, adopt a balanced approach that keeps people in the conservation equation, and allow you to find your own intellectual and emotional path.

If you are a typical urban dweller, you spend about 85 percent of your time indoors in artificial environments with controlled light, humidity, and temperature. It could be you have disconnected with nature. If so, you've disconnected with yourself, not uncommon in today's crazed world. The problem is, it's hard to listen to nature through the blare of a television set except for the precious but minuscule moments of nature programming on PBS. Then there's our daily duel with Texas' urban traffic, where all you see are vistas of rolling hardware on asphalt and concrete. It's hard to listen through the increased complexity of our lives, too, as we plunge deeper into the information society.

This book is designed to help you, with a minimum of fuss and hopefully a lot of fun, to reconnect with nature right here in Texas. As you reconnect, I hope you will begin to develop a generational mind-set. I hope you will become aware that the nature you're connecting with is in real trouble, right here in Texas, never mind the rain forests. We are really talking about the earth your children's children will inherit. There are places in Texas where you may begin to experience personally a shift of values to your own conservation ethic. A conservation ethic cannot be mandated. Each individual must come to it in his or her own way. You must go to the land itself, and look, and listen. There is much to see, hear, and do in Texas.

It will be helpful for you to know what to look for, how, and when, because if you have not lived in wilderness areas, you won't be attuned to finding the communities of plants and animals common to a specific habitat. You may wish to acquire field guides that are specific to areas and species. Their many listings reflect the complexity of nature. But don't let this inhibit you. Each little bit of natural knowledge will be fun to master, and no one is asking you to become an expert naturalist. This book is just a primer. I hope you go far beyond its offerings, because there is much more to be learned about conservation in Texas than can be covered in one book.

I organized this book to focus you on a number of key conservation accomplishments, to give you an insight into the conservation history of each selected area, to brief you on specific habitats, and to give you some idea of what to look and listen for in selected areas. Sites have been selected from each of the ten ecological areas of Texas to help you experience the beauty and diversity of our state. The sites include state, national, and private preserves.

Texas is rich in wild and beautiful things to see, especially birds and wildflowers. Many animals are common to large areas of the state, such as white-tailed deer, various rabbits, squirrels, raccoons, armadillos, bobcats, many common species of birds, and all manner of reptiles. To list every creature you might possibly see in each area would be redundant and far too cumbersome. I list only animals and plants of special interest to each area highlighted, including some that are rare, endangered, or threatened.

WHY BOTHER TRYING?

An acquaintance once remarked, while flying in a small aircraft over the seemingly never-ending tapestry of Central Texas, on what he perceived to be the irrelevance of the work being done by The Nature Conservancy. His conservation ethic was not too well developed. Unfortunately, more than a few Texans share his point of view. Many have taken the Book of Genesis literally, where it records, "God said unto them, Be fruitful and multiply, and replenish the earth and subdue it: and have dominion over the fish of the sea, and over the fowl of the air, and over every living thing that moveth upon the earth." Like Don Moors, chief of the Galveston Field Branch in the National Marine Fisheries Service Habitat Conservation Division, has said, "We appear to be extremely good at destroying habitat and not so good at replacing it." The part from Genesis that we seem to have a lot of trouble with is the "replenish" part—because once gone, species can't be recreated, at least not by mortals.

To my indifferent traveling companion, the why of conservation is incomprehensible. "We are here to subdue the earth. Texas is inexhaustible, as any fool can plainly see from a small aircraft." If there was a tiny tear in the tapestry of Texas ecosystems, you couldn't see it from his Cessna. We had been flying for hours and, to his way of thinking, had seen a beautiful mosaic of farm fields, lots of cattle and oil rigs, and only a few people. That's the way it should be in Texas, he pointed out. With so much land uninhabited by people, so far from major population centers, why bother with protecting any of it? After all, 95 percent of Texas is in private ownership, mostly by ranchers and farmers who have the most to gain from wise use of their land.

In one important sense, he was right. Much of Texas' natural biodiversity has indeed been protected by the enlightened stewardship of farmers and ranchers. But immensely important ecosystems are in danger throughout the state, along with the tapestry of life that they comprise. These ecosystems stretch beyond the fence lines of private landowners and even beyond political boundaries. The abrasions, rips, and unraveling threads of ecosystems such as our Blackland Prairies, rivers, lakes such as Caddo, wetlands, Pineywoods, South Texas Plains, Hill

Almost all white-tailed deer fawns found seemingly abandoned are not. Never disturb them or pick them up—a doe is nearby to provide a mother's care.

Country, and even our huge Chihuahuan Desert are obvious to even the untrained eye. Only our Devils River remains relatively pristine. Out of twelve million acres of Blackland Prairie, only five thousand acres remain; the lush South Texas Plains are almost all in agriculture, with the few surviving specks suitable for wildlife strung out like miniature green jewels along the polluted Rio Grande. On our border, Mexico looms as an environmental disaster—and a potential conservation opportunity.

Texas has a heritage of extraction, of dominating nature, a heritage that is all too clear to any student of Texas history. Extraction—of oil, gas, coal, other minerals, and water—has been a mainstay of the Texas economy. So have agricultural operations for food crops and livestock production. So has development for manufacturing and commerce for towns and cities.

From the days of the Chisholm Trail, we have dominated the nation's cattle industry. Today we are major producers of cotton and large-scale producers of grains and other food crops. With some few exceptions, the Texas agricultural industry now seeks sustainability of the natural resources required to grow crops.

The world's population could double from today's 5.5 billion to 11 billion by the time my grandson has had any grandchildren of his own, 2030 or so. The question will become one of carrying capacity, the environmentalist's term for the number of individuals of a species that an ecosystem can support for some specified time period, and of sustainability. How much arable topsoil is left in the major agricultural areas of Texas? How much nitrogen and phosphorus can we throw on the land? Will our aquifers and annual rainfall provide enough water? Will fertilizers pollute our dwindling water supplies?

We cannot continue to extract all of nature's riches with impunity. It doesn't take a scientist, or even particularly good eyesight, to see the degradation of our environment and the decline of the native plants and animals that inhabit it. The fact is, Texas, along with the rest of our planet, is in trouble. There is no truly pristine wilderness left in or near Texas. Every square inch of our state has felt the impact of humanity. To the credit of most Texans and our visitors, our "Don't Mess with Texas" campaign is being heeded. There is much less visible debris than in years past. Sadly, it's still far too easy to leave your human imprint, even unintentionally.

I suggest a Conservationist's Code:

1. Don't take flower or plant samples, not even roadside flowers.

2. Leave everything as you found it.

3. Take out everything you brought in with you.

4. Don't mess with Texas by littering.

5. Stay on paths or trails whenever possible.

6. Always obtain permission to enter private land. Texas has some of the strictest trespass laws, and many landowners are more than willing to enforce them.

7. If you do identify a threatened, rare, or endangered species, please tell a conservation professional—not the world at large. Unfortunately, there are those who make an illicit living from stealing rare Texas flora.

8. Don't disturb nesting birds.

9. Don't pick up cuddly little animals such as fawns or rabbits.

10. Don't introduce nonnative species without professional guidance.

11. Much of the year in much of Texas, there is a high fire hazard: be very careful of starting fires.

12. Be wary of feeding wild things: gators can become too tame, birds too dependent, deer too addicted, skunks too close!

13. Don't pick up artifacts such as arrowheads.

It comes down to simple concepts like understanding, caring, respect, and taking responsibility to save the best of Texas. It is within each of us.

THE VANISHING WATERS OF TEXAS

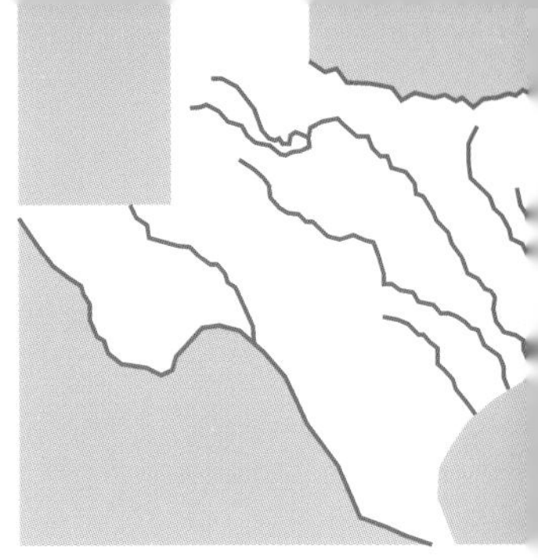

CHAPTER 2

Two miles north of St. Marks we crossed the Blanco, a mountain torent of purest water, narrow and deep; there is the finest spring of springs (for they are not less than 50 in a distance of 200 yds.) I ever beheld. These springs gush from the foot of a high cliff and boil up as from a well in the middle of the channel. One of these, the first you see in going up the stream, is near the center, the channel is here 40 yds wide, the water 15 or 20 feet deep, yet so strong is the ebullition of the spring, that the water is thrown two or three feet above the surface of the stream. I am told that by approaching it in canoe, you may see down the chasm from whence the water issues. . . . Great numbers of the finest fish and occasionally an alligator may be seen sporting in its crystal waters.

WILLIAM A. MCCLINTOCK
at San Marcos Springs, *Journal of a Trip through Texas and Northern Mexico in 1846–1847*

Also sporting in these lovely springs, fortunately not only for the other inhabitants of the ecosystem but also for the humans above, was a small, inconspicuous lizardlike amphibian, today called the San Marcos salamander, and a minnowlike fish, the San Marcos gambusia. If McClintock had spotted either one, he may have considered it as bait to catch the "finest fish" he could see in the crystal-clear waters; he may well have served bass filets with the now endangered native wild rice then found in abundance. These species, accompanied by a fountain darter and a Texas blind salamander, constitute the endangered five that led to the passage of legislation signed into law by Governor Ann Richards on June 11, 1993, to establish the Edwards Aquifer Authority.

The Edwards Aquifer is home to a number of other curious creatures, including two kinds of blind catfish too small to fry, rare mollusks, numerous crustaceans, and beetles. Many of the aquifer's invertebrates

OPPOSITE PAGE
The Llano River flows through billion-year-old Precambrian rock formations of the granite uplift area of the Hill Country. For most of its course, it is lined with oaks and pecans, which typify the Edwards Plateau.

are distinguished by their blindness and lack of pigmentation. These creatures have been isolated in the subterranean world for thousands of years so that many distinct species have evolved almost cave by cave.

While we will examine the closely studied southern segment of the Balcones Fault Edwards Aquifer, keep in mind that there are two other major aquifers in the Hill Country, the Edwards Trinity Plateau and the Trinity Group. Three minor aquifers complete the groundwater resource: Hickory, Marble Falls, and Ellenburger–San Saba. Overall, Texas has nine major aquifers and twenty minor ones occurring under more than 80 percent of the state. Fully half of our water consumption comes from groundwater. Almost three-quarters of the more than six million acre-feet of typical annual groundwater usage is for crop irrigation, while municipal use accounts for about 20 percent. Manufacturing, mining, steam electric generation, and ranching operations are also key consumers. In many areas of the state, the quantity of groundwater withdrawn has exceeded the recharge of aquifers.

Thankfully, the springs described by McClintock still flow with much the same ebullience as in 1846, some now capped and studied at the Edwards Aquifer Research and Data Center complex at Southwest Texas State University in San Marcos. Center director Dr. Glenn Longley confirmed to me that these are the springs described by McClintock.

According to Longley, the fauna of the Edwards Aquifer consists of at least forty troglobiotic species such as snails, worms, beetles, crustaceans, salamanders, and catfish, many endemic. These rare, threatened, and endangered species depend on the natural processes and functions of the southern Edwards Aquifer system.

The Edwards Aquifer was formed 95 million to 125 million years year ago during the late Cretaceous period when Texas was covered by a shallow tropical sea. Alternate periods of submergence and exposure provided a network of caverns, and the entire region was uplifted as the seas receded. Subsidence of the Gulf of Mexico and extensive faulting during the Miocene epoch, 12 million to 15 million years ago, resulted in the dipping of the Edwards toward the Gulf Coast. This caused increased water flow down toward the Gulf. The area's geologic history explains why there are many marine and brackish species present, even species found elsewhere only in the Caribbean. Adding to the diversity, many surface species escaped into the aquifer during the last ice age. The diversity of aquifer fauna was further broadened by the convergence of distinctly different physiographic regions with different geologic structures, periods of isolation, and connections between storage pools.

The key ecological processes that must be maintained include the continued supply of organic matter, source of nutrients and energy; natural patterns of water entrance *above historic low levels;* and unchanged water-quality characteristics of both the water entering the formation from the recharge zone and fresh water in the artesian zone that could experience temperature changes or be contaminated. The main threat to the aquifer system is caused by overdrafting of groundwater for agricultural irrigation and municipal use.

The establishment of the Edwards Aquifer Authority came barely in time not only to conserve the critters but also to preserve the quality of life of almost two million humans. Pumping on the aquifer will be limited for the first time in state history, settling this decades-long water rights controversy among ranchers, farmers, urbanites, and environmentalists. In the rest of the state, landowners have the right to pump as much as they want so long as it's not proven the water is being wasted. Texas law is based on old English water law, called the right of capture. This right is typically exercised by those with the most power, land, and money. The only exception is when groundwater can be classified as an underground stream, which is the case in the southern Edwards Aquifer.

The Edwards Aquifer Authority legislation is only a beginning for better conservation and the establishment of market mechanisms, but we should remember that this new law has not eliminated the possibility of federal intervention in the future. The bill limited total annual aquifer usage to 450,000 acre-feet, and the total must be reduced to 400,000 acre-feet in fifteen years. These usage restrictions would seem to be within the scientific limits determined by Dr. Longley in his 1991 report *Status and Trends of the Edwards Aquifer in the San Antonio Region*. Dr. Longley points out that it is "sobering to note that during the 1947–1956 period recharge was not much above 500,000 acre-feet in any year and was significantly below that for most of the period. . . . It's easy to visualize what type of conditions may occur if we have another drought as severe as the one that ended in 1956." The argument that we will run out of water, to me the most persuasive environmental argument of all, did not provide a basis for commonsense reconciliation of the issues.

According to professors Stanley N. Davis of Stanford and Roger J. M. DeWiest of Princeton, every person uses up to 5 million gallons of water during his or her lifetime. In their landmark work *Hydrogeology* (1991), they up this individual total to 10 million gallons when the per-person share of industrial, agricultural, and recreational usage is calculated. The professors compare this with usage by indigenous people: "In contrast, an individual living under primitive conditions might easily survive a lifetime with 50,000 gallons and would be able to maintain personal cleanliness with an additional 50,000 gallons."

Davis and DeWiest explain that profligate use of water in cities and towns occurs because water is cheap: "At a cost of a few cents per ton, water can be used to transport most industrial and domestic wastes. Vast quantities of water are used for nothing more than heat exchange purposes. . . . Cities in the western United States sell processed water that is used to keep lawns green through hot, dry summers. In some communities more than half the water that is sold is used for lawns and flower gardens."

The Texas High Plains already has more than 50,000 irrigation wells drilled neatly into the Ogallala Aquifer, the largest aquifer in Texas and the United States. Think of the Ogallala as a huge swimming pool filled with wet gravel, perched upon the bedrock of the Texas Caprock Escarpment. The formation is of interlayers of sand, caliche, silt, clay, and wet gravel ranging in thickness from 150 to 300 feet. Erosion escarpments on the east and west and on the Canadian River breaks have confined the aquifer. The southern boundary of the Ogallala is just north of the Pecos River, which completed the aquifer's isolation when it cut off the ancient flow from the Rocky Mountains. You can visualize the Ogallala as an island of water under the Texas High Plains.

The groundwater of the Ogallala, which took millennia to charge from Rocky Mountain runoff, supplies 75 percent of all such water in Texas. Since it can now be recharged only from surface-water percolation, it is finite—on its way now to being drained because pumping throughout these many years has removed more water than rain can replace. A Department of Commerce forecast predicts that by 2020, at the current rate of depletion, Texas will have pumped out two-thirds of its Ogallala reserves. If drained, the Ogallala will take six thousand years to refill. It's true, the aquifer should last another few generations. So why worry now? Who cares about your grandchildren's grandchildren?

As the succeeding chapters focus on the ten fundamentally different ecological areas found in Texas, portions of rivers are mentioned in separate sections, though most rivers run through several ecosystems. Since groundwater sources, aquifers, springs, creeks, rivers, lakes, estuaries, the Gulf Intracoastal Waterway, and the Gulf marine systems also span ecological areas, this chapter summarizes the overarching water-related issues.

OPPOSITE PAGE
A "torent of purest water" flows from the Edwards Aquifer near Austin, a treasure of inestimable value. This spring is one of thousands protected by conservation-minded private landowners in Texas.

Although we live in fear of major oil spills in our estuaries and river systems, the effects of most of these spills are short lived and as nothing when compared with the impact of all the dredging, plowing, and other transformations of the land.

The cycle of evaporation, condensation, and precipitation that keeps us all alive on this planet was working in our favor in Texas in the early nineties. Our aquifers were being recharged, our reservoirs filled to the brim, every stock tank overflowed. We were getting more than our share of the global stock of atmospheric water, estimated at any one time to

be the equivalent of a one-inch-thick layer covering the earth, the one inch that keeps us alive. In fact, all terrestrial life is sustained by the 1 percent of fresh water that we can access. This actually is a lot of water. The catch is that only a tiny fraction falls on your head, and precious little falls west of the hundredth meridian, where evapotranspiration returns most water back to the atmosphere, where we can't get at it without a rain dance. Also, we must remember that fossil groundwater is finite.

The hydrologic cycle can just as easily work against Texas, bringing terrible droughts. Rural Texans have always understood the enigma of evaporation and transpiration observed by Solomon in Ecclesiastes: "All streams flow into the sea yet the sea is not full, though the streams are still flowing." We know mesquite trees suck up water through their deep roots and transpire it right back into the atmosphere before our very eyes. This propensity to waste water is typical of other phreatophytes, such as willow, ash, and cottonwood, and has a major impact in arid and semiarid regions of Texas.

The many springs that burble up from the Edwards Aquifer drainage under my Granada Springs ranch in western Kerr County are a constant source of mystery and joy to me. I'm not the only one so affected; history, literature, and modern advertising abound with the religious, medical, and marketing superstitions attributed to spring waters. Many of us believe wonderful things about bottled spring water. The fact is, spring water quality is often lower than that of groundwater or processed sources and usually higher in dissolved solids, which are more subject to pollution. But to me, in a most basic sense, the flows of Granada Springs represent the source of all life. To stay near them for a spell is renewing, like immersing yourself in a great opera or poem. Looking downstream, I can see the miraculous effect of the spring's water being pumped through green plants, capturing the energy of the sun through photosynthesis, giving back food and oxygen as it removes carbon dioxide. Sitting by a spring, whether it's seeping or gushing, is an excellent way to build up your conservation ethic and to understand the land ethic, too. I have attempted to protect these springs, which were once threatened by development, for I can imagine the contribution they make as their flow winds its way down Turtle Creek to the Guadalupe to San Antonio Bay, past Matagorda Island and into the Gulf, becoming part of a million acre-feet of annual runoff.

In its scenic 200-mile meander, the lifeblood of Granada Springs helps nurture a series of riverine and riparian systems supporting plant and animal habitats and hundreds of thousands of humans. More than 300,000 people visit the twenty-five-mile stretch of the lower Guadalupe below Canyon Dam each year just for recreation. So, my small flow plays its part in the full spectrum of life, from species survival and subsistence to sport and silliness. Don't get me wrong; we need to be silly every once in a while, and there are few better ways than tubing.

Although hundreds of impoundment lakes have been created by damming the Guadalupe and scores of other Texas rivers, this book mentions only a few, usually in connection with a natural area. Other reference books, such as *The Sportsman's Guide to Texas* (1988), list the significant impoundments and the fish that can and should be caught in them, but this is a book about conservation. As useful as dams and reservoirs are to the needs of the urban many, and there is no denying this, they are still the principal threat to the biological hardiness of our rivers. The physical transformation of rivers through the widespread efforts of the Corps of Engineers has also resulted in an ecological transformation. Riverine temperature and nutrient patterns are disrupted, and agricultural runoff takes its toll of biological diversity, as does the effluent of urban areas. The result is an impoverishment of the ecosystem, a thinning of life, bottomland hardwoods and wetlands submerged forever.

Dr. Larry Master of The Nature Conservancy (TNC) has studied this phenomenon and found that in North America 28 percent of amphibian species and subspecies, 34 percent of fish species, 65 percent of crayfish, and 73 percent of mussels were imperiled in degrees ranging from rare to extinct. The comparable figures were 13 percent for terrestrial mammals, 11 percent for land reptiles. As a state that relies heavily on dams and that has a large desert area, Texas riverine systems are even more impaired.

THE RIVERS OF TEXAS

Only a few of the state's 80,000-mile total of rivers and streams can be discussed here, those that reveal a special conservation concern. However, as a canoeist myself, I can testify that many of our rivers provide a wonderful conservation education experience.

The CANADIAN RIVER rises in the Sangre de Cristo Mountains of northeastern New Mexico near Taos. The Canadian River Valley slashes an average of 600 feet through the High Plains ecological area, cutting a swath up to thirty-five miles wide. Locals use the term "breaks" to describe this rugged terrain. It is an apt term. The Canadian is not your typical recreational river, but its course across the Panhandle helped change the course of history. Its periodic raging floods leave behind quicksand, making it dangerous to cross.

The RED RIVER is second only to the Rio Grande in length and legends, forming much of the northern border of Texas. Even modern writers are confused about its headwaters, which are in the High and

Rolling plains, not the mountains of New Mexico. It flows to the southeastern tip of the Texas Panhandle's Oklahoma border; here, the Red River becomes the border. Near Texarkana,the Red becomes the Texas-Arkansas border for a few miles before sweeping southward through Louisiana.

The main river system in North Central Texas is the TRINITY, which has its headwaters in the Rolling Plains. In three channels that come together below Dallas, its 5.8 million acre-feet of water begins the voyage to the Gulf. The Trinity's lower course was developed for navigation around 1900, and every once in a while this possibility is advanced again by those who dream of barges docking in downtown Dallas. Such a scheme was proposed as recently as 1980, despite the fact that it would be an environmental disaster. The Trinity's water is highly polluted. Major efforts are in place to prevent further toxic and harmful effluents. This can be done; the effluence from the Dallas manufacturing plant for which I had responsibility for many years was actually much more pure than tap water and, for that matter, most bottled water. Perhaps one day the Trinity will be rediscovered for what it was, one of the most beautiful and bountiful rivers in Texas, with much wildlife and ecosystems bursting with rare and lovely diversity. Such a mammoth job will require a remarkable partnership to accomplish, an assignment for the conservation-minded of the next century.

Not far from The Nature Conservancy's Blacklands Prairie Clymer Meadow preserve in Hunt County is an easy-to-miss wetlands area. From this modest beginning, the SABINE RIVER ultimately discharges 6.8 million acre-feet a year into the Gulf of Mexico—the largest flow of any Texas river. The river, named for the Spanish word for cypress, was once churned by stern-wheelers all the way to Logansport, Louisiana, just north of present-day Toledo Bend Reservoir. Much Blacklands cotton and Pineywoods timber came down this river. The river forms the Texas-Louisiana border from Logansport to Sabine Pass. The river is scenic in a remote, swampy way, with centuries-old cypress, spotlessly white sandbars, and an eerie sense of wildness.

The NECHES RIVER, second only to the Sabine in discharge, is named for an Indian tribe. It contributes more than six million acre-feet to the Gulf annually. This river is critical to the biodiversity of the Pineywoods, flowing as borders to two national forests, the Angelina and Davy Crockett, where it is marked as a canoe trail. It is also a principal corridor through the Big Thicket National Preserve. A spring wildlife viewing trip is preferred to a fall trip, since you are assured of higher water levels and will see many beautiful flowers and plants.

The beautiful BRAZOS RIVER, so important to ancient and modern Texans, once had its beginnings on the Texas–New Mexico border

The Guadalupe River begins its 250-mile, million-acre-feet flow to the Texas coast from aquifer springs near Kerrville. This is one of the most scenic rivers in the state, heavily used for recreation.

in Parmer County with a bounteous flow of water from the Ogallala Aquifer. No springs flow today in Parmer County. The spring waters were high in sodium bicarbonate, silica, and fluoride and very alkaline, but drinkable. This area is rich in Paleo-Indian artifacts, and just a few miles to the west, in the Brazos drainage at the Blackwater Draw archeological site, are found the oldest artificial wells in the Americas at six thousand years old.

The SAN BERNARD RIVER doesn't receive the recognition it should for its important contribution to the Gulf wetlands ecosystem. Unlike its mighty neighbors to the north and south, the Brazos and Colorado rivers, the San Bernard rises in the coastal plain on its own with a meek 124-mile flow. But it is rich in springs, and no one has yet thought to dam it, making it still vital to Gulf Coast fisheries and migrating birds.

The headwaters of the COLORADO RIVER in Dawson County once gushed with large springs, as noted in the 1600s by Spanish explorers who gave the river its name, "Colorado," meaning reddish. Archeological sites in Dawson County document fifteen thousand years of human habitation. Thus begins the largest river entirely within Texas, stretching 600 miles to the Gulf of Mexico. The Colorado is also the state's most dammed river, with the two largest dams being those at Lake Buchanan and Lake Travis. The Highland chain of lakes begins at Buchanan, forming constant-level scenic lakes such as Inks, LBJ, and Marble Falls in beautiful Hill Country settings. Above Lake Buchanan there is a striking area that runs through dramatic limestone cliffs, past Gorman Falls, one of the most spectacular waterfalls in Texas, located at the point where Gorman Creek spills into the Colorado. The falls are now part of Colorado Bend State Park. Bald eagles have taken up winter residence in a stretch of the Colorado just as it enters Lake Buchanan. This area has been carefully preserved by ranchers on both sides of the Colorado, including Ed Auler, owner of Fall Creek Vineyards at Tow.

Frederick Law Olmsted described the GUADALUPE RIVER near Sisterdale in his 1857 *Journey Through Texas:* "The Guadalupe was even more beautiful here than below, quick and perfectly transparent. I have rarely seen any resort of wood-nymphs more perfect than the bower of cypress branches and vines that overhang the mouth of the Sister creek at the ford near the house. You want a silent canoe to penetrate it; yet would be loth to desecrate its deep beauty. The water of both streams has a delicate, cool, blue-green color; the rocky banks are clean and inviting; the cypresses rise superbly from the very edge, like ornamental columns." I take considerable comfort from the fact that if one could find a writer of matching eloquence, much of the Guadalupe's course can be so described today. This river is one of the critical resources to be conserved as part of the ambitious Nature Conservancy project, the Hill Country Bioreserve, discussed in the chapter on the Edwards Plateau.

Most of the rugged hillsides surrounding Rocksprings, headwaters for the NUECES RIVER and center for Angora goat raising, have been closely nibbled and clear-cut for timber. This is tough country to sustain life, to which humans, goats, grasses, and trees can testify. What was assumed to be an endless supply of water from recharge to the Edwards limestone aquifer here is jeopardized, since water that once was given time to seep into the aquifer by ground cover now just runs off. As a result, the once plentiful springs of the Nueces headwaters are drying up one by one. A famous spring just northeast of Rocksprings is Devils Sink Hole, which fifty years ago had a substantial spring flow and since the 1880s was a source of water on cattle drives. Today there are only pools of live, fresh water but no discernible flow. Devils Sink Hole is of great importance biologically, as it is the summer home to several million Mexican free-tailed bats and a number of troglobiotic species, at least one of which is endemic. The area is now under the guardianship of the Texas Parks and Wildlife Department (TPWD) as a state natural area and future park. The picturesque headwater forks join near Uvalde, where the river flows out of the Balcones Escarpment into the South Texas Plains.

Although the PECOS RIVER arises in the Sangre de Cristo Mountains of New Mexico, it receives a nice bonus from Delaware Creek, which rises in Culberson County, Texas, and joins the Pecos just at Red Bluff Lake. Below Pandale, the last 55 miles of the river is very remote, with canyon walls climbing higher and higher on either side. Rapids often form at canyon mouths, especially at Cold Water Canyon. The Pecos eventually joins the Rio Grande, where even today, the canyon seems deep. Sadly, the incredibly beautiful scenery of this junction is mainly under the waters of immense Lake Amistad. The 67,000-acre reservoir, a cooperative project of the United States and Mexico, has 850 miles of shoreline extending 25 miles up into the Devils River Canyon, 14 miles up the Pecos, and 74 up the Rio Grande, negatively affecting the local ecosystem but providing water resources and recreation.

The DEVILS RIVER has one of the largest base flows of any Texas river because of the many springs that supply it. Some decline in spring flow has been attributed to irrigation pumping in the northern recharge area. During normal rainfall much of the river's flow is runoff from the rugged surrounding terrain—draws that are usually bone dry. This is, after all, the eastern border of the Chihuahuan Desert.

In the 1600s, Juan de Oñate gave us the name we *norte americanos* use for the mighty RIO GRANDE, but our neighbors to the south still say "Río Bravo." For 1,248 miles of its total length of 1,896 miles, it is the international border between the United States and Mexico, and both countries share the responsibility for saving it. In the last twenty years the river has been pummeled by *maquiladores,* factories built from El Paso–Juárez to Brownsville-Matamoros to take advantage of low-cost Mexican labor and slack environmental laws. In 1993, America Rivers proclaimed the Rio Grande one of the top ten endangered rivers, and press pundits coined the phrase "Sewer Grande."

At El Paso, the American Dam directs the United States' share of the water into the American Canal, which connects back up with the river downstream of the International Dam. Meanwhile, Mexico siphons off its liquid allotment into the Acequia Madre, and both countries soak up the water for agriculture. There is often only dry rock river bed between the ruins at Fort Quitman and the confluence of the Río Conchos

To most, the phrase "desert spring" would evoke at best a sheltered pool of liquid succor. This bold spring flows within Texas Parks and Wildlife Department's Devils River State Natural Area, helping sustain the Chihuahuan Desert river's near-pristine water quality.

between October and January. This is wild canyon country, through which only the merest traces of roads pass on the U.S. side beyond the metroplex of Ruidosa and Candelaria.

At Presidio-Ojinaga, the Río Conchos, which flows out of Mexico's Sierra Madre Occidental, saves the Rio Grande and thus greatly enhances the ecosystem of which the Big Bend Ranch State Natural Area and Big Bend National Park are part.

The Rio Grande rises on the eastern face of the Continental Divide in Colorado. The primary sources are at about twelve thousand feet in the Cordilleran ice fields. Tributaries such as Spring Creek, South Fork, and others join it as it first heads east then plunges south for the length of New Mexico. It picks up power from Galisteo Creek, Jemez River, Rio Puerco, and Rio Salado, then makes its turn to the southeast to run for the Gulf of Mexico. After its wild gyration at the Big Bend, the river picks up more water from the Pecos and Devils rivers at Amistad Reservoir. Between the Amistad and Falcon reservoirs, five Mexican rivers and three U.S. trickles flow into the river. Thus three-fourths of the river's water comes from Mexico in its waltz through Texas.

Cooperation is building between the newly formed Texas Natural Resource Conservation Commission, the U.S. Environmental Protection Agency (EPA), TPWD, and the International Boundary and Water

Commission working with Mexico's Comisión Nacional del Agua and Comisión Internacional de Limites y Aguas (CILA). Multinational teams are forming partnerships, working hard and well together, and the mid-nineties should show progress on Rio Grande water quality issues. At stake is the survival of the second longest river in the United States.

Below Falcon Dam the river cuts through the semiarid South Texas Plains, then through subtropical terrain as it nears the coast through the Valley, and finally oozes into the Gulf of Mexico south of Boca Chica, exhausted after its 1,900-mile journey, only a shadow of its former self. The sad, ugly trickle you see when crossing over to Matamoros is where Richard King and other steamboat captains plied the river in the 1860s.

THE BAYS AND ESTUARIES OF TEXAS

When we go down to the low-tide line, we enter a world that is as old as the earth itself—the primeval meeting place of . . . earth and water, a place of compromise and conflict and eternal change. For us as living creatures it has special meaning as an area in or near which some entity that could be distinguished as Life first drifted into shallow waters—reproducing, evolving . . . we come to perceive life as a force . . . strong and purposeful, as incapable of being crushed or diverted from its end as the rising tide.

RACHEL CARSON

1955, as quoted by Paul Brooks in *The House of Life: Rachel Carson at Work*

The shore is an ancient world, for as long as there has been an earth and sea there has been this place of the meeting of land and water. Yet it is a world that keeps alive the sense of continuing creation and of the relentless drive of life. Each time that I enter it, I gain some new awareness of its beauty and its deeper meanings, sensing that intricate fabric of life by which one creature is linked with another, and each with its surroundings.

RACHEL CARSON

The Edge of the Sea, 1955

Thomas Duke of Technical Resources, Inc., and William Krusczynski of the U.S. Environmental Protection Agency collaborated on a 1990 report to a conference on the environmental status of the Gulf of Mexico, pointing out that 50 percent of the Gulf's coastal wetlands were lost between the late 1700s and the 1980s. They state: "Ecologically, coastal wetlands provide many essential functions, structures, and shelter for a myriad of plants and animals. The quality and acreage of these wetlands have been severely reduced through natural processes such as subsidence, erosion, and rising sea level as well as by human activities, including construction of canals and channels, dredging, spoil disposal, draining and filling, and release of toxic substances and sewage."

It's a good thing that these places of "compromise and conflict and eternal change" are tough, because these ecosystems function under the harshest and most demanding circumstances asked of any, particularly on the Texas coast. To the credit of many partners including private landowners, the U.S. Fish and Wildlife Service, EPA, TPWD, TNC, the Texas Coastal Management Program, the Texas Chemical Council, and the Texas Mid-Continent Oil and Gas Association, we can see a slowing of the deadly trends of the sixties. Before enactment of the Texas Solid Waste Disposal Act of 1969, many industrial wastes were discharged directly into the estuaries and tidal wetlands.

We can't question the value of wetlands, defined as areas saturated by water at least seven days a year, that have mucky or peat-based soils, and that support specified plant life. The term "wetlands" is broadly applied, from our playas to our extensive tidal marshes. In addition to helping filter toxic wastes, excess nutrients, sediment, and other pollutants, wetlands also help prevent erosion and reduce flooding by storing storm water. The forty-eight contiguous United States have lost 50 percent of their wetlands since Washington crossed the Delaware. In 1993, the Clinton administration continued President Bush's "no net wetlands loss" program, which, according to EPA administrator Carol Browner, actually loses about 300,000 acres a year. The Clean Water Act of 1972 requires anyone seeking to fill a wetland to obtain a permit from the Corps of Engineers, which is submitted to the Environmental Protection Agency for review. Since we still have about 100 million acres of wetlands worth saving, some agricultural and development interests don't seem to be overly concerned with the conservation issues. But we must conserve them; wetlands are irreplaceable biological systems of irrefutable value to humankind.

The Trinity–San Jacinto estuary, better known as Galveston Bay, at 600 square miles, is the seventh largest in the United States. More than 30 percent of Texas fishery landings are associated with this vital estuary, and at the same time it is a key Gulf port, with more than 250 million tons handled annually. Significantly, 30 percent of U.S. petroleum refining and 50 percent of the country's chemical production are located here. And not least, the nation's fourth largest city is perched thirty-six miles up Buffalo Bayou. Clearly, Galveston Bay is an estuary system under siege.

In late 1994, the Institute for Southern Studies released a study that correlated strong environmental protection with long-term economic health. All fifty states were surveyed in forty categories related to both ecological and economic vitality. Texas finished forty-ninth on the environmental yardstick, fortieth on the economic.

One of the major dangers to the Texas estuaries is the reduction of freshwater inflow, an essential driving force of ecosystem health. The three key roles of freshwater inflow are reduction of salinity, mixing, and delivery of nutrients and sediments from the watershed. Reduction of salinity is the major function because salinity is, according to Robert R. Stickney in *Estuarine Ecology of the Southeastern United States and Gulf of Mexico* (1984), "crucial to the survival, optimum growth, spawning, larval rearing, movement, and general well being of various important estuarine species."

The criticality of freshwater inflow is well illustrated in the Matagorda Bay system, in Texas second only to Galveston Bay in size at 400 square miles. Unlike the other major estuary systems in Texas, there has been relatively limited urban and industrial development in this area, therefore allowing abundant natural resources. The bay's aquatic habitats include saltwater marshes, brackish ponds, marshes, and open water. All are dependent on clean, fresh water if they are to remain productive.

With the exception of the Colorado delta, the emergent wetland habitats of major Texas river delta estuaries—including the Guadalupe, Lavaca, Trinity, Neches, San Jacinto, and Nueces—have declined dramatically since the thirties. The marshes of the Colorado delta have accreted, actually gotten larger, but this is attributed to major deposits of sediments after hurricanes. The general trend is the replacement of vegetated areas by areas of shallow, open water habitat or barren intertidal flats.

The Whooping Crane, one of North America's most imperiled species, overwinters at Matagorda Island and the Aransas National Wildlife Refuge. Surface water originating as Edwards Aquifer spring flow helps maintain premier wintering habitat conditions for the Whooping Crane on barrier islands and in coastal marshes and tidal flats. Other rare shorebirds and hundreds of thousands of migratory waterfowl share the coastal habitat sustained by flow from the aquifer's karst springs.

The estuarine ecosystem is the essential link in the marine food web from tiny organisms to shrimp, oysters, crabs, flounder, redfish, trout, and other valuable marine resources. Shrimp is the most profitable catch, estimated in 1983 to be 78 percent of the weight and 91 percent of the value of Texas commercial landings.

The Texas coast has been identified as one of the most critical areas in the United States with respect to freshwater inflow, and water supply problems are expected to become increasingly severe as we approach the twenty-first century. There is a positive relationship between freshwater inflow and the production of fish dependent on estuaries on the Texas coast. Estuaries that receive the constantly strong flow from East Texas rivers contribute more to the commercial fisheries than those down the coast. The issue always comes down to dams such as those proposed for the Guadalupe and San Antonio rivers, which prompted a study by

The Southeast Texas flood of fall 1994 ruptured pipelines in the San Jacinto River, cascading crude oil downriver on the same course as this tanker in the Houston Ship Channel and threatening sensitive Galveston Bay.

TPWD that was able to demonstrate the major disruption of the ecology of the San Antonio Bay system that would have occurred if the dams had been built.

It's clear that there are many competing demands for the coasts and estuaries. It's also clear that those making the demands must work together in a responsible way. The coastal wetlands and estuaries cannot absorb all our waste indefinitely.

THE GULF INTRACOASTAL WATERWAY

When the wind "blew like stink" offshore I would often sail my ketch, *La Scala,* into the welcome shelter of the Gulf Intracoastal Waterway (GIW) to navigate the coast, vying with barge traffic for the relative calm of the channel. On other occasions, to find the barges' perspective, I've piloted push-boat barge combinations of almost a thousand feet, gaining great respect for those who handle these behemoths safely.

Spring flow from the Edwards Aquifer is essential to preserve the quality of the coastal aquatic habitat such as that found at San Antonio Bay. This bay is part of the second largest bay system in Texas and borders Aransas National Wildlife Refuge.

Having grown up on the Intracoastal Waterway in Florida, I have an affinity for it and its many good purposes. But there is no doubt that the GIW has caused the loss of much estuarine habitat in Texas. We have about a thousand miles of dredged channels. To maintain these channels and add new ones, we remove more than 50 million cubic yards of bottom material each year. An estimate made in 1973 stated that if dredging in the Houston Ship Channel remained constant, the capacity of existing spoil disposal areas would be reached in 26.4 years, an estimate we'll be able to verify soon.

We know dredging can destroy bottom habitats, alter habitats when soil is disposed of, and degrade water quality. We also know that major channels such as the GIW can serve as conduits for the spread of exotic aquatic plants and pollutants. Of major concern is the proposal to extend the GIW into the Laguna Madre of Mexico, south of the mouth of the Rio Grande. This would not only immediately devastate some of the Gulf's most critical estuarine systems but also put greatly increased pressure on the U.S. segment, particularly the Louisiana and Texas coastal wetlands. Barge and other traffic could be expected to increase in ratio to how far down the Mexican coast the GIW was extended.

To residents of the Texas Gulf Coast, there is continual evidence that something is going wrong. Dolphin deaths have been on the increase; the turtles are disappearing. Hundreds of thousands of fish were killed in the Gulf off the northeast Texas coast in May and June 1994, possibly by algal blooms. More than one hundred rare Kemp's ridley turtles were reported dead in the first five months of the year.

According to Larry McKinney of TPWD, more than 50 percent of the Gulf's shellfish beds are typically restricted in any given year or closed completely because of pollution. Algal blooms, known as red tides, seem more prevalent, and we are more aware now of the 3,000-square-mile dead zone off the coast of Texas and Louisiana, probably increased in size by the Great Flood of 1993. Despite all of this, the Gulf still produces a bounty of 2.5 billion pounds of seafood each year.

Sail out into the Gulf and you can really sense and see the degradation firsthand, especially the increase in debris and in fishing pressure, both commercial and recreational. Hundreds of miles out, I have often encountered the nets of long-line fishermen, cut loose and kill-drifting their way across the Gulf. The United Nations Agenda 21 conferences on global fisheries reported that fishing nations admitted their fleets have diminished stocks of the world's edible marine fish to a level unimaginable only a few years ago. Catch rates throughout the world began a serious decline in the nineties, and we have had to protect our reef fishing in Texas by putting strict limits on size and numbers of popular fish caught, such as red snapper. Distant-water fishing countries—such as the United States, China, Russia, and Japan—with advanced, long-range vessels, are taking their toll in the Gulf. I cannot but believe the Gulf, vast as it is at 615,000 square miles, is today overfished. One of the things that is needed is research into critical habitat issues, quantification of economic values, fishery interactions, and improved fishery statistics.

One Gulf crossing experience led to a very positive conclusion, although it did not seem that way the moment it happened. I was sailing at night, no lights visible anywhere, at about 27°54' north latitude and 93°36' west longitude, or 170 nautical miles south of Sabine Pass, when the depth sounder, set for 20 fathoms (120 feet) surprisingly sounded its alert. As I should have been in 600 feet of water, I was nonplussed and immediately put *La Scala*'s bow into the wind to lose way. I feared I had come upon some strange obstruction and a grounding was imminent. A quick check below of my charts cleared up the mystery. We were crossing over the 56-square-mile Flower Garden Banks, which crest at a depth of about 60 feet. These are beautiful coral reefs formed on salt domes and are covered with colorful fish. Today the reefs are protected as part of a network of eleven marine sanctuaries in the coastal waters of the United States. These sanctuaries are maintained by the National Oceanic and Atmospheric Administration. The number of sanctuaries in the system is expected to double by the year 2000, protecting a valuable yet hidden part of America's rich biodiversity. The Flower Garden Banks are the northernmost coral reefs in the world and remind me of those in the Red Sea. I am certain the Gulf holds more surprises for us in biodiversity not yet measured, resources, and a capacity for sustainable use if we can keep it healthy and productive for future generations. It will depend in large measure upon our collective conservation ethic.

"MANY A DENSE THICKET"
THE PINEYWOODS

CHAPTER 3

Thank heaven there will long be many a dense thicket, where bears and panther, wolf and wild cat, may find refuge; many a prairie where gentle doe and timid fawn can feed in peace; many a broad league of primeval forest, where stalwart oaks and lofty pines will rear their lofty heads proudly, and in safety from the desecrating axe—whose virgin soil, uncontaminated by cotton, cane or corn, unscathed by plough, mattock, will generously nurture a thousand varieties of wild flowers, that fill the eye with beauty and the air with fragrance.

PHILIP PAXTON
Piney Woods Tavern, 1858

Eloquent words from a pioneering explorer, right on all counts except the time it has taken us to desecrate much of the Pineywoods, especially Paxton's Big Thicket. However, there are trees left, and a thousand species of wildflowers, so it's still worth visiting, especially if you're of the urban many. Trees are the story of the Pineywoods, as you would guess, mainly the variegated greens of the pines, but also many kinds of oak, ash, elm, hickory, and sweet gum that, in combination, make the area so beautiful throughout the year.

Among the first trees to flower in the early spring are varieties of wild plum and pear. My favorite time is early April, timing the drive to Caddo Lake so that the elegant white dogwoods decorate the hills and a few redbuds surprise. The showy dogwood is a treasure of East Texas, and to me it stands out most dramatically against the deep piney greens when its limbs are covered in frothy white blossoms. Then, with a hike in the crisp, pine-scented air, too slowly city cares will ease, gradually abated by nature's spring harmonies. This is a place to renew your

OPPOSITE PAGE
Henry David Thoreau's statement "You cannot perceive beauty but with a serene mind" evokes Caddo Lake's cypress and moss-bedecked tranquility. Caddo was saved by a partnership of individuals, landowners, agencies, and conservation organizations.

conservation ethic, to pause and smell, not yet the headiness of Tyler roses, but the spring pines, to see the new sap-green foliage, to listen to both sweet silence and sweet birdsong.

The Texas Pineywoods are characterized by rolling hills and rich bottomlands with tall hardwoods and biologically diverse wetlands. The highly weathered soils, deep loam or sandy, have been developed over ancient marine sedimentary material. The open longleaf pine woodlands once dominated many parts of southeastern Texas. Most of the longleaf and beech-magnolia forests have been cut and the woodlands are now in plantations of loblolly and slash pine; many natural communities were destroyed in the process. In addition to the longleaf pine and beech-magnolia forest, rare animal and plant species such as the Red-cockaded Woodpecker and Texas trailing phlox have become endangered.

The Pineywoods are part of an ecological area of approximately sixteen million acres that extends into Louisiana, Arkansas, and Oklahoma. Texas Pineywoods elevations range from 50 to 500 feet. Average rainfalls are the highest in Texas, from thirty-five to fifty inches; temperatures and humidity are high. The area is replete in ecotones, also called edges, where different habitats run together. Edges are usually rich in plant and animal life and often have a variety of soils and geologic characteristics. They have greater diversity because of overlapping species and habitat components. The Texas and Louisiana chapters of The Nature Conservancy are collaborating on a major cross-border project, identified as the Pineywoods Bioreserve, to help protect some of the remaining diversity.

CADDO LAKE

Caddo Lake lies across the northeast Texas boundary with Louisiana. It's renowned for its Spanish moss–covered cypress, which holds its place of grand distinction with the redwoods and sequoias of California. Even though bald cypress can grow in uplands, it thrives best in flooded areas. In the 1890s, cypress, known as "wood eternal," was in great demand for its long-lasting qualities. Cypress swamps were first cut, then drained for agriculture over much of the South. Cypress trees are opportunistic, one of the first trees to take root in new land, and all swamps are relatively new by geological standards. The trees grow well if not shaded out by a canopy and if they don't get their feet too wet at first. Once established, they like varying levels of water and can live for hundreds of years.

Of the five classifications of wetland systems, Caddo represents three: riverine, lacustrine, and palustrine. Riverine freshwater wetland consists of stream and river channels, such as Big Cypress Bayou. The lacustrine system includes freshwater lakes and ponds, like Whistleberry Slough.

The palustrine system contains emergent marshes and forested wetlands, like those in Kitchen's Creek and Alligator Thicket.

The hydrology of the Caddo area is key to its very existence. When the marsh is too dry, pine seedlings take root. Since pines grow faster than cypress, they quickly take over and the cypress seedlings lose out. Conversely, flooding kills off the pine seedlings, giving the cypress a head start on life.

It is estimated that many of the cypress trees seen in Caddo Lake are hundreds of years old. The age of Caddo's cypress trees becomes important when we hear that the lake was formed by the historic New Madrid earthquakes, which vibrated many of the southern states in 1811–1812. (New Madrid is about sixty miles south of St. Louis.) Modern Richter-scale estimates exceed 9.0 points for this massive quake series, which actually did create Reelfoot Lake in Tennessee. But current theory is that the New Madrid quake served only to deepen Caddo Lake in places, enhancing its ecological richness, beauty, and usefulness.

It is believed Caddo Lake was formed by a natural occurrence taking place over hundreds, perhaps even thousands of years. Known as the Great Raft, millions of trees felled by nature washed down the Red River, causing flooding and creating wetlands wherever they clogged the waterway. The Great Raft forced water back into Caddo's tributaries. By 1836, Henry M. Shreve had snag-boated his way through the raft to present-day Shreveport. The raft above Shreveport opened on its own to admit steamboats up the Red River to Caddo Lake and Jefferson in the early 1840s. The removal of the Great Raft eventually drained the lakes and swamps of northwestern Louisiana. Caddo Lake was the only exception, and it would have drained away too, had it not been for a dam built in 1914, which was subsequently rebuilt. Today more than 40,000 acres of lake and cypress swamp remain, making it one of the most beautiful ecological areas in the world.

Although much of Caddo has been conserved, there are still many challenges. Fred Dahmer, author of *Caddo Was . . .* (1988), has lived in the Caddo area more than seventy years. He has spent much of his life fighting for the lake, the last twenty-five years in a pitched battled against Daingerfield Reach, a U.S. Army Corps of Engineers canal project that would have connected the Red River with the Lake o' the Pines, chewing a huge hole through the romantic beauty of Caddo Lake. The canal would have had a tremendous impact, necessitating the cutting of 10,000 to 12,000 acres of trees. Obviously, the canal was an awful idea that would have destroyed the Caddo ecosystem, and it's amazing how far such projects can go when politically driven, usually by some narrow special-interest group.

Until late 1992, fewer than five hundred acres of this biologically rich

Deliberation marks the Great Egret's stalking style, here waiting for a minnow to make a fatal error in a quiet Caddo cove. Texas Parks and Wildlife now manages seven thousand acres here as a state park and wildlife management area.

land was within state park boundaries, and Caddo Lake was very much a threatened ecosystem. For years, well-meaning state, federal, and private organizations tried to find a way to conserve more of the lake and swamp, but nothing ever seemed to be accomplished.

Caddo was, and is, a place accustomed to being left alone, truly isolated from many of the problems caused by humans. Even private owners with strong land ethics didn't invite outside help. But without outside partners, Caddo's way of life was destined to disappear altogether. Irreplaceable hardwoods were being cut at an alarming rate, often illegally by tree thieves. Timber rustlers are still a Pineywoods threat, illicitly whittling away $12 million a year in trees. Pileated Woodpeckers were being shot for sport. Habitat was shrinking for rare, threatened, and endangered plants, fish, and animals. The quality of life of Caddo Lake, the natural beauty that brought people there in the first place, was deteriorating rapidly.

Maybe it's not altogether coincidental that the Pileated Woodpecker was a symbol of warfare in American Indian cultures, perhaps because its measured hammering resounded like warlike drumbeats through the lake. These fastidious-looking red, white, and black birds are the largest

The measured drumbeats of feeding Pileated Woodpeckers are as much a part of the Pineywoods experience as the pines themselves. No matter how many you've seen, your next sighting of America's largest woodpecker will still startle.

of our woodpeckers, and at Caddo Lake, their senseless shootings inspired Robert McCurdy to finally take action.

In 1990, Caddo landowner McCurdy realized he needed help in preserving the Caddo ecosystem. McCurdy owned 471 acres up Kitchens Creek and on Goat Island on the north side of Caddo, and he spent much time there in his homemade shelter. When I first met McCurdy, in October 1992, he had just spent the night in this shelter, but it was no longer his. His donation to TNC of his 471 acres started a domino effect, the second tile being a bargain sale of another 589 acres to TNC. Soon the Conservancy had options to buy an additional 5,000 acres, and the Caddo Lake project was well on its way.

A mosaic of land had to be pieced together, small parcel after small parcel, to assemble this preserve. More than forty landowners of twenty-eight tracts were linked in the process. A key Nature Conservancy acquisition was the 3,600-acre Chew Estate, some of it purchased, some donated. Many partners were involved in the 7,000-acre conservation effort, with money donated from Ducks Unlimited and the U.S. Fish and Wildlife Service, in addition to donations of land and money raised by TNC.

"My interest in this when it all began was the waterfowl," said McCurdy. "This is one of the great roosting grounds for migratory waterfowl and also wood ducks. The lake's fingers and sloughs contain a lot of flooded water oak, an abundance of acorns. That's one of the principal feeding grounds for the ducks." McCurdy continued, "I hope Caddo can someday return to the spooky, mysterious wildness that haunted me."

The area will be known as the Caddo Lake State Park and Wildlife Management Area. It is to be operated by the Public Lands Division of the Texas Parks and Wildlife Department, but because partial funding came from waterfowl stamp income, waterfowl hunters and fishermen will be guaranteed access forever. Part of the state's investment will be reimbursed through the North American Wetlands Conservation Council.

Start a tour of the park with the exhibits in the visitor center, where information is furnished on Caddo flora. Plan time to walk the interpretive trails and nature trails. Canoe rentals are available in the state park, and canoeing is the best way to experience Caddo. As you canoe eastward from the original Caddo State Park, then north into the new preserve areas, notice the contrast between what is built up on the right bank of Big Cypress Bayou versus the almost primeval condition of the swamp on your left. You'll see loblolly and shortleaf pines mixed in with oaks, hickories, and other hardwoods.

An ideal way to develop your own sense of the new TPWD management area at Caddo Lake is to pack a picnic, then follow the main channel through Hell's Half Acre to Devils Elbow; you are now tracking through the center of the new preserve. Swing down through Alligator Bayou, where you may pause for your floating picnic, then on to Potter's Point, the eastern border of the preserve, where it reaches its highest ground. Someday, this will become one of the loveliest camping areas in Texas. Thanks to Robert McCurdy, Shaun Hamilton of The Nature Conservancy, Andy Sansom of Texas Parks and Wildlife, and thousands of other conservation-minded individuals, your great-grandchildren will be able to hear the music of the pines and the song of the water.

NATIONAL FORESTS OF EAST TEXAS

The Big Slough Wilderness, sadly, isn't big enough or deep enough for Ivory-billed Woodpeckers anymore, but it's still a special spot, with places that have never been logged and places for adventurous canoeists to nose into. Flower lovers may spy a water spider orchid, the rare green rein orchid, or uncommon green adder's mouth. But you won't see the ivorybill, thought extinct in this wet wilderness for many years.

Close to Big Slough, in the Ratcliff Lake Recreation Area of the Davy

Crockett National Forest one recent spring, I lingered near a mossy mound of bricks, unprepossessing but terrifyingly evocative of what had occurred here a little less than a century ago. This was the site of the Central Coal and Coke Company (4Cs) sawmill, which sang its song of wood against metal between 1902 and 1920 to the tune of 350,000 board feet a day. By 1917, the mill had processed all economically accessible timber that was greater than twelve inches in diameter. By 1920, the last whine of the saw-blade song was heard, the timber gone.

Although our national forests have many rare and endangered plants and animals, including the endangered Red-cockaded Woodpecker, on the more than 600,000 acres in Texas, much of the controversy that has swirled about the Spotted Owl in the Pacific Northwest has been avoided. The National Forest Service can take some credit here, as can our commercial timber interests, the TPWD, responsible conservation organizations, and enlightened politicians.

Our four national forests—Angelina, Davy Crockett, Sabine, and Sam Houston, which average more than 150,000 acres each—are located on land that nobody wanted in 1934, land that was for the most part logged or farmed-out barrens, or sloughs that were impossible to timber. Some of it had even been abandoned as worthless, and some confiscated for tax delinquencies. In 1934, the U.S. Forest Service began buying land and persuaded the Civilian Conservation Corps to conduct a massive reforestation program that lasted a decade. Now these forests contain three of the largest trees of their species found in the United States: a black hickory in Sabine, a barberry hawthorn in Angelina, and a black tupelo in Sam Houston. Two other trees share national honors, an American hawthorn in Angelina and a littlehip hawthorn in Sabine.

The multiple-use concept of the Forest Service requires that all uses of the forest—timber harvesting, mining, wildlife preservation, soil conservation, grazing, water uses, hunting, fishing, camping, hiking, recreation, and, yes, conservation—be given equal consideration. A study of six national forests in the Southeast, funded by the Wilderness Society, showed that gross annual timber sales totaled $32 million, less than a tenth of the $379 million in gross economic benefits associated with recreation and tourism. Under the leadership of Interior Secretary Bruce Babbitt and new chief Jack Ward Thomas, the Forest Service is making great progress toward a "whole ecosystem" conservation approach, similar to the bioreserve concept.

While the Forest Service is the official guardian of the national forests, Texas Parks and Wildlife also plays an important role. The TPWD has wildlife management areas within the forests, including Alabama Creek (Davy Crockett), Bannister (Angelina), and Moore Plantation (Sabine). It has restocked eastern Wild Turkey, which disappeared from the area in the forties because of land clearing, hunting, and egg predation by feral hogs.

Since the area was logged level before the thirties, even its wildest areas can lay claim to being only second- or third-growth southern forest. But don't kid yourself, the areas within these national forests that have been designated by the U.S. Congress as wilderness areas are *wild*. In all, more than 36,000 acres have been set aside or allowed to return to a wilderness state, and primitive hiking and camping in these areas, especially in the spring and fall, rank among the state's finest outdoor experiences. Just standing with your eyes closed in deep woods and inhaling the spicy scent of pine blended with floral and fern and woodsy essences will make you wish you had smelled the last of your city. And when your eyes open to a beauty I can't begin to describe, you may never leave!

Here another story began, one that has many heroes and will have more as our conservation ethic deepens. It is a story of enlightened companies that know that properly managed forests are one of the world's most important renewable natural resources. Such companies also understand the need to protect the unique natural vegetation, biological diversity, and wildlife of the forest through the concept of multiple use. Temple-Inland alone has acquired 1.85 million acres of forest, making this company the largest private landowner in Texas. Temple-Inland has invited The Nature Conservancy and other groups interested in forest ecosystems to participate on an advisory board to evaluate its practices.

Glenn A. Chancellor, an executive with Temple-Inland Forest Products Corporation and past president and executive committee member of the Texas Forestry Association, has been in forest management for decades. He says the company plants 25 million seedlings annually in reforestation programs. Chancellor recognizes that Temple-Inland has a major responsibility to "manage its forests in an environmentally appropriate way while satisfying the demands of its customers." This company's actions represent an excellent example of the balance that must be struck between economics and ecology. Chancellor reports that more than seven thousand acres of Red-cockaded Woodpecker habitat have been protected by the company and that special care is taken to conserve the increasingly rare bottomland hardwoods and river corridors that crisscross Temple-Inland holdings.

OPPOSITE PAGE
The 4Cs National Recreation Trail rambles through twenty miles of the heart of the Davy Crockett National Forest. Stroll the trail in early April to experience your private dogwood festival.

As far as I can determine, an important forest-products economy is coexisting with ecosystems that are basically healthy. No one questions that there is more work to be done to conserve the biological diversity of the Pineywoods. But the good news is that I believe there is a tacit commitment from all parties involved to create a Pineywoods bioreserve stretching into Louisiana that will conserve the best of this "last great place."

DAVY CROCKETT NATIONAL FOREST

Ratcliff, settled in 1875 by a thirty-two-wagon train of Georgians, is now a tiny village buried in national forest. But in 1910, more than seventeen thousand loggers and their families were living here, working to supply the 4Cs sawmill. All of this is hard to imagine as you hike the twenty-mile 4Cs National Recreation Trail through Davy Crockett National Forest in late March or early April. Your journey leads you under an incredible, seemingly endless bower of dogwood blooms, where light refracts from iridescent petals like starbursts against the intense green of the pines. To the north, in Palestine, a dogwood festival is in progress, but the real show is blooming here in the Pineywoods. The trail begins at the Ratcliff Recreation Area, itself a delightful camping and picnicking location, complete with interpretive trails. Woodpeckers are the birds of choice along the trail. You are likely to hear the forest-vibrating rattle of a Pileated or even spot a Red-cockaded. Vireos, nuthatches, and warblers flit through the spring woods, and the hawk you spot will likely be a Red-shouldered, as these like to hunt over the bottomland hardwood corridors. The trail climbs to a marvelous panoramic view of the forest at 600-foot-high Neches Bluff.

SAM HOUSTON NATIONAL FOREST

The length of the Lone Star Trail from one side of Sam Houston National Forest to the other will give you some idea of what more than 150,000 acres can encompass—140 miles of wonderful ecological diversity. In fact, a 26-mile stretch of the trail, which begins at FM 945, has been designated a national recreational trail because of the biological diversity on the edges of Double Lake and in the Big Creek Scenic Area. The Big Creek Scenic Area greets the wildlife viewer with a variety of forest life all the way from swamp rabbits and squirrels to armadillos, raccoons, and white-tailed deer. Migrating warblers and butterflies flash through the trails. Toads, frogs, and salamanders populate the clear stream that runs through the area.

ANGELINA NATIONAL FOREST

The 1964 U.S. Wilderness Act defined wilderness as an area "where the earth and its community of life are untrammeled by man . . . where man himself is a visitor who does not remain . . . which has outstanding opportunities for solitude or a primitive and unconfined type of recreation." The act, more poetic than most congressional tomes, well describes the two magnificent wilderness areas within Angelina National Forest, Upland Hill with 12,650 acres and Turkey Hill with 5,286 acres. The TPWD has the responsibility for establishing and enforcing hunting and fishing regulations within these areas, and Turkey Hill is within the Bannister Wildlife Management Area. Both areas have extensive longleaf pine communities, which are a delight to stroll through.

In the bottomlands, your spring stroll will be under a leafy canopy, and the Turkey Creek bottoms are lush with what seems to be almost all species of the hundreds of trees and flowers of the Pineywoods, including such rare delights as Indian pinks and wild iris and not-so-rare but strikingly beautiful spider lilies. White-tailed deer have made a great comeback in East Texas, nowhere so evident as in this area, where tracks reveal a large population. Some say too large and predict a die-off of the deer herd in the mid-nineties.

Another one of a total of seven recreation sites within the forest is a lovely area called Boykin Springs. All 300 acres are great for spotting the Red-cockaded Woodpecker along with Pine Warblers and Bachman's Sparrows. Pitcher plants can be discovered throughout the year. The 5.5-mile Sawmill Hiking Trail originates in Boykin and ends at Bouton Lake. More than ten species of warblers can be found nesting along the trail in the spring. About halfway along the Sawmill Trail is a waterfall that typically displays a parasol of wild azaleas. A loop off the trail will take you to another old sawmill, the Aldridge, which was the 4Cs of this area, responsible for most of the deforestation in the early 1900s.

A special area is located just three miles from the bottomland inundated by the creation of Sam Rayburn Reservoir, southwest of the lake. These are oak and hickory woodlands known as the Black Branch Barrens. This area has not been disturbed and is noted for its rare plants. The Black Branch Barrens cover about half a square mile and feature small, stunted blackjack and post oak trees scattered across the prairies and glades. Nature Conservancy and TPWD botanists have identified a number of plants that are rare in East Texas, including the flowing white orchid Navasota ladies' tresses, bright yellow golden hedge hyssop, and the lavender gayfeather. Rare plants recorded include Drummond's sandwort, least daisy, San Saba pinweed, Nuttall's milk vetch, western dandelion, and Texas saxifrage. The key to this special place is that the trees and shrubs are not only stunted but also far enough apart to provide areas with little shade, favoring the growth of prairie species, in contrast to the surrounding heavily wooded areas. The Nature Conservancy ranks such barrens as threatened around the world.

SABINE NATIONAL FOREST

There are five recreation areas within the Sabine National Forest, a special one being the Ragtown area in the northern section (off FM 3184 on Forest Route 132). This area is located on a high bluff facing east, making it a marvelous place for a dawn cup of coffee. A nature trail wends through the forest of beech, oak, and pine.

Hidden along the western bank of Toledo Bend Lake, buried within the Sabine National Forest is another special wilderness area, 11,946 acres called Indian Mounds. American beech and southern magnolia

A nectar secreted along the top edge of the yellow-green leaf of the rare pitcher plant attracts insects. Minute, downward-pointing hairs inside the leaf tube allow entrance but never egress. A liquid at the base is quite effective at digesting the insect prey of this carnivorous plant.

trees thrive here, although the species are listed as threatened by the Texas Natural Heritage Program. Forest flower lovers will delight in the violets and Carolina jasmine of spring, and you're likely to spy a rare wild orchid such as coralroot or green adder's mouth. April flower seekers may hit floral gold by coming upon the rare yellow lady's slipper orchid, which so resembles its name in shape and royal golden color. This is the largest and showiest orchid in East Texas and western Louisiana, according to field botanist and writer Geyata Ajilvsgi.

Indian Mounds Wilderness is the principal battleground for the ongoing confrontation between the forest-products industry, environmentalists, and the U.S. Forest Service over a beetle about half the size of an uncooked grain of brown rice. Widespread infestations occur about every seven to ten years, and 1993–1994 were peak years. That these southern pine beetles are devastating to pine trees is unchallengeable. I grew up in pine country and remember my forester friends speaking in awed tones of tall pines killed in four or five days by these 50-million-year-old insects. The glistening, chocolate-brown beetles fly through the Pineywoods until they connect with an aged or lightning-weakened tree. They then exude pheromones to bring in a hundred thousand or so hungry friends, all boring into the bark, eating the cambium between the bark and the wood, forcing out resin as they dine. The resin drys to a hard white glob, known to foresters as popcorn. Popcorn trees can be easily spotted, and are doomed.

In 1985, the year the wilderness areas of East Texas were so designated by Congress, southern pine beetles chewed up $50 million worth of

Pineywoods timber. Common sense tells me that the beetles may spread to commercial pine forests outside the wilderness areas despite buffer zones cut by the Forest Service. The issue is that legal action resulting from environmental impact statements for these wilderness areas prevents the USDA Forest Service from cutting to control the infestation within the protected areas. Done at an earlier stage, this works very well; the beetles can gain the upper hand if they are allowed to infest large tracts.

Some environmental groups, including the Sierra Club, Texas Committee on Natural Resources, and the Wilderness Society, want to stop the Forest Service from cutting any trees in wilderness areas. To me, the logic is flawed. These forests are not true wilderness but rather second or third growth, and the beetles do threaten the livelihood of private landowners and forest industry employees. Dr. Ron Billings, principal entomologist for the Texas Forest Service, agrees and has attempted to get the USDA Forest Service to modify the effects of the environmental impact statement that currently restrict prompt and timely beetle control within wilderness.

The beetle battle rages on, with no one giving an inch. A conservationist who believes in sustainable natural resources (and the forests are this planet's best example of same) would hold the position that early control efforts make sense. The pine beetles are a problem today because there are too many pine trees, and the bugs are simply eating their way toward a balanced ecosystem, one that existed 150 years ago. But the ecosystem has been irreversibly altered by humankind, for our other needs, and these needs must be factored in.

THE BIG THICKET NATIONAL BIOLOGICAL PRESERVE

The Big Thicket has been referred to as the biological crossroads of America. It was designated a United Nations biosphere reserve in 1981. It is rich in diversity and, because of the edges throughout the thicket, is a real testing ground even for trained biologists and botanists. The Big Thicket is bounded by blackland prairies and post oak savanna on the north and west and on the south by the coastal plain with its coastal and tropical species. Many animals and plants from different regions live together here. Further intriguing the experts are numerous relict plants, once spread throughout the South's mixed forests but now pretty well limited to survival in the Big Thicket because of its special soil and climate conditions, such as relative humidity averaging 75 percent and annual rainfall ranging from fifty inches in the north to sixty inches in the south.

The Big Thicket lies in a basin, the Neches River on the east and the Trinity River on the west, with only about 300,000 acres remaining of the original 3 million. It is a place where visitors can gain an appreciation of the concept of plant associations.

The principal plant associations found in the Big Thicket include sweet gum–oak floodplain, known as bottoms; palmetto-oak flats, which are found buried deep in the southernmost part of the Thicket in wild, inaccessible areas; bay–gallberry holly bogs, where some of the rarest of the flowering plants can be found in these complex, diverse habitats; longleaf–black gum savannas, grassy flat areas with the magnificent longleaf pines widely spaced; and longleaf-bluestem uplands, where the few remaining stately longleaf pines struggle for existence.

We owe the Ice Age for much of the patchwork of habitats of the Big Thicket. Glaciers pushed many plants and animals from the southwestern deserts, central plains, eastern forests, Appalachians, and southeastern swamps into the area. After the glaciers retreated, many species continued to live in pockets of suitable habitat within the Thicket, and consequently the area is considered North America's best-furnished ecological laboratory.

Wildlife once abundant in this area included black bear, cougar, red wolf, even the jaguar, the endangered Red-cockaded Woodpecker, the Ivory-billed Woodpecker (now extinct in North America), and the Carolina Parakeet (also extinct). Large flocks of Passenger Pigeons used to visit the Thicket each fall; the last large flights were in the 1880s. In 1914, the last Passenger Pigeon died in the Cincinnati Zoo. Thicket meat hunters managed to kill their share of the pigeons, usually by clubbing them to death on their night roosts.

Today, 300 species of birds frequent the Thicket, along with 50 species of reptiles, 60 types of mammals, 200 types of trees and wild shrubs, and more than 1,000 species of other flowering plants. The Thicket even has plants that eat insects, and four of the five kinds of carnivorous plants found in the United States are found here: pitcher plant, bladderwort, butterwort, and sundew.

One of the great attractions of the Big Thicket is the once abundant Red-cockaded Woodpecker, which may become an important part of the Thicket's salvation since it is protected under the Endangered Species Act. Clear-cutting and pine-plantation planting seriously depleted the population. The Red-cockaded Woodpecker needs large, mature pine trees. The bird's strategy is to drill many holes below and even around the den hole. The resulting resin flow, produced only by certain mature trees, then confounds the bird's enemies, especially when the resin is fresh and gummy. A key, then, to the survival of the Red-cockaded Woodpecker is the existence of large, mature pines, especially the longleaf.

Forested corridors follow many of the rivers and streams that wind through the Thicket, connecting some of the preserve areas. Each unit within the preserve has something special to offer. But perhaps the most special thing of all is what happens to your mind when you are immersed in the Thicket. The word "mysterious" is often used to describe the Thicket, but I think it's the wrong word. "Mysterious" often means unnatural. This is one of the most natural places in the world, and maybe that's the problem with those of us who spend so much of our time in cities. We really cannot comprehend the natural richness of the Thicket and tend, therefore, to view it as unfathomable, magical, cryptic, even scary. When you're deep in the Thicket, your city instincts become discordant, and that *is* a strange feeling. You should always be prepared in Texas with sunscreen and insect repellent, and in the Thicket you will need a compass too. You can get completely turned around—lost except for the fact that you can eventually walk out in any direction—and the sensation is one of near panic, the reaction of a person well out of tune with nature. The Thicket is an ideal area to sharpen your conservation ethic, since it is so fragile, so precious, and irreplaceable.

One instinct you'll find hard to overcome is the impulse to kill a poisonous snake, such as a copperhead in the wooded areas or a moccasin by the waterways. The first time a Texan lets such a snake live in peace is, for most of us, a singular event. And resist the temptation to wander off the trails and paths. The environment is so fragile that even your tracks will do damage.

That portion of the Big Thicket protected within the federal nature preserve is only about 85,000 acres, scattered through eight units and four water corridors. This preserve came about, after a half-century battle between conservationists and commercial interests, in 1974 when our nation's first national biological preserve was created. In the early nineties, the House Interior Committee approved a bill to enlarge the Big Thicket National Preserve by almost 16,000 acres. This land was located within the Davy Crockett and Sabine national forests. The acreage was to be obtained in two ways: more than 10,000 acres would come from three timber companies, and the rest would be purchased from private landowners.

As part of your new conservation ethic, remember to respect the rules of the Big Thicket National Preserve. All plants and animals are protected within the preserve. You are not allowed to collect *any* specimens. Pack out whatever you pack in and do not litter. Fires, vehicles, and pets are not allowed in the backcountry portion of the Thicket.

Units with developed facilities are scattered throughout the preserve area and include Turkey Creek Unit, with a fifteen-mile trail running north-south, which begins at FM 1943 and goes through a former pine plantation. The trail takes you through an area of incredible diversity, including representatives of southwestern desert plant life and subtropical species. On the northeast is a boardwalk (accessible to handicapped persons) through the carnivorous plant area called the Pitcher Plant Trail.

One of the rare plants found at TNC's Sandylands Sanctuary is the Texas trailing phlox, endemic to southeastern Texas. The plant is on the federal endangered species list.

This trail enters an open savanna that is home to the four carnivorous plants and many of the wildflowers of the Big Thicket. The pitcher plant (family Sarraceniaceae) is most evident when its showy, solitary yellow flower blooms in late March and early April. Its long, funnel-shaped leaves are what the botanists call a pitfall trap. The plant's nectar attracts insects to the opening, and once inside, downward pointing hairs on the inner surface of the tube prevent escape. The pitcher plant then digests the hapless insect, giving the plant increased vigor and rate of growth. The plants are much more rare now because so much suitable habitat has been lost to drainage ditches, livestock grazing, and fire suppression. In the absence of fire, taller plants spread into the wetlands and shade out the pitcher plants. When I last visited the Pitcher Plant Trail, I noted that the National Park staff had burned right to the edge of the savanna containing the largest population of pitcher plants, even scorching a few in their effort to save the many.

Boating and canoeing are available at locations along the Neches River, Pine Island Bayou, Village Creek, and Turkey Creek, and fishing is allowed.

Three Indian tribes are usually associated with the Big Thicket: the mound-building Caddos from 800 B.C., the cannibalistic Atakapans, and the peaceful Alabama-Coushatta, newcomers who didn't arrive until around 1800. In 1854, the state purchased 1,110 acres in Polk County as a reservation for the Alabama, which you can visit today. It's a worthwhile visit, offering a chance to gain American Indian insights into the Pineywoods, to learn about their culture, and to watch the artisans at work. This tribe is known for its intricately woven pine-needle basketry.

OPPOSITE PAGE
This longleaf pine at The Nature Conservancy's Sandylands Sanctuary relied on fire for its start in life. Prescribed burnings in the sanctuary suppress an understory of grasses and shrubs that may have prevented the pine's seedling from growing.

ROY E. LARSEN SANDYLANDS SANCTUARY

This Nature Conservancy preserve is situated in the Big Thicket along an 8.5-mile stretch of Village Creek, a major tributary of the Neches River. Canoeing Village Creek in the spring is a lovely way to tour the sanctuary and to see areas inaccessible by land. Sandylands Sanctuary encompasses the topographical transition from stream and riparian forest to upland pine habitats and includes excellent examples of the floodplain, baygall, and successional pond communities. The preserve has an accessible trail system and complements the Big Thicket National Preserve. The coarse, sandy soil drains water quickly, creating ideal habitat for longleaf pines, cactus, and other fire-tolerant plants. A range of plant communities is found here; bald cypress, tupelo, and baygall are common along the river. There is a great diversity of wildflowers within the preserve, particularly in the spring after a prescribed burn. The preserve is a critical spring waystation for northbound neotropicals and year-round range for a descent of woodpeckers, including Northern Flicker, Red-bellied, Golden-fronted, Red-headed, Downy, Hairy, and the endangered Red-cockaded. Winter months bring others to this ideal woodpecker habitat.

The very existence of the sanctuary speaks to the key point of partnerships that involve private land ownership, conservation groups, and state and federal agencies. Arthur Temple, founder of the giant forest-products company Temple-Inland, used to drive through the Big Thicket just to see the huge old-growth trees. But he was torn between his love for the trees and a distaste for selling forest lands to the federal government as the Big Thicket preserve was being formed. His solution was to make a memorial donation of land to The Nature Conservancy in the name of a friend, Time-Life board chairman Roy E. Larsen. In 1993, Temple-Inland donated 3,400 acres of land and conservation easements to almost double the size of the sanctuary. This addition provided a horseshoe-shaped buffer around the Sandylands Sanctuary. Temple-Inland will research restoration of longleaf pine habitat in the area, complementing the work being done at Sandylands.

The sanctuary is a core preserve in The Nature Conservancy's huge Pineywoods bioreserve project. The conservation story will be won or lost here based on the interaction of the Forest Service with private landowners. Today there is an opportunity for change, and more than a million acres in some of the most diverse areas can be managed for both the economy's and the environment's benefit.

East Texas native Ike McWhorter of The Nature Conservancy staff has been involved in restoration of the longleaf pine communities for many years, which I think makes him as important to the Big Thicket as the longleaf pine he so jealously protects. The longleaf pine ecosystem has a number of other systems embedded within it, such as floodplain forest, baygall, and succession ponds. The Sandylands Sanctuary is unusual in this respect. The longleaf pine community here is one of the driest of such systems in East Texas. It's called the longleaf pine sandhill. This longleaf system relies on fire to maintain its character. Fire controls hardwood and shrub encroachment and maintains the open savanna. TNC uses prescribed burning to keep the area open and to allow an understory of grasses and herbaceous species, which can survive only in a fire-maintained environment and can't survive under a dense canopy of hardwood trees. The fire doesn't kill off the mature hardwoods; there will always be a mix of hardwoods, particularly in the bottomlands, which normally don't burn.

There are several rare species of plants in the Sandylands, including *Gaillardia aestivalis* var. *winkleri,* commonly called white fire wheel; *Silene subciliata,* known as scarlet catchfly; *Amsonia glaberrima,* known as smooth bluestar; and *Phlox nivalis* ssp. *texensis,* called Texas trailing phlox, which is on both the federal and state endangered species lists.

RARE BIRD ALERT

Up-to-date information on rare-bird sightings for the Pineywoods may be obtained by calling the rare bird alert number for the upper Texas coast, also known as the Lone Star Rare Bird Alert or the Texas Rare Bird Alert, 713-992-2757 (sponsored by the Houston Audubon Society). Additional information for the remaining ecological areas of the state is provided in the report.

"A SEA OF PALE GREEN" THE POST OAK SAVANNA, BLACKLAND PRAIRIES, AND CROSS TIMBERS

CHAPTER 4

We came to-day upon the first prairie of any extent, and shortly after crossed the Trinity River. After having been shut in during so many days by dreary winter forests, we were quite exhilarated at coming out upon an open country and a distant view. During the whole day's ride the soil improved, and the country grew more attractive. Small prairies alternated agreeably with post-oak woods.

FREDERICK LAW OLMSTED
A Journey through Texas, 1857

THE POST OAK SAVANNA

The Post Oak Savanna that Olmsted entered was one of the earliest regions of Texas to be settled by Americans. This area is approximately 8.5 million acres and is a transitional area between forest and the Blackland Prairies to the west. There is not a clear line of demarcation, but as you drive from east to west out of the Pineywoods the oaks become more evident; you are traveling along a forest-to-prairie continuum, most often canopied but varied because of the intermixing of forest, savanna, wetlands, and prairie. The flora features mid-American oak-hickory forest, and today there are many more trees than in 1900; many of the new additions are mesquite.

At the Pineywood edge the communities are so interwoven that it is difficult to separate them. An example of the transition diversity is Little Sandy, a private 3,800-acre tract of virgin bottomland near Hawkins. The tract boasts at least one national record tree (the bottomland oak) and three state record trees (the black gum, green ash, and Shumard oak). To delight the botanist, this bottomland has the thickest growth of palmetto seen in East Texas. The land has been protected by a conservation easement granted to the U.S. Fish and Wildlife Service because of its unique natural habitat.

OPPOSITE PAGE
The Nature Conservancy's Lennox Woods preserve shelters one of the best remaining old-growth mixed pine and hardwood forests in America and the many rare species of plants and animals found there. Never logged, it includes post oaks (similar to this one) nearly 300 years old and even a loblolly pine aged 140 years.

Elevation in the Post Oak Savanna ranges from 300 to 800 feet. Annual rainfall is thirty-five to forty-five inches, with the rainy season in May and June. The distinctive soils of this area have paid a dear price for being so attractive to farmers. Much of the area has been cultivated, and soil erosion is rampant.

The Texas Post Oak Savanna is an important part of a vast expanse that once intertwined with the prairies all the way to the Great Lakes and into Canada. Nature Conservancy botanists estimate that oak savannas once covered 30 million acres of the midwestern United States. Only about 1 percent remains.

Private landowners will be the key to the needlepoint stitching that must be accomplished if the ecosystem is to survive. Many private farms and timber lots contain degraded savanna that can be restored as buffers without interfering with economic uses of the land. The Nature Conservancy believes that as much as 5 to 10 percent of the original savanna can be restored.

Savanna settlers came from Missouri, Georgia, Alabama, Mississippi, Tennessee, and Kentucky in the 1830s and began growing corn and garden produce. However, cotton soon became king as settlers moved in from lands to the east already depleted by cotton farming.

David Diamond of the Texas Natural Heritage Program explains the relationship of the Post Oak Savanna and the Blackland Prairies: "The prairies are more fertile, yet initially were harder to plow because they were clay soils, and so they were not plowed as quickly as the Post Oak Savanna. A lot of the savannas were plowed. They grew cotton or other crops, and the soil wore out quickly because it wasn't as fertile as the Blackland Prairies. Later on, when the prairies were plowed, the Post Oak Savanna went back into rangeland of some sort and today is no longer plowed.

"Not all the Post Oak Savanna—and to the west, the Cross Timbers—were plowed, because in many areas it was hard to remove the timber and the soil wasn't quite as fertile. Once the settlers got to the Blackland and figured out how to plow it, the prairies were soon almost all in cultivation. It wasn't just a sea of grass in the Blackland Prairies, and it wasn't just a sea of savanna in the Post Oak Savanna and the Cross Timbers. There were grass and woods in the prairies, and there were grass and woods in the savanna and Cross Timbers." Dr. Diamond explains that the plowing of the prairies made them productive croplands. Speaking of the owners, he says, "You've got to put the land you own to use; you've got to make money to pay taxes and send your kids to college, have a nice house, and so on. But I think it would not hurt society to go ahead and conserve what remains of the Blackland Prairies and restore some viable, functioning prairies and savannas and Cross Timbers, too."

LENNOX WOODS

This 366-acre Nature Conservancy preserve is located in the Post Oak Savanna ecological area in Red River County, about ten miles north of Clarksville on Pecan Bayou. The preserve was donated to TNC by the Lennox family of Clarksville and the Lennox Foundation. Lennox Woods is an excellent old-growth woodland containing mockernut hickory, shortleaf and loblolly pine, and a variety of oaks, including white oak, post oak, water oak, willow oak, bur oak, southern red oak, and overcup oak. There's a post oak nearly 300 years old and a loblolly pine that's 140 years old. The preserve contains dry upland forest that slopes gradually downward to a flat bottomland containing Pecan Bayou, an intermittent watercourse that forms the current southern boundary of the property. The preserve contains the best remaining example of mesic upland mixed pine-hardwood forest, a forest once characteristic of northeastern Texas, southern Arkansas, northern Louisiana, and extreme southeastern Oklahoma. The preserve has not been logged, and it boasts a long list of rare species of plants and animals. Rare mammals include river otter and eastern big-ear bat. Rare birds include Bachman's Sparrow, Piping Plover, American Swallow-tailed Kite, Merlin, Peregrine Falcon, Bald Eagle, Wood Stork, Red-cockaded Woodpecker, and interior Least Tern. Ongoing botanical surveys have turned up scores of rare plants, including two species previously unknown in Texas, hooked buttercup (*Ranunculus recurvatus*) and caric sedge (*Carex artitecta*).

This preserve also protects an old-growth, bottomland hardwood forest associated with Pecan Bayou. Since there is no upstream dam, the bottomland forest remains viable with a relatively natural hydrologic regime. Several old oxbow sloughs provide habitat diversity within the bottomland. In addition to its old-growth character, this bottomland forest remnant shelters the state's only known population of Arkansas meadow rue (*Thalictrum arkansanum*).

Lennox Woods is an extraordinary example of an undisturbed, old-growth forest with rich herbaceous flora. It has tremendous ecological significance. Lennox Woods is also a fine example of individual and community action, which, with TNC, preserved an important ecological site. A great deal of pride and interest in the well-being of the preserve are obvious in nearby communities.

LAKE SOMERVILLE STATE RECREATION AREA

The White-eyed Vireo scolded in greeting from the dense yaupon thicket, his yellow eye circles, like reading glasses, a sure field mark to differentiate him from the federally listed Black-capped Vireo I sought. The thick undergrowth of native yaupon is one of the features of lovely Lake Somerville, nested in the undulating Post Oak Savanna

The Bald Eagle has made a dramatic comeback in most of North America, and Texas winters are now graced by large and increasing populations. Many utility power plant lakes such as the one at Fairfield Lake have become popular eagle rookeries, where the magnificent birds of prey are easy to locate even for amateur birders.

near Brenham. Early Anglo settlers used yaupon leaves to make a passable tea.

There are two park units at Lake Somerville, one at Birch Creek, with 3,140 acres, and the other at Nails Creek, 2,830 acres. The park is right on the edge of where the Gulf Prairies ecological area gives way to the Post Oak Savanna. As always, the edge helps explain why the park has such an abundance of different types of animals and plants, as the prairies are interspersed with dense groves of blackjack, post oak, hickory, and other hardwoods.

Late winter and early spring add more than sixty birds to the watch list, including spectacular Bald and Golden eagles. Ospreys and Sandhill Cranes plus brightly colored spring migrants such as Painted Buntings are found here, and this is a good time to find both Red-breasted and White-breasted nuthatches.

This park offers one of the longest and loveliest trails in the TPWD system. The 22.6-mile Somerville trailway wends through some five thousand acres of post oak environment and is underutilized except by white-tailed deer, coyotes, squirrels, raccoons, foxes, feral hogs, cottontail rabbits, and other mammals. The summer months will reward hikers with cool, shady, canopied trails and lots of Turk's cap, partridge pea, Indian blanket, purple bindweed, prickly poppy, and bright clumps of orange trumpet creeper. In April and May the trail is awash in the vibrant floral palette of scarlet and orange Indian paintbrush, brilliant yellow swaths of coreopsis, pink evening primrose and phlox, and, you guessed it, bluebonnets. A rainy winter assures a breathtaking wildflower display.

Just a little more than two miles beyond the Nails Creek trailhead, you reach a hiker-only trail that leads northeast around Flag Pond, past the primitive Mill Pond campsite. Flag Pond is usually covered in fall with flocks of egrets, Great Blue Herons, geese, and even White Pelicans; you can gain a good viewing prospect from the levee on the north side of the pond.

FAIRFIELD LAKE STATE PARK

This is one of the state's largest Bald Eagle rookeries, and eagles are readily seen all winter long since the lake plays host to more than twenty annually. A tour is offered from November through February. During a recent late February visit, we watched what park rangers believed was the last of the majestic winter Texans, a mature Bald Eagle, pack up and head north. Nearby tanks sported rafts of Canvasbacks and several varieties of diving ducks, such as Bufflehead and Lesser Scaup. The best eagle viewing in this 1,400-acre state park is from a tour boat operated by park personnel, but the eagles can also be viewed with scopes and binoculars from the shoreline. Look across the lake from the boat launch area toward the warm-water discharge of the Texas Utility power plant. Reservoirs serving power plants as heat exchangers are especially attractive to the fish-loving Bald Eagles. More than eight hundred now migrate to Texas between October and November. A bird-watcher trail has been installed, replete with feeders and benches angled back for easy glimpsing. White-tailed deer can also be seen throughout the oak-hickory forests and around the lake. Try any of the more than six miles of hiking trails among the dogwoods in the spring for a beautiful walk. An unusual feature of this lake is that it contains a good population of redfish.

PALMETTO STATE PARK

In sharp contrast to most of the rest of the Post Oak Savanna, this park looks more like a southeastern swamp, and it sounds like one, too, as Pileated Woodpeckers commonly drum visitors into the park. Texas continues to surprise by inserting a tropical site within a prairie ecosystem. Palmetto State Park is situated in the Ottine Swamp and takes its name from the dwarf palmetto, which grows wild in the park. The park is a classic ecotone, where eastern plants meet western, and this edge produces the expected diversity of wildlife, especially birds, with 240 species recorded within the park confines. On a late winter visit just before a norther blew in, I watched a skein of Sandhill Cranes circle the park, gaining altitude to overfly the front. This is a maneuver accompanied by much crane communication, a haunting, almost alarming sound. The green tree frog and Gulf Coast toad are abundant, and reptiles include the green anole (chameleon) and ground skink. It's a beautiful place for a picnic, featuring an enchanting hiking trail decorated by ferns and palmettos that wanders 1.7 miles among the 264 acres.

THE BLACKLAND PRAIRIES

O, the glorious beauty of that scene. Fancy would in vain attempt to paint it! Below, stretching for twenty-five miles in length, and twelve in breadth, lay a sea of pale green, hemmed in by timber of a darker hue; flowers of every variety, shade and form, interspersed over the surface; a dark green belt of verdure here and there, making the ravines and water courses, and groves of trees, or clumps, or single trees, scattered in such perfect arrangement over the whole, as to seem as though some eminent artist had perfected the work.

W. B. PARKER
summer and fall 1854, notes taken during the expedition commanded by Capt. R. B. Marcy, *Through Unexplored Texas*

The Blackland Prairies ecosystem extends from San Antonio to the Red River and overlaps the Post Oak Savanna. But the tallgrass prairies as described by Parker, undulating in the almost constant winds of the plains, are mostly gone, save for a few carefully preserved remnants, which, if you hold your head just right, let you imagine what the men of Marcy's expedition saw a century ago. Parker quotes from an ox driver on the expedition, "Oh, if I was only a *lawyer*, how I could talk about such a sight as this, but I haven't the *larnin'* to say what I want." Parker notes that "any man who could gaze upon and not admire a scene like this, must be wanting in the very elements of the division between human and animal." Parker was speaking to the conservation ethic, to why today The Nature Conservancy has made such a vigorous effort to preserve at least the remnants of the original prairie. In the spring, maybe even a lawyer would have the instinctive larnin' to stand in awe of the wild prairie flowers and tall grasses.

When Texas entered the Union, it was the largest prairie state, and 12 million acres of prairie were located in the Blackland area alone. Like all the prairie communities of North America, and like the buffalo and plains wolf, the native grasses are almost all gone. The awesome, original Blackland Prairies, through which Indians pursued antelope less than two hundred years ago, are now reduced in Texas to less than

5,000 acres. Although the tallgrass prairies flowed from Texas all the way into Canada, encompassing some thirteen states and more than 142 million acres, the physiographic region we now call the Blackland Prairies stops at the Red River.

The prairie has four dominant species: big bluestem (turkeyfoot), little bluestem, Indian grass, and switchgrass. All begin growth in the spring and mature in late summer and early fall. Big bluestem can reach heights greater than eight feet and is excellent for grazing. After all, the prairie once fed millions of buffalo.

The Blackland Prairies consist of three basic types of communities. The upland areas with loamy soils are covered with tall dropseed, switchgrass, and sedges. The clay-soil uplands and clay lowlands feature grama grass, switchgrass, and Indian grass. The rest of the uplands throughout the area support plant communities of big bluestem, little bluestem, and Indian grass.

The original prairies saw much fire, started either naturally by lightning or by Indians seeking to drive game, principally buffalo, in a hunt. With the coming of the white people fires were controlled, but without fire the prairie, paradoxically, can be destroyed. This destruction comes from the invasion of woody plants, trees such as mesquite, and brushy undergrowth. Prescribed burns, among other management tools, are used to maintain the last few remnants of prairie.

The once vast expanse of prairie could not withstand the human hand holding a plow. The plow cut the tallgrass roots like Delilah sheared Samson's hair and strength, because it was the root structure, deeper than the tallgrass was high, that sustained the prairies. The small patches that remain were preserved as hay meadows by the original settlers. Those settlers knew from experience how nutritious these rich native grasses were, so they reserved the meadows for grazing and hay production. Botanists estimate that there were from 200 to 300 native plant species in the prairie, with some varieties waving eight feet in the air sustained by root systems sixteen feet deep.

The subterranean elements of the prairie are as diverse as those above. These are soils that are deep and black, a clay deposit filled with organic matter. Soils have intricate profiles, defined not just by chemical composition but also by linkages analogous to those of the human body. As a human transforms food, soils transform earth, air, fire, and water to provide sustenance for all life. Wendell Berry writes with insight about our soils in *The Unsettling of America* (1977), "It is the nature of the soil to be highly complex and variable, to conform very inexactly to human conclusions and rules. It is itself easily damaged by the imposition of alien patterns. Out of the random grammar and lexicon of possibilities—geographical, topographical, climatological, biological—the soil of any one place makes its own peculiar and inevitable sense. It is impossible to contemplate the life of the soil for very long without seeing it as analogous to the life of the spirit."

Soil scientists have identified more than fourteen thousand soils, each with its own distinctive profile, made up of layers called horizons. The soils of the Blackland Prairies are special; found only here and rich in carbon dioxide is an assemblage of horizons perched high upon bedrock, which once nurtured a rich diversity of grasses over millions of acres of prairie.

When humans disturb the prairie by plowing we not only tear up the root system but also start killing off the microorganisms, bacteria, and fungi, making the soil sterile. We don't realize how incredibly infertile a great deal of farmland has become. There is a lot of land in North Texas that never should have been plowed. Add the problem of erosion, and we wind up with land totally worthless for agriculture.

Native grasslands have all but disappeared in the United States. While the agricultural yield that resulted in the prairie's destruction has been extremely beneficial, creating the world's breadbasket, we must beware the loss of diversity. The wild grasses contain the genetic materials to protect our grazing lands as sustainable natural resources forever.

Within a few hours' driving distance from the Dallas–Fort Worth metroplex is one of The Nature Conservancy's national conservation efforts, the Tallgrass Prairie Preserve, northwest of Tulsa in Osage County, Oklahoma. This is one of the last great stretches of tallgrass left in America. It's more than a sea of grass. It's a complete ecosystem, a cycle of life that requires at least the 32,000-acre preserve to function.

This is a massive effort to recreate the living prairie, complete with the buffalo that were abundant more than 160 years ago. The seed stock of buffalo, some 300 head, was donated by Ken-Ada Ranches, International, of Bartlesville, Oklahoma. This is a complete herd, from calves to breeding stock, and is expected to grow to 1,800 by the year 2000. Towering bluestem grass, blankets of prairie wildflowers, and the raptors of the plains are thriving on the prairie there once again. In addition to TNC efforts and public support, corporations like Miller Brewing Company, Kerr McGee, and the Williams Companies have committed time, talent, and millions of dollars to preserve the natural functions of the Tallgrass Prairie.

The Tallgrass Prairie Preserve features self-guided nature trails that are ideal outdoor laboratories for learning prairie ecology. This is a place of majestic beauty, especially when the rising sun sets the grasses ablaze in waves of gold. It also has an interesting history of use, since about 1000 B.C. by the Caddos up to its recent occupation by the Osage nation.

Fire is the friend of prairies, stemming the incursion of woody plants, brush, and trees and providing fertilizer for new growth. Fire ecology is one of The Nature Conservancy's most important tools in maintaining its tallgrass preserve systems.

When Congress killed the high-physics superconducting super collider in 1994 The Nature Conservancy proposed a prairie restoration project for the ten-thousand-acre site near Waxahachie. The restoration would take decades and utilize seeds from TNC's protected Blackland Prairie sites. It would be the largest prairie restoration project in the United States, and eventually buffalo could be reintroduced.

Today, prairies don't get the support that other ecological areas receive, because from the road, the land is just not that attractive, making it hard for us to become emotionally attached to it like we can to a desert, forest, mountain, or even a swamp. Sunday drivers don't see a lot of scenic trees in the prairies, and the wildflowers are not consistent. Prairies generally have to be enjoyed up close and personal.

I was introduced to the wonders of Texas native prairies by prairie specialist Madge Lindsay (now head of Outreach and Promotions for TPWD Nongame and Urban Programs), who first took me into the tallgrass when The Nature Conservancy was buying Clymer Meadow. At the time, her enthusiasm puzzled me. I kept thinking, "Grass is for mowing and for livestock. Just why are we about to invest several hundred thousand dollars on just grass when other areas really need us?" Madge led me by the hand into shoulder-high turkeyfoot and made a convert for life. It takes experience and time out on the land to appreciate the rich color, beauty, texture, and usefulness of prairie grasses.

CLYMER MEADOW

Clymer Meadow is 311 acres of unplowed Blackland Prairie in Hunt County near Celeste. A $500,000 grant by Karen and Tim Hixson made possible its acquisition by The Nature Conservancy. The prairie community here is dominated by little bluestem and Indian grass with tall dropseed, big bluestem, switchgrass, and eastern grama grass. Although the spring flowers are lovely, especially after a burn, the best time to see the grasses is in the fall when most of them are flowering in varying shades of brown and orange. The first time I saw Clymer in the fall I thought of Willa Cather's words in *My Antonia:* "More than anything else I felt motion in the landscape; in the fresh, easy-blowing morning wind, and in the earth itself, as if the shaggy grass were a sort of loose hide, and underneath it herds of wild buffalo were galloping, galloping." It's not hard to imagine the vast herds of buffalo that used to roam here.

Small, water-filled depressions known as hog wallers are found along ridge tops and contain a rich variety of aquatic fauna. (The scientific name for these depressions is "gilgai," but I prefer the more descriptive "hog waller," as one can easily imagine that an animal has dug the depression to "waller" in it.) The draws contain woody plants such as cedar elm. The soils are predominately deep, well-drained clays, and those of the ridge tops belong to either the Heiden or Houston Black series. There are close to three hundred species of native plants to be found on this small patch.

My favorite time at Clymer is in late April and early May after the prairie has been burned, when the native grasses are still dormant. Clearing out the dead areas allows more sunlight to reach the ground, bringing life to the grasses, forbs, and wildflowers. The burns are tough going for TNC fire management teams. Members wear bright yellow, fire-resistant "banana" suits and packs with five-gallon water containers, back breakers for those who have to walk a long way. Quite a bit of equipment, including a large-capacity pumper standing by, has to be assembled to ensure efficacy and safety.

The burns remove dead vegetative litter from previous years and battle back the constant assault by woody plants that have taken over so much of the former Blackland Prairie area. There is evidence that periodic fires increase the diversity of prairie species by creating microdisturbances that allow seeds from different species to infiltrate. Burning stimulates growth of the grasses and encourages them to take off by inducing germination. The burns leave decomposing natural fertilizer that returns rich nutrients to the soil. These nutrients then lead to grand bursts of color. Giant relatives of the bluebonnet bear up under the unappealing name "scurfy pea," along with colorful beacons of at least three different prairie paintbrushes (in magenta, cerise, and, rarely, lemon yellow) hovering over gold swatches of bladderpod and the shimmering pinks of evening primrose interspersed with the delicate chartreuse brushes of prairie parsley. A slow, careful stroll reveals exquisite blooms, including crimson woolly loco, yellow trumpets of puccoon, lacy fleabane daisy, the sky blue of prickleleaf gilia, dainty flax, and wispy threads of bee blossom. Scattered through the meadow are white star-shaped windflowers and winking blue-eyed grass. On the meadow borders, you can find the black beads of Eve's necklace, which in the spring is replete with exotic cascades of rose-colored blossoms. In June, forbs are prominent, including purple coneflower, rosinweed, blue sage, basketflower, various brown-eyed Susans, and gayfeather. Yet later, Mexican hats pop up as miniature reddish orange sombreros, skirted by delicate lavender blossoms of many varieties of aster. And I'm always struck by the presence of soaring hawks and falcons.

HAGERMAN NATIONAL WILDLIFE REFUGE

Just off to one side of a gaggle of at least a thousand Snow Geese, a smaller goose fed unconcernedly. I wiped the lens of my binoculars and peered again into the brightly lit landscape. No doubt about it. The back and neck of that little goose were an iridescent blue, and the bill lacked the grinning patch so characteristic of the Snow Goose. This trip to Hagerman, handy to the DFW metroplex, had just paid off handsomely because, although Ross' Geese visit the refuge occasionally in the spring, fall, and winter, the blue phase is considered extremely rare.

This popular 11,320-acre refuge was created in 1946 by an agreement with the U.S. Army Corps of Engineers and includes 3,000 acres of marsh and water and 8,000 acres of uplands and farmland. It provides food, roost, and shelter for a variety of resident birds and animals such as quail, songbirds, squirrels, bobcats, white-tailed deer, raccoons, and beavers. For the city dweller, migratory birds are the show, since the refuge is a winter home of thousands of ducks and geese and an important spring-summer migration path for shorebirds. More than 313 species of birds have been recorded on the refuge, with only 40 considered accidental.

The most numerous migrant is the Canada Goose, with populations ranging from 10,000 to 15,000 in the winter. Every time I've visited the refuge I've also seen large populations of Snow and White-fronted geese and a few Ross', but only that single blue phase. There is a four-mile tour road that makes viewing armchair easy. Several fields and roads are available for hiking. Try the Harris Creek Trail, looping for almost a mile through several habitat types including bottomlands and upland prairie. In the wintertime, if you drive back into the marshy areas formed by earthen dikes, you'll almost always see wild Mallards, pin-

Blackland Prairie, as it responds to an early spring burn, is lush green just beginning to be sprinkled with the carpet of wildflowers soon to follow. This is TNC's Clymer Meadow in Hunt County, one of the few remaining native prairies in Texas.

tails, and Green-winged Teal. In the fall and spring diving ducks such as Redhead, Canvasback, scaups, and Ring-necked stop over to refuel. The spring also brings Shoveler and Blue-winged Teal, returning from their long migrations. Shorebirds migrate through in the summer, with July often being spectacular. The marshes are drained in summer to promote the growth of natural foods and allow for the planting of other high-energy foods. The refuge grasslands are being restored by periodic burning and the planting of native grasses and forbs.

Resource management programs on the refuge are directed at preserving and improving habitat for wildlife. About six hundred acres are cultivated for waterfowl feed, including high-energy milo and corn for migrants. You'll notice a lot of green winter wheat, on which are perched thousands of head-down geese. Late-winter geese seem to prefer stoking up on high-protein grasses, which lean their bodies and develop strength for the long haul north to nesting grounds.

THE CROSS TIMBERS AND PRAIRIES

These Cross Timbers are a very singular growth. The one we had now entered is called the Lower Cross Timbers, and is about six miles wide; then eighteen miles from the outer edge of this one, we should enter the Upper and larger. They extend almost due North and South, from the Canadian to the Brazos. The timber is a short, stunted oak, not growing in a continuous forest, but interspersed with open glades, plateaus, and vistas of prairie scenery, which give a very picturesque and pleasing variety.

W. B. PARKER
Through Unexplored Texas, 1854

This seventeen-million-acre area is also a transitional region, a natural extension of the Post Oak Savanna and the Blackland Prairies into the Rolling Plains. Most of the flora and fauna of the Cross Timbers and Prairies have ranges that extend into the Great Plains or eastward toward our Pineywoods. The terrain is rolling and hilly, deeply cut with rivers, most notably the beautiful Brazos. Rainfall is twenty-five to forty inches annually, with April, May, and June being the wettest months.

Today this is mainly ranchland interspersed with open savanna and dense brush, and covered with prairie tallgrasses and midgrasses, blackjack and post oak. The soils are loamy or sandy with acid surface layers in the Cross Timbers portion (prairies have basic to neutral soils). As on the Blackland Prairies and Post Oak Savanna, most of the native vegetation of the Cross Timbers has been altered by plowing and overgrazing. The original grasses were the little and big bluestems and Indian grass. The most prevalent grasses now are silver bluestem, Texas wintergrass, and buffalo grass.

The north-central prairie on the western edge of the Cross Timbers tells us why most of our native grasslands won't last until 2000. This open, rolling grassland was once dominated by midgrasses such as sideoats grama and little bluestem. Now, mesquite, lotebush, and other woody plants have taken over the grasses because livestock have grazed too thoroughly. As with the Blackland Prairies, the absence of fire has allowed the takeover, since fire controls the spread of the woody invaders.

POSSUM KINGDOM STATE PARK

This lovely, 1,615-acre park is located on the southwestern shoreline of Possum Kingdom Lake, a deep, clear lake of almost 20,000 acres. The drive to, and a stay at, Possum Kingdom will contribute to your conservation education and give you a good feeling for the Cross Timbers. In late winter and early spring look for bluebirds, goldfinches, pyrrhuloxia, and always robins.

Below the lake, the Brazos River continues. A canoe tour of this historic river is one of the finer environmental and historical trips in Texas. The river, "where it loops and coils snakishly from the Possum Kingdom dam down between the rough low mountains of the Palo Pinto country," is eloquently revealed by John Graves in his *Goodbye to a River* (1960).

Professional canoe outfitters can gain access to the river at Fortune Bend, an ideal spot to begin a short ten-mile cruise downriver to FM 4 at the Dark Valley Bridge. Call the Brazos River Authority (817-776-1441) at Waco to obtain current flow information for the time of any canoe trip. Almost any river anywhere in Texas can be very dangerous in times of heavy rains, and canoeists will particularly want to know about the releases at Possum Kingdom dam.

Below the dam, the Brazos twists and writhes upon itself. Great Blue Herons are on lonely stakeouts; kingfishers, Loggerhead Shrikes, and the occasional gadwall will keep you company. Although croplands keep you mindful of civilization, it's easy to let your mind drift back a century or two in this part of the river. This stretch of the river was smack in the middle of the eastern fringe of the Comanchería. The TPWD makes it reasonably easy for you to acquire a trout for lunch from releases just below the dam, and a friendly gravel island makes an elegant picnic landing. Never trespass off the river. The folks hereabouts are understandably touchy about their landowner rights. You would be too, if you owned land along such a scenic waterway.

The drive to Fortune Bend is lovely. At times the road swings close to the river and can surprise you with flocks of Wild Turkeys and closeups of Red-shouldered and Red-tailed hawks. I recently checked on the spring migrations of Cedar Waxwings and robins, which I found in unbelievable numbers in February in the backcountry around the Shut-in and Schoolhouse mountains. The convivial, colorful waxwings, with their distinctive crests and bandit masks, like the abundant winter berries of Central Texas trees and shrubs. The birds flowed like wood smoke through the bleak late-winter landscape, reminding me of ashes swirling up from a long ago Indian campfire.

LAKE MINERAL WELLS STATE PARK

Only four miles from downtown, this 3,009-acre park is a prime example of the Cross Timbers ecological area, crisscrossed by deep canyons, with rolling, hilly terrain throughout, studded with post oak, blackjack oak, and mesquite, and the bottomlands are scattered with pecan, Texas oak, Texas ash, cottonwoods, and American and cedar elms. The deep canyons are thick in brush habitat, and the dry upland woodlands contain the expected Ashe juniper, sugarberry, elbow bush, and sumac. All of this has good access by way of twenty-one miles of trails.

The rock-climbing area allows visitors to get up close and personal with the geological setting for the park, which consists of sandstone and shale deposited more than 300 million years ago during the Pennsylvania period.

This can be a productive birding site, especially if you canoe up into what locals call Lost Lake, above the 646-acre Lake Mineral Wells. You may spot Wood Ducks and Hooded Mergansers in winter, Common Yellowthroats, Marsh Wrens, and even Soras in the fall migration. In the summer look for nesting Yellow-crowned Night-Herons, Canyon Wrens at their extreme eastern limit in Texas, and Wild Turkeys. In all, some 170 species of birds have been recorded inside the park. Canoeing also gives you a chance to spot gray fox, raccoons, opossums, fox squirrels, white-tailed deer, and, with a lot of luck, ringtails and coyotes.

FORT WORTH NATURE CENTER AND REFUGE

Metroplex residents are privileged to have access to one of the finest urban natural areas in America, a 3,500-acre gem with more than twenty-five miles of hiking. The Fort Worth Nature Center and Refuge is the largest city-owned nature center in the United States. Physiographic areas include bottomland hardwoods, typical Cross Timbers forest, prairie, marsh, limestone ledge, and the east fork of the Trinity River. Thus, the visitor can identify principal features of the major ecosystems surrounding the DFW metroplex. Staff members refer to their natural areas as "the only refuge in town."

This nature center was inspired by Fort Worth birders who watched with horror as the city systematically cleared brushy habitat from city parks, in the misguided spirit of neatness. In 1964, the Fort Worth Parks and Recreation Advisory Board announced that 380 acres on upper Lake Worth would be designated a wildlife refuge and that this tract, known as Greer Island, would "be retained in as nearly its natural state as possible." This may have set the all-time speed record for local government action. In 1967, the area was extended to more than 3,000 acres.

The nature center trails meander through a diversity of habitats and include a boardwalk over the lake, a good place to see migratory ducks and other waterbirds, especially in the fall. Spring migrations bring a variety of songbirds, including warblers and buntings.

RARE BIRD ALERT

This number is for the North Central Texas area, officially called the Metro Rare Bird Alert for North Texas: 817-329-1270 (sponsored by the Dallas County Audubon Society, the Harris County Audubon Society, and the Fort Worth Audubon Society).

"LIKE AN OCEAN IN ITS VAST EXTENT" THE ROLLING AND HIGH PLAINS

CHAPTER 5

Like an ocean in its vast extent, in its monotony, and in its danger, it is like the ocean in its romance, in its opportunities for heroism, and in the fascination it exerts on all those who come fairly within its influence. The first experience of the plains, like the first sail with a 'cap' full of wind, is apt to be sickening. This once overcome, the nerves stiffen, the senses expand, and man begins to realize the magnificence of being.

COL. RICHARD I. DODGE
The Hunting Grounds of the Great West, 1878

When you cross the ninety-ninth meridian in Texas, you enter the Great Plains environment where early explorers and travelers had much to overcome. Beyond the ninety-ninth, rainfall drops sharply all the way to the West Coast, although there are refreshing exceptions. West of the ninety-ninth meridian, annual rainfall averages twenty inches and, in some Texas locations, drops to twelve inches or less. Complicating plains life is the much higher rate of evaporation in the summer, up to fifty inches in the High Plains. For Texas purposes, the ninety-ninth is where East meets West.

European explorers—whether Coronado from heavily wooded Spain or Anglos such as Long, Marcy, and Gregg—were discombobulated without ready access to both trees and water. Accounts of Coronado's *entrada* into the High Plains have several references to lost men, "no track left." All this land offered was—land. Captain Marcy spoke of the "dreary monotony of the prospect; it was a vast, illimitable expanse of desert prairie—the dreaded 'Llano Estacado' of New Mexico; or, in other words, the great Zahara of North America."

This chapter combines the Rolling Plains and High Plains ecosystems because the systems knit together and intertwine at the Caprock

OPPOSITE PAGE
The U.S. Conservation Reserve Program is helping to conserve more than a million acres of the Texas Panhandle, critical not only to slowing erosion but also to providing habitat for migratory waterfowl. Programs at Rita Blanca National Grassland include leases for cattle grazing.

Escarpment. The High Plains caprock simply perches upon the Rolling Plains, making it a unique part of the physiographic pattern of the southern Great Plains. The Rolling Plains cover about 24 million acres, the High Plains 20 million.

The Great Plains were formed by the wearing down of the Rocky Mountains and are underlain by outwash, debris that was carried away from the mountains by fast-flowing streams, burying the ancient marine landscape beneath several hundred feet of rocks, sands, and other sediments, forming an alluvial quilt. These streams eroded, redepositing the sediments as they zigzagged across the ancient sea bed and forming the dramatic landscape we see today, chock full of geologic surprises. The meandering rivers created the Ogallala Formation, which over millions of years soaked up a quadrillion gallons of water. The surprises are the awesome canyons *below* the flat surface of the plains, deep, violent slashes created by stream erosion. The most prominent of these canyons, in sequence from north to south, are Palo Duro, Tule, Quitaque, Casa Blanca, and Yellow House. You can drive almost up to many of these canyons and not realize they are there. The Texas Natural Heritage Program calls them "escarpment breaks" and assigns them to an ecological subregion distinct from both the High Plains and Rolling Plains. I hope "sub" was an unintentional pun.

The surface of the Ogallala Formation is covered by caliche, a whitish calcium carbonate–cemented layer, a few inches to a few feet thick. The Pecos River, rising from the lovely Sangre de Cristo Mountains of New Mexico, eroded into the Ogallala Formation south and west of the caprock until it cut off the aquifer from its sources in the mountains. Eventually, erosion on all sides was halted by the resistant caliche, forming what we call the Caprock Escarpment on the east and the Mescalero Ridge on the west. The eroded area east of the escarpment is known as the Rolling Plains. The remaining mesa or High Plains ranges from 3,000 to 4,000 feet above sea level.

THE ROLLING PLAINS

From Red River to this point, nothing can surpass the facilities of the country for stock-raising, sufficient to mark Texas as the great stock-yard of our country in the future. Water is plenty, the whole country being intersected with creeks and rivers, and although the season was unprecedentedly dry, we met with no scarcity even on our narrow line of march. . . . After breaking up camp, we gradually ascended in a northwest course, over rolling country, covered with buffalo grass and mesquite timber.

W. B. PARKER
July 16, 1854, notes taken during the expedition commanded by Capt. R. B. Marcy, *Through Unexplored Texas*

Captain Marcy was on the move again, headed west into the Rolling Plains, crossing that east-west demarcation line at the ninety-ninth meridian, which almost precisely divides Texas in half. Marcy had just met with the famous Indian agent Major Robert S. Neighbors. No doubt they talked much of Comanches, for they were well inside the Comanchería, among the gently rolling hills and prairies of this ranch country. More than two-thirds of this ecological area is still rangeland, and the large spreads of the Swenson (S.M.S.) and Waggoner ranches are still operating.

Ranch incomes have been supplemented in many cases by oil and gas revenues. Much of the original prairie grass was improved (as the agricultural scientists call it) for pasture or cleared for oilfield pads. Today, the potential for biological restoration of these pad sites is being studied, and some restoration work is under way. This would be a costly, long-term project, but we have at least learned that future oil exploration and production can take into account the needs of the environment.

Parker's notes also accurately reflect the fact that this area is the birthplace of many Texas rivers. The Colorado, Concho, and Red rivers have their trickling origins in the western part of the Rolling Plains, in the breaks of the Caprock Escarpment, and the Brazos sustained many a settler here. These rivers and their systems sliced their way through the soft clay and sandy soils to give the ecosystem its rolling character.

If Parker had had the knowledge and equipment, he would have found that the rivers host many endemic creatures, including the Harter's water snake, which lives only in a few places along the Colorado and Brazos river systems where rapids flow. Bird hunters in the area have to be careful not to mistake a Snowy Plover, inbound in bad light, for a dove. However, there's no mistaking the rare interior Least Tern that may be found here.

Early settlers supplemented their diet with persimmons, mulberries, wild plums, grapes, currants, juniper berries, hackberries, and prickly pears. They grubbed root vegetables such as Indian potatoes, onions, radishes, and Jerusalem artichokes. Comanches mixed marrow from the bones of the buffalo with crushed mesquite beans (from which I've made flour). Buffalo meat was a staple. Killing a buffalo on foot took skill and cunning. Since Comanches did not have access to water or the inclination for agriculture, the acquisition of the horse from careless Spaniards became their key to plains survival, then dominance. By the end of the seventeenth century the horse was out of the barn, so to speak, and the Comanche became "the horse people." One account states that the Antelope Comanche collective, consisting of two thousand people, controlled fifteen thousand horses.

Fortunately for the Comanche, buffalo were plentiful. The Comanche defined the concept of sustainable natural resources long before any European figured it out or thought it important. Even the hooves of buffalo were used for dishes, powder horns, and spoons. Today, much is made of the transfer of technology in a global economy. The Comanche demonstrated this notion more than three hundred years ago, not only rustling horses from the Spanish but also confiscating intellectual property such as the concept of tack and improved weaponry.

In this part of Texas, the issues of farmers, ranchers, and conservationists come together; all want clean air, water, fertile soil, and the opportunity to pass what has been an abundant natural heritage on to future generations.

Obviously, buffalo cannot be returned to the immense herds of the past—the prairies are mainly gone. Gone also are the main natural predators, the Indians and the gray or plains wolf, so we cannot recreate the elements of the ecosystem that sustained the buffalo. To me, seeing a remnant herd of buffalo, even on a huge expanse of prairie such as The Nature Conservancy's Tallgrass Prairie Preserve in Oklahoma, is a firm reminder of how quickly and how profoundly humans can alter an ecosystem.

Today the Rolling Plains is paisano country, and these cuckoos are noted for speed afoot. Biologists discovered that the roadrunner has a salt gland in its beak that helps control its body temperature in the desert and a patch of skin on its back that acts as an exceptional heat conductor to keep it warmer during the infamous blue northers of its habitat. Like the antelope, it has been running around since the Pleistocene, a well-adapted creature.

The Rolling Plains ecological area is about 24 million acres and is an extension of the Great Plains of the central United States. In fact, the high breaks of the Caprock Escarpment harbor relicts of Rocky Mountain flora and fauna that once were much more widespread throughout Texas. Juniper woodlands found on the steep breaks of the canyons have their own mouse, the Palo Duro mouse, a variation on the pinyon mouse of the Rockies.

In Texas, the gray wolf has been extirpated, but there's still an abundance of coyotes. Gray wolves were reintroduced into Wyoming and central Idaho in 1994. Coyotes are more active early in the morning and at sunset but will often hunt in the daytime. Although they are less social than wolves, I have often observed them in packs. My thinking is that when plenty of rodents are available, coyotes are comfortable hunting alone or with a mate, but to hunt larger prey, they form packs. This isn't because coyotes are gang-style predators; it has more to do with the coyote's cowardly ways, and the pack is for group defense. There is

little evidence that coyotes kill deer or cattle, but they do prey on sheep and goats. Coyotes are universally disliked by ranchers, and all manner of death-dealing devices have been aimed at them, including M-44 registers firing sodium cyanide capsules, toxic sheep collars, traps, and bullets, sometimes fired from airplanes. Huge sums of money and a massive collective effort have been expended in Texas to control coyotes, but in the more remote reaches of the High Plains, your ears will tell you the coyotes won, their wild evening chorale ringing out across the plains.

Early plains explorers such as Josiah Gregg (Commerce of the Prairies, *1844) relied on "quantities of wild* turkeys, *which are frequently seen ranging in large flocks," for camp meals. The Rio Grande Wild Turkey is once again abundant in Texas, thanks in large measure to private landowner conservation.*

Unlike the resilient coyote, other plains residents such as horned lizards (known as horny toads) have not fared well. Two of the three horned lizards in Texas are now protected. The three species include the Texas horned lizard, the mountain short-horned lizard, and the unprotected roundtail horned lizard. The Texas horned lizard, though in serious decline, may be found statewide. The roundtail horned lizard is found only in the Rolling Plains, High Plains, and Trans-Pecos. The Texas horned lizard's decline is thought to be due to a shortage of ants because of pesticides marshaled against fire ants; it takes 200 ants a day to keep a horny toad happy. Texas Parks and Wildlife Department enforcement personnel are serious about the horny toad's threatened-species status.

In Marcy's time, turkeys roamed, prairie chickens stole corn crops, hawks and ravens scoured the sky, the endangered Texas poppy mallow was abundant, and native grasses waved tall. As in the Blacklands, most native grasses have been replaced by cultivated crops and pasture grasses. Where the pastures that replaced the native grasses are left to their own devices, mesquite spreads rapidly, as does snakeweed and prickly pear. Some of the old stands of mesquite make wonderful dove roosts, and on some of the clay-loam soils, a little critter called the Texas kangaroo rat forages. These cute brown and gray rascals burrow at the base of mesquites. They are a continuing mystery to biologists since they are desert-adapted mammals, well out of their range in the relative moist of the Rolling Plains. Are they relicts, or have they simply expanded their habitat range into more amenable conditions? No one knows.

The land slopes up from about 1,000 feet at the edge of the Cross Timbers to 3,000 feet in the western reaches. Rainfall diminishes as you drive west, from twenty-eight inches to eighteen inches. The Rolling Plains have had to rely mainly on the good environmental work done by private landowners, as there is a surprising lack of TPWD, U.S. Fish and Wildlife, and TNC conservation in this ecological area or in the High Plains.

COPPER BREAKS STATE PARK

For the traveler driving west into the heart of the Rolling Plains, the 1,933-acre Copper Breaks State Park is one of the first natural-area opportunities. Juniper breaks and grass-covered mesas are cut through by draws that reveal several geological formations of the Permian age. The colorful natural formations in the park are red beds of the mid-Permian age formed more than 230 million years ago. Copper deposits in the area gave the park its name. The red shales, clays, and alternating layers of gypsum are characteristic of Permian red-bed canyonlands to the northwest. According to Lynn Pace, a regional resource specialist for TPWD, when the state acquired Copper Breaks it was a farming and ranch operation that included an old field. The TPWD is reestablishing the native vegetation including sand bluestem, Indian grass, blue grama, sideoats grama, little bluestem, and various species of wildflowers including Engelmann daisy, sometimes called cutleaf daisy. The cheerful, yellow, eight-rayed flowers are a standout on the plains from April into the fall. This is a good place to watch for spring bird migrants, especially in the trees around the main lake, and there's decent birding during the winter waterfowl migrations.

If you follow the Pease River westward from Copper Breaks, you'll be traveling through increasingly rugged country, more than 28,000

acres of which is protected by a state wildlife management area (WMA) less than ten miles north of Paducah. Matador WMA is normally open to hunters in season, but at other times of the year your TPWD conservation passport is all you need to obtain a reservation to enter. This is four-wheeler country, and easing through the WMA in search of mule and white-tailed deer is quite an adventure. A favorite time for me at Matador is in April and May, as it is on a songbird migration path. I can assure you your birding will not be overburdened by other people. This is lonesome country.

Native vegetation is on display at Copper Breaks State Park, starring a variety of wild grasses and the prolific Engelmann daisy. Red beds of the mid-Permian outline the juniper breaks and mesas of the park.

CAPROCK CANYONS STATE PARK

Strangely, the sense of past comes upon me most strongly in this astounding place. I know that ten thousand years ago the Folsom people butchered a very big buffalo, from a now extinct species, on the bluff above what is now called Lake Theo. Stone scrapers and characteristic Folsom projectile points were scattered about a spring that now is under the lake, a freely flowing, large spring at which these same Folsom folks

Leroy Williamson climbed through the transition zone from Rolling Plains to High Plains to expose this view of Caprock Canyons State Park. The escarpment area provides some of the best-quality wildlife habitat in this part of Texas.

camped. Bones and stones buried by the sediments that washed down the draws from the steep bluffs of the escarpment tell of a gradual drying, perhaps an earth warming long before white people's carbon dioxide emissions, and of population decline. As the generations passed, with ever drier climates, the hunting and gathering cultures emerged, much to the discomfort of smaller creatures such as squirrels and rabbits. Alibates flint arrowheads and pottery marked permanent settlements in these canyons.

More recently, Apaches and Comanches enjoyed the largess of the spring-fed streams that once bubbled through these canyons, pouring out from a massive slate of quartermaster gypsum. Comanche petroglyphs decorate sandstone slabs not far away, at Double Mountain Fork Canyon, and more are hidden away in other secretive arroyos.

Just a hundred years ago, cougars, bears, gray wolves, buffalo, and prairie chickens were plentiful in these canyons, as were wild grapes and plums. Many of the springs are now dry, certainly in the summer. The former spring-fed streams can be found by their cottonwood, willow, hackberry, salt cedar, and tough mesquite. The land still supports the exotic, out-of-control aoudads, as well as native deer, badgers, coyotes, porcupines, cougars, bobcats, ringtails, Wild Turkeys, Scaled Quail, rabbits, and ground squirrels. In fact, the escarpment area contains some of the finest wildlife habitat in the entire Rolling and High plains ecosystems, as there is still water in some canyons. Scrub Jays, Canyon and Rock wrens, and bushtits are year-round attractions. Migrating birds follow these riven canyons and flock to Lake Theo. In the winter, birders can sometimes spot a Golden Eagle, often Mountain Bluebirds, Golden-crowned Kinglets, and waterfowl. More than 175 different species of birds have been sighted in the park. Places like the Tule Narrows were unquestionably sacred to prehistoric humans, and although it's hard to imagine, when the Ogallala was brimming, there were falls, and the sound of roaring water may have conjured a water spirit or two to the ancients.

The park's elevational relief is about 1,000 feet, from 2,180 in the east to 3,180 feet in the west as the terrain climbs from the Rolling Plains to the High Plains. This then, is the boundary of our next ecological area, sculptured by tributaries of the Little Red River into a badlands scenario that you'll never forget.

The park has many facilities, including primitive camping areas on the North and South Prong canyons and sixteen miles of trails through its 13,906 acres. May is my favorite month to hike up one of the canyons to photograph flowers and just enjoy the Indian blankets and creamy flowering yuccas.

THE HIGH PLAINS

The Comanches having all disappeared, we resumed our March, and soon emerged into an open plain or mesa which was one of the most monotonous I have ever seen, there being not a break, not a hill nor valley, nor even a shrub to obstruct the view. The only thing which served to turn us from a direct course pursued by the compass, was the innumerable ponds which bespeckled the plain, which kept us well supplied with water.

JOSIAH GREGG

describing Moore County, *Commerce of the Prairies,* 1844

When you have climbed the almost thousand feet up from Lake Theo to the North Prong in Caprock Canyons State Park, you've made the transition from Rolling Plains to High Plains. You've scaled the escarpment featured in so much of the early plains literature.

The High Plains are dotted with pools of rainwater called playas,

The playas of the Texas Panhandle are critical oases for millions of migratory waterfowl, and the good news is that duck populations in particular were on the rebound in fall 1994. More playas are being restored by farmers to provide income-producing hunting habitat.

clay-lined depressions that collect runoff water. They number more than 20,000 even today. These playas are capable of overwintering more than one million ducks.

A hundred years ago, a carpet of short grasses, such as blue grama, galleta, and buffalo, easily accommodated millions of buffalo and large herds of pronghorn antelope, which were pursued by gray wolves, then by Comanches. There were immense wintering flocks of Sandhill Cranes, geese, and ducks that came to the playas. Male Lesser Prairie-Chickens puffed out their orange-red neck sacs and boomed to attract females to ten thousand or more playas. In truth, these last creatures are still using the playas, only not in such large numbers. Until 1994 most species of ducks were less abundant than they were in the mid-fifties and were well below desired levels.

The problem here is destruction and degradation of habitat, not hunting. It's hard to find a Texas duck hunter today, although there are many who profess to be. It's not hard to find a birder, though. They are 50 million strong and support the North American Waterfowl Management Plan (NAWMP) signed in 1986 by the Canadian Minister of Environment and the U.S. Secretary of the Interior. Mexico became a partner through a memorandum of understanding signed in 1988 by the directors of the three federal wildlife agencies. That makes the NAWMP a policy statement of three nations undertaking the restoration and maintenance of abundant stocks of waterfowl in North America. The plan has set goals for achievement by 2000, pegged to levels recorded during the seventies. Then, breeding populations averaged 63 million ducks, including 8.3 million Mallards and 5.6 million pintails, with total populations averaging 100 million nationwide.

Now we come back to our playas. The creators of the NAWMP recognized the importance of migrational and wintering habitats, so a concept plan was devised to create the Joint Venture for the Playa Lakes Region. The Joint Venture was conditionally approved in 1988, with all objectives consistent with those of the NAWMP and a goal to create partnerships of responsible state and federal agencies, dedicated organizations such as The Nature Conservancy, Audubon Society, and Ducks Unlimited, and private landowners, individuals, and businesses. The Playa Lakes Region includes almost 90 million acres, with 44 percent in Texas, the state with the most responsibility. The region is the main winter range of the Short-Grass Prairie population of lesser Canada Geese and a substantial number of Mallards. About half the midcontinent population of Sandhill Cranes winters here, the other half migrating through playa routes.

Playas were formed by slumping of the surface into cavities where the caliche had dissolved. They are the drain holes of the High Plains. As clays accumulated in depressions, the playa bottom soils became almost impervious, although they will usually dry out in the scorch of summer. When full, water spilling over the edges causes the playa basins to grow outward in an annual ring phenomenon like tree rings, which continues today. Blankets of bright yellow coreopsis are often seen around playas, because of the moisture. Early plains settlers poked wads of coreopsis into their bedding to discourage bedbugs. For many reasons, the playas in Texas are less hospitable than one hundred years ago. Cultivation has eroded the surrounding uplands, and the sediments flow into the playa to form a pipe through the clay soil, creating leaks. Many of the playas that were modified to form basins for agricultural pumping have been abandoned, and the original playas don't receive the enriching flow of water that grows goodies for waterfowl. About 10 percent of playas have been so modified and could easily be converted into waterfowl havens.

The decrease in usable playas causes undesirable concentrations of waterfowl, which can lead to the rapid spread of stress-related diseases such as avian cholera. This disease is chronic in the High Plains. To their credit, energy companies have really cleaned up open pits and other practices that would affect waterfowl health.

The College of Agricultural Science at Texas Tech University has studied vegetation management in the playas for wintering waterfowl. Texas Tech urges farmers in the area to utilize their playas for waterfowl hunting leases, much like ranchers who derive extra income from deer leases. When feeding in playas, ducks prefer seeds from plants that germinate in moist soil conditions. That's why the playa needs to be flooded after it has naturally dried out. When this happens barnyard grass, willow smartweed, and pink smartweed—preferred dining for ducks—will grow.

The playa initiative will have great benefits for much nongame wildlife. The High and Rolling plains are alive with all manner of birds, 100 migrant species as well as many natives such as Orchard Oriole, Western Meadowlark, mockingbirds, Scissor-tailed Flycatcher, Ash-throated Flycatcher, and Common Nighthawk. To my delight this is also raptor country, with many birds of prey commonly in evidence, especially during their migrations. These include the Red-tailed Hawk, Mississippi Kite, Swainson's Hawk, Ferruginous Hawk, and Golden Eagle. Migrating swarms of Horned Larks and Lark Buntings are often seen in the spring, like dust devils two-stepping across the plain.

One of the tools used by farmers in the area is the Conservation Reserve Program (CRP), a provision of the Federal Farm Security Act of 1985. The act seeks to convert highly erodible land to permanent vegetation and encourages landowners to improve wildlife habitat. More than ten million acres of farmland in the prairie pothole regions of the United States has been protected under the CRP since 1985, land that was at serious risk of erosion. Hundreds of thousands of acres of prairie potholes and other wetlands have been restored as a result. The population of breeding ducks in spring 1994 was 100 percent greater than the average of the last forty years and 20 percent more than in 1993. As you might surmise, all this breeding will result in the largest flights of ducks in years arrowing into the Texas Panhandle and beyond.

Texas farmers are concerned that the CRP will not be reauthorized by Congress in 1995–1996. While undoubtedly some farmland has found its way into the program that should be in cultivation, most of the land enrolled should never have been cultivated. Nationwide, the CRP is credited with saving 700 million tons of soil a year. Just the ten Texas plains counties of Gaines, Terry, Swisher, Dallam, Bailey, Cochran, Yoakum, Martin, Runnels, and Wheeler each have at least 25 percent of available cropland in the Conservation Reserve Program, totaling more than 840,000 acres. Reauthorization of the CRP would be good news for ducks, duck hunters, bird watchers, and farmers alike.

Texas Tech urges a program that will reestablish the diverse native habitat. The High Plains populations of introduced pheasant, native kit fox, quail, and Lesser Prairie-Chicken will appreciate the CRP initiative.

The Prairie Dog Town Fork of the Red River just keeps eroding away layers of sedimentary formations, demonstrating how ancient, east-flowing rivers carved Palo Duro Canyon State Park into the caprock.

So will conservationists, since the native plant communities are aesthetically pleasing while they protect and sustain one of our state's most precious long-term assets, West Texas soil. Not so pleasing is the vegetation that invades barrens and overgrazed range, such as broomweed, a.k.a. snakeweed. To the urban many of the highway, fields of broomweed with their clusters of little yellow blossoms may appear decorative, but livestock and deer shun it, and bird hunters hate it because their dogs' sense of smell is thwarted by its pungent, Pineywoods aroma. Known as "escoba de la vibora" to Mexican herbalists, dried bundles of the flowering stems can be steeped in a quart of boiling water for thirty minutes, then cooled. Add this to a hot bath for aching muscles after a day afield, as it will reduce inflammation. Some recommend a tea; I don't.

There are many unique areas within the High Plains, such as sand-dune shin oak patches that harbor the sand-dune sagebrush lizard. The tallgrass prairie finds its way along the Canadian River, itself a wonder at all times of year but resplendent in the fall.

The Canadian River valley still has abundant Scaled and Bobwhite quail, Lesser Prairie-Chicken, Wild Turkey, and white-tailed deer. Cottonwood, hackberry, elm, and scrub oak help make the area colorful in the fall when waterfowl are plentiful. A great place to see the Canadian in the fall is at the Gene Howe Wildlife Management Area. It is also the place to see and hear the booming of male Lesser Prairie-Chickens during their mating season.

As is often the case, an exotic had become, by the early 1840s, a major feature of the plains wildlife—the fabled mustang, descendant of Arabian-stock domestic horses introduced by the Spanish. Most of the wild horses of eleven western states were gone by 1971, and there are no wild horses in Texas anymore. The Wild Horse and Burro Act of 1971 was passed to save the wild horse, and it did. Now it appears this protection has been too thorough, with many areas being grazed beyond carrying capacity, and management has become a costly problem in many western states other than Texas. It's also a political problem, since the wild horses have a strong, activist constituency that often works against the herd health of the very animals it seeks to protect.

Another Asian exotic invaded the High Plains following the newly planted grain fields of the early 1900s—the pheasant. The TPWD had to help the pheasant across the wild Canadian Breaks, but it is fair to say they made it into Texas on their own. These exotics have been most welcome, unlike the aoudad sheep that are now doing serious damage to native mule deer habitat in the canyons of the High Plains.

An upside-down wonderland is hidden in the Llano Estacado, the mostly unknown beauty of the canyon country. I won't argue whether it is high or rolling plain, for it's neither. What this country is, is awesome, and it's a shame that only a few handfuls of it are conserved for posterity. One such handful is the sixteen thousand acres of Palo Duro Canyon, which could have become the third magnificent national park in Texas fifty years ago but for a lack of support.

PALO DURO CANYON STATE PARK

My initiation to this astounding, 800-foot-deep slice through nearly 300 million years of geological time was as one of the first allowed into the park to camp after a flood. The Prairie Dog Town Fork had subsided from a torrent that had closed the park, demonstrating how it made the canyon by eroding yet more of the sedimentary layers down to Permian red shale. Easing slowly along the creek banks, I could read the much more recent history of the park in the tracks of a multitude of animals including coyote, beaver, rabbit, ringtail, and many Wild Turkey. Eastern Bluebirds, considered prophets of the future by the original human inhabitants of these canyons, and pesky Scrub Jays flashed bright blue

Much of the wild diversity of the High Plains is still conserved within canyons such as Palo Duro, sanctuaries for plants and wildlife below the harsh llanos.

Dunes from "a place no one goes." Leroy Williamson said he saw only one pickup truck in the several hours it took him to locate and photograph this dune north of Monahans, just at the corner of New Mexico and Texas.

against the red shale and green relict forest. Bushtits, Canyon Wrens, and Rock Wrens jittered about the camp area, and as dusk faded, the resonant hoots of a Great Horned Owl sounded. Once the sun slipped behind the canyon ridge hundreds of feet above, it was soon owl dark. As in many other areas, Bald Eagles are returning to Palo Duro in the winter, and Mountain Bluebirds sometimes escape harsher weather farther west to vacation here.

As the Comanches were hazed out of the caprock canyonlands in 1874, they left behind nesting Golden Eagles high on the cliff faces. Of all the goodbyes they said to the wild things of these broken canyons, parting with the sight of these majestic raptors must have pained them the most. Despite unrelenting onslaught, including strafing from airplanes and poisoning, the Golden Eagles have hung on, and new nesting pairs are being reported.

The dunes of the High Plains shelter some rare desert relicts, including the sand-dune sagebrush lizard, and there are unique tallgrass meadows along the Canadian. But these are not rarities found in the canyons, and as I noted earlier, magnificent scenery alone does not earn conservation support when there is so much biodiversity to be guarded elsewhere.

MOUND LAKE

As breathtaking as the canyonland appears, the playas hold the key to protecting biodiversity (especially migrating waterfowl), until they freeze over. Then, saline lakes such as Mound Lake, one of the largest saline lakes in the High Plains at almost 1,300 surface acres, furnish critical, wildlife-saving habitat. Mound Lake is a substantial wetlands ecosystem, long recognized as a major resting, roosting, watering, and breeding area for migratory and neotropical birds and other wildlife in the High Plains. It is a major Sandhill Crane winter roost, and has been during all of recorded history. During the peak months, from October through March, it's common to see more than 70,000 Sandhill Cranes at one time. Flights of ducks are common from autumn through spring, and spectacular flights of waterfowl use the lake when playas and other fresh-water areas are frozen.

The lake is located within a blown-out depression that has penetrated the caprock right into the Ogallala Formation and is, therefore, stabilized at groundwater level. Because of the severe evaporation in the area and fluctuations in the aquifer level, the lake will vary from almost dry to full, which is an average of two feet deep. The good news is that the Ogallala Aquifer appears to be stable and even increasing in the Mound Lake area.

Mound Lake also features a shoreline buffer zone of dune ridges covering about 1,200 acres. These 40- to 100-foot dunes have not been tilled and remain in native prairie dominated by grama and buffalo grasses, a rarity in the High Plains and, indeed, in all Texas.

MULESHOE NATIONAL WILDLIFE REFUGE

Nearly six thousand acres provide a winter home for more than 100,000 Sandhill Cranes in addition to large roosts of geese and ducks. The area is also on the migration route for a variety of shorebirds, which are best seen near the beach areas of the many lakes. Golden Eagles can be spotted in fall and winter. Coyotes and bobcats are occasionally seen from the roads.

"THE WHOLE COAST IS VERY FLAT" THE GULF PRAIRIES AND MARSHES

CHAPTER 6

We discovered a river mouth through which fresh water was flowing into the sea, but we did not reach it because there were no more than 2 fathoms a league offshore. To this one, I gave the name Rio Dulce. From here we went another two leagues in which there are 11 quite small mottes and as many as four large ones. . . . A little before arriving at Rio Dulce, we anchored in 3 fathoms, mud bottom, south of these mottes. The whole coast is very flat, as I have said, and therefore the thickets stand out.

ENRIQUEZ BARROTO
Diary, Tuesday, April 15, 1687

Barroto, in his circumnavigation of the Gulf of Mexico, had reached Texas Point at the mouth of the Sabine River; he was among the first Europeans to view the High Island chenier and what is now Sea Rim State Park. His single-sail, shallow-draft, sixty-foot vessel, called a piragua, enabled him to sail or even row into the Texas coast much closer than any previous explorer.

I enjoyed referring to his diary when I drove down the coast one recent Christmas. The gray rains slashed down on a drab, foggy Galveston Island as I began my trip through flat, barrier-island-protected marshes rippling off to the horizon, browned by winter but still emerald speckled. The heart of the area along the Gulf is the deltas of four major rivers, the Brazos, Colorado, Guadalupe, and Nueces.

The Coastal Bend of Texas is the hottest spot in the nation for winter birding, and the annual Audubon Christmas Bird Count is a major event attended by birders of consummate skill, great eyesight, and expensive equipment vying for life-list additions.

OPPOSITE PAGE
A pair of adult Whooping Cranes soar across their territory at Aransas National Wildlife Refuge. In 1994, three young whoopers sweated out the summer heat, never leaving the refuge, a first in U.S. Fish and Wildlife Service records.

The weather did not augur well; it's hard to see a Least Tern when you can't see at least the hood of your truck. Although the weather stayed drizzly, at the end of three days I recorded more than one hundred species of birds, imbibed the tangy bouquet of healthy salt marshes, listened to the gentled wash of Gulf waves miraculously free of debris as they played against well-stabilized barrier islands, and even spotted a rare Black-throated Blue Warbler, an escapee from Castro's Cuba.

This area is rapture for the raptor lover. From a Galveston Island subdivision, where I came upon a large flock of Sandhill Cranes grazing under the watchful eye of a Northern Harrier, to the Rio Grande Valley, guarded aloft by a cast of White-tailed Hawks, I was rarely out of sight of a raptor.

Although we collectively have made a lot of progress in the past thirty years, our coastal plain and marshes still have plenty of room for environmental improvement, and the Lower Rio Grande Valley is also threatened. Do take this as a report of hope, of an improving quality of life for people and wild fauna and flora. It's not yet time for congratulations, but it is time to point to the many, many conservation accomplishments in these areas, led by private landowner initiatives, massive expenditures by major industrial companies, dedicated public employees (especially those of the USFWS), and the assistance of private conservation groups such as Ducks Unlimited and the Audubon Society.

The Gulf Prairies and Marshes feather into the South Texas Plains, but there is a clear edge of transition. This is best represented by Padre Island, one of the longest barrier islands in the continental United States, and the salt marshes associated with it. Just across the Laguna Madre, which separates Padre Island from the mainland, the ecological pattern changes to the South Texas Plains, chiefly because of climate-induced vegetational shifts. Like many other edges in Texas, it's just a short drive from one natural region to another. Sometimes, it's just a step.

The Gulf Prairies and Marshes encompass an arc 50 to 100 miles wide from the Sabine River at the Louisiana border 367 miles to the mouth of the Rio Grande. Except for the barrier Padre Island, the last 100 miles of the lower Gulf Coast are associated ecologically with the South Texas Plains. The Gulf coastal plain rises gently from sea level to around 200 feet. It is geologically new, with the oldest part, around the Beeville-Goliad area, featuring reddish, sandy soils and large areas mantled by Reynosa caliche. Deep clays and loamy soils, island silt, and sand are typical. Much of the flora is in tallgrass and midgrass prairies and cordgrass marshes. The coastal prairie is low-lying, averaging 150 feet in elevation, and crossed by many rivers flowing to the Gulf. Rainfall varies from fifty-five inches near the Sabine River to twenty-five inches at Baffin Bay. The coastal marsh itself is a narrow belt of low wetlands. The fauna is very diverse, with more than three hundred species of birds relying on this area for food and rest on their spring and fall migrations. The plain includes two types of wetlands—marine and estuarine—including tidal marshes.

Spanish records tell us that there were extensive open prairies of little bluestem, Indian grass, and sedges on the uplands between the many rivers. The bottomland hardwoods were abundant, with sugarberry, pecans, elm, and live oaks. Now, most of the land has been plowed and cut into farms and ranches.

An exception is the Welder Wildlife Foundation, created by Robert Hughes Welder. During his lifetime, Welder was frequently quoted for his concern over the increasing scarcity of wildlife. In the foundation's report on its first twenty-five years, Welder is said to fear that his descendants would not have the pleasure he had enjoyed since childhood of hunting, fishing, and nature study. The report stated, "He had seen small farms with their pastures, feedlots, and fence rows merged into large farms with complete mechanical cultivation, with no fence rows and no pastures, no trees, and no place for game to hide, reproduce, or secure food."

Exotic invasion has also taken its toll. As the land was overgrazed, Macartney rose and Chinese tallow proliferated. Mesquite and huisache also took advantage of the overgrazing, sweeping in to infiltrate thousands of coastal prairie acres. As a result, Texas bitterweed, the Houston toad, and Attwater's Greater Prairie-Chicken are in deep trouble.

The barrier islands and spits from the Bolivar Peninsula to Boca Chica protect an intertidal zone of salt marshes and flats, which are the building blocks of the food web of the Gulf. The salt marshes above sea level are covered by cordgrasses (*Spartina*), which fix the sediment and produce a peat substrate, which in turn nurtures much plant diversity—making Texas marshes one of the most productive areas on earth.

There are three principal types of salt-loving grasses on the Texas coast: smooth cordgrass, marshhay cordgrass, and saltgrass. Smooth cordgrass (*Spartina alterniflora*) is coarse and large and grows to four feet. The leaves are about one-inch wide at the base, then taper to a point. This grass thrives in areas with tidal action. It actually absorbs salt, both as a nutrient and to control transpiration. When its salt content is too great it secretes excess salt on the leaves—look for the crystals.

Marshhay cordgrass (*Spartina patens*) reaches only two feet and has fine leaves resembling kite string. This is usually the dominant grass of a salt marsh, and it provides most of the cover for marsh life. Composting has become fashionable with people who have developed a conservation ethic, but female alligators have long used the chemical concept. They build their nests from this specific grass, and as it decomposes, it produces heat that incubates the eggs.

Saltgrass (*Distichlis spicata*) is not only short in height (less than one foot) but it is also short on food for most marsh inhabitants except insects. It has narrow leaves along the stem, and it can be identified from a distance by its straw color.

Unvegetated tidal flats are found on the fringe of the salt marsh, and although you'll not see much plant life here, these flats are home to a wide variety of organisms, including microalgae and macrophytic algae, which are food for suspension feeders and deposit feeders, which in turn are fed upon by predators such as crabs, whelks, shrimp, and eventually by the scavengers. As you go up the food web, fish and shorebirds join in the tidal-flats banquet.

By the sixties, the Texas coast had become one of the unhealthiest places in the United States: the coastal air, water, land, wildlife, and humans were suffering from a rapidly deteriorating environment. Despite all the progress made by responsible corporations such as Amoco, Conoco, Dow, Enron, Mobil, and other companies that have invested hundreds of millions of dollars in environmental improvements, there are still threats to our fragile coast.

Today, the national wildlife refuge system protects more than 90 million acres in more than four hundred units. It is this system and its hard-working employees that has come forth to protect critical areas of our coastal ecosystem. The first Texas refuge was established on December 31, 1937, and originally encompassed 47,261 acres on Blackjack Peninsula.

The protection of our coastal wildlife treasures has been a partnering effort between federal, state, and private organizations. Although the Fish and Wildlife Service is federally funded, often the wheels of government cannot move quickly enough to acquire a critical bit of habitat when available. The same is also often true of the efforts of the Texas Parks and Wildlife Department. The Nature Conservancy has emerged as a key partner with both state and federal agencies in the acquisition of critical habitat. The Conservancy can first supply the requisite scientific diligence and then buy land without delay. This puts TNC's privately raised money at risk and incurs a continuing stewardship cost until the land is repurchased (if ever) by the state or federal governments or by a conservation buyer who will guarantee the protection of biodiversity. Obviously, there is the cost of money plus the cost of administration, scientific work, and stewardship, and The Nature Conservancy expects to recover these costs at the time of sale. Even with these added costs, by the way, the usual result is a lower cost to us taxpayers because the land was typically bought at the right time at the right price. The Conservancy is motivated by the need to protect biodiversity, not profit—the monies involved could earn a far greater return in normal market investments.

Acting as a private partner, The Nature Conservancy has played a part in the acquisition program of Texas' national refuges. Ronald G. Bisbee, refuge manager of Brazoria, San Bernard, and Big Boggy national wildlife refuges, recalls the original planning team that in 1976 laid out a master plan for coastal wetlands protection on the Texas coast. A principal player in the plan's development was Tom Smith, director of realty for Region 2 of the Fish and Wildlife Service, based in Albuquerque, New Mexico. When Smith and his group of public and private conservationists drew up the plan, calling for the acquisition of around 300,000 acres, few actually believed it could be accomplished. The obstacles were many and daunting, for the work had to be accomplished in concert with the petrochemical, agricultural, and development interests on the coast, with limited staff and money. In the seventies the environmental contribution of the nation's wetlands wasn't widely known or appreciated. Tom Smith has been described as quiet and unexcitable, and there were those who lacked faith in his ability to drive this massive effort. What they overlooked was his total commitment to saving a seriously impaired ecosystem, one of the most threatened in North America and, at the same time, one of the most important.

Another hero of the coastal wetlands conservation effort is Claude Lard, recognized in 1993 by The Nature Conservancy with its Lifetime Public Service Award. Lard's distinguished professional career began in 1948 and led him from the deserts of southwestern Arizona to the coastal plains of Texas. In each of his assignments with the USFWS he had a significant effect on the environment and wildlife. He served as a supervisor of national wildlife refuges in Texas and headed up the effort to preserve more than 300,000 acres of coastal prairies and marshes. He has been the recipient of numerous conservation awards, including the Outstanding Service Award from the USFWS and the Meritorious Service Award, the highest professional award conferred by the Department of the Interior.

Smith and Lard pointed The Nature Conservancy toward high priorities, and acquisitions began immediately. Today, there is not a national wildlife refuge in Texas that hasn't benefited from TNC's work. The Conservancy has played a part in protecting more than 200,000 acres of biologically diverse landscape.

Also working in harmony with the plan was the Texas Parks and Wildlife Department, and in the past fifteen years the department has acquired 60,000 to 70,000 acres incremental to the USFWS acquisitions, including properties at Brazos Bend, Varner-Hogg, Sea Rim, Galveston Island, Brazoria County, Bryan Beach, Mad Island, Matagorda Peninsula, Goose Island, Matagorda Island, Mustang Island, and other wildlife management areas such as Murphree, Alabama Creek, Angelina Neches, Moore Plantation, North Toledo Bend, and Peach Point.

Bisbee reminisced, "Our relationship with The Nature Conservancy has been great. For example, we have had major additions at San Bernard National Wildlife Refuge thanks to TNC. Actually, this goes back to 1976, when the Fish and Wildlife Service, along with TPWD biologists, and TNC scientists identified all the major chunks of a plan to acquire more coastal marsh. Just as we were finishing that plan we identified about 2,400 acres just west of San Bernard, and TNC was able to go in and pick that up quickly. They bought it and held it for us. The Fish and Wildlife Service had some trouble getting the governor's approval, so it was five or six years before we were able to buy the land from TNC. TNC did the same thing on Anahuac Refuge, acquiring a large parcel. It's been a great relationship as far as I'm concerned."

When I first met Ron Bisbee it was the first day of the second duck season of the year, and he was busy patrolling San Bernard, one of the primary wintering grounds for most of the Central Flyway waterfowl. Bisbee explained that his three refuges were still relatively young and that he was still primarily "managing for wildlife"—public facilities would come later in his program. Bisbee said that these refuges and other nearby salt marshes are the ancestral wintering grounds of lesser Snow Geese. Populations of 10,000 to 60,000 may be on the refuges in December and January. Within several hundred yards of where Bisbee was explaining the marsh ecology, a gaggle of thousands of these nattering geese was roosting, along with a colorful mélange of other waterfowl.

Controlled waterfowl hunting is permitted in this and other refuges by special permit, but as I circled Moccasin Pond, nearby geese seemed most undisturbed. They knew they were in a protected area, free to roost without fear of steel shot. The users of steel shot, however, were entitled to the hunt; their duck-stamp money is a principal source of revenue for the refuge system.

Hunters, notably waterfowl hunters, and anglers lent support to the refuge plan. A significant effort was mounted by the Gulf Coast Conservation Association. The association was founded by Walter Fondren and Perry Bass, who provided essential funding to start the TPWD Palacios fisheries facility, which is not only restocking trout and redfish but also helping to restore snook, permit, and tarpon to Texas coastal waters. The association's efforts paid off in 1980 with the passage of a law that banned netting of sportfish such as trout and redfish in the estuarine systems of the coast.

Today, longtime coast residents report that the bay and estuary fishing is better than it has been in their memory despite terrible freezes in 1983 and 1989. One explanation is the voluntary program started by Dow Chemical in 1985, establishing a redfish rearing pond at one of its plant sites, complete with a canal dredged into the Gulf to help control water temperature.

San Bernard National Wildlife Refuge is carved out of the ancestral waterfowl wintering grounds, and it is common to see populations in excess of ten thousand Snow Geese. Snow Geese nest north of the Arctic Circle, and the long, ragged formations of their migratory flights often climb past 20,000 feet.

The loss of coastal marshes along the Gulf of Mexico during this century has been dramatic, with Louisiana losing about sixty square miles every year and the Texas coast showing signs of great stress. Officials of the U.S. Fish and Wildlife Service's National Wetlands Research Center, in Lafayette, Louisiana, told me in 1993 that a healthy salt marsh may produce seven times as much protein as a wheat field. (The National Wetlands Research Center has a Texas field research station at Corpus Christi.) In addition to absolute loss, marsh pollution is affecting the health of this critical resource. The Gulf coastal wetlands make up half of all coastal wetlands in the United States.

Staff at the National Wetlands Research Center work with the Gulf Coast Joint Venture partnership, part of the North American Waterfowl Management Plan. The Gulf Coast Joint Venture encompasses coastal wetlands and adjacent agricultural areas of Alabama, Mississippi, Louisiana, and Texas. The plan was created in 1986 and joined in 1988 by Mexico. It is a partnership of local citizens, private companies, conservation organizations (such as The Nature Conservancy, Ducks Unlimited, and the National Audubon Society), and government agencies. The governmental members include the Texas Parks and Wildlife Department, the U.S. Fish and Wildlife Service, and the National Fish and Wildlife Foundation.

The plan "responds to plummeting waterfowl populations in North America," according to Gulf Coast Joint Venture literature, which cites declines over the past few decades of 52 percent for pintail, 27 percent for Mallards, 41 percent for Blue-winged Teal. The goal of the plan is to "restore the continent's waterfowl populations to the level of the 1970s by the year 2000." Along the entire Gulf Coast, biologists have identified 4.5 million acres of important waterfowl habitat. Initial goals for the Gulf Coast Joint Venture are to protect, enhance, restore, or create 1.5 million acres of wetlands and to have a spring flight of thirteen million ducks and more than one million geese. Of the six initiative areas, three involve Texas: the Chenier Plain, the Texas Mid-Coast, and Laguna Madre. The other areas are Mississippi River Coastal Wetlands, Coastal Mississippi Wetlands, and Mobile Bay, Alabama.

Many Gulf Coast Joint Venture projects are under way. In Louisiana and Texas many private landowners flood harvested rice fields October through March to provide waterfowl feeding and nesting sites in heavily hunted areas. Since more than 80 percent of all Gulf Coast wetlands are privately owned, citizen and business involvement is crucial. The response by farmers, ranchers, and Gulf Coast businesses has been excellent. One of many examples is Conoco, with its donation in 1991 of 150-acre Atkinson Island in the middle of the Houston Ship Channel to the TPWD for use as a protected wildlife habitat, creating an oasis for migratory birds.

Naturalist John Dyes, a former technical services engineer for Marathon Oil, had the luxury of spending a year studying the wading birds of the Texas coast, yielding a work entitled *Nesting Birds of the Coastal Islands* (1993). He takes the reader from the February gathering through the July dispersion to the September migrations of Great Blue Herons, Great Egrets, and the other herons, egrets, and cormorants. He tells of the White Ibises, social animals that join the colonies to select an area where they can nest as a group. Dyes has a conservation message for us about Little Pelican Island, down the Intracoastal from Atkinson: "With a decreasing amount of prime wildlife habitat due to an expanding human population, the constant building of new industrial and harbor facilities, and the need, every few years, to dredge the Gulf Intracoastal Waterway, Little Pelican Island must have sanctuary status." Close by, North Deer Island is protected as a national wildlife refuge.

The Gulf barrier islands form a precarious crescent along the coast. These islands are new in ecological terms, only about three thousand to five thousand years old, and they are very fragile. They are constantly in motion, freestanding in the Gulf, subject to overwash, dune movement, and inlet formation. Storm waves bear great quantities of sand as they wash and push over the barrier islands, the source for new dunes and plant communities. On the very southern border of this ecological area, the climate is desertlike, and wind becomes the most important rebuilder of the barrier islands.

The Texas coast features some of the best naturally stabilized barrier islands and spits in North America, including (in sequence down the coast) Bolivar Peninsula, Galveston Island, Follets Island, Matagorda Peninsula, Matagorda Island, San Jose Island, Mustang Island, Padre Island, and Brazos Island. Most of the barriers have wide, flat beaches, and those accessible to automobiles are heavily used as surfside throughways. The well-stabilized dune systems are covered with grasses such as sea oats (a prolific dune stabilizer), sesuvium, cordgrasses, wild indigo, phlox, railroad vine, and goatsfoot morning glory. These plants are the lifeline of the dunes and should not be walked or driven upon, or picked for their beauty. Erosion accelerates when vegetation is ruined by trampers, pickers, and grazers. With their vegetation destroyed, dunes soon blow out, and the next thing you know, your dune is in the lagoon.

SEA RIM STATE PARK

Sea Rim State Park is aptly named because its 15,109 acres and 5.2 miles of coastline are in a zone of great biological importance. This is where salt tidal marshlands meet the Gulf, a stretch of over 2 miles. The rest of the coastline consists of sandy beach and dunes between the beach and marsh. The inland marshes are usually filled with all types of marsh birds, typical marsh flora, lots of alligators, and even more mosquitoes. I'd suggest a boat if you are serious about this part of your conservation education. Much of the land on the inland side of the access road is protected within the McFaddin National Wildlife Refuge.

For those like me, who enjoy the special pleasure of the winter beach, this is the best time of year. In the winter the sun sets down the beach and rises over the Sabine River; both directions seem confusing at first until you understand how the coast curves here. The emptiness, broken only by wintering seabirds, the feeling of timelessness, the keenness of the winter wind, and the surge of the surf contribute to an aesthetic experience worth the trip. You can drive certain sections of the coast, including some of Sea Rim, staying alert for the infamous Beaumont clay, rich in bone fossil remnants but a trap for your car. Pleistocene fossils are frequently found here after storms: teeth from prehistoric mammoth, bison, camels, and horses; sloth claws and bones; turtle shells.

Laughing and Ring-billed gulls are everywhere, as are terns from Least to Forster's, Royal, and Caspian with its oversized, bright orange bill. This is a shorebird beach, with a congregation of plovers: Black-bellied, Semipalmated, and, every once in a while, the endangered Piping,

A rare freeze tames the voracious biting insects of Sea Rim State Park, and a walk on the Gulf's edge into the dawn light becomes a transcendent experience, happily shared with shorebirds.

although I see this more frequently at Mustang Island to the south, where they nest. Least Sandpipers, dowitchers, both Long- and Short-billed, and Long-billed Curlews with their down-curved probes decorate the winter beach, darting in and out of the slick, gray, gently rolling Gulf surf.

The highway north from High Island was undercut a number of years ago by a hurricane and, because it is crumbling across a stretch of several miles, is closed to traffic. The eroding road poses a serious threat to the McFaddin Wildlife Refuge's freshwater marshes, since the Gulf's longshore currents at this point cut deeply into the coast, breaching the barrier to saltwater intrusion. Repair of this road and barrier may take years, not only because of costs but also because of bureaucratic delays. That McFaddin is critical to the environment and the Gulf economy is unquestioned. It is the centerpiece of this upper Texas coast conservation complex, including Sea Rim, TPWD's Murphree Wildlife Management Area, and the federal Texas Point Refuge. In the Murphree WMA alone, more than 13,000 acres are home to a variety of waterfowl as well as alligators, river otter, muskrat, beaver, nutria, and fish. The largest Canvasback duck population in Texas can be found wintering in the Lost Lake Unit, a wonderfully active marsh. Waterfowl are best spotted before and following hunting season, when viewing is cur-

Indigo Buntings, exhausted from flight across the Gulf into a northerly wind, take a breather at High Island. This photograph was taken during one of the island's famous fallouts, when oak mottes can be covered with bright-feathered migratory songbirds.

tailed. Alligators are most easily seen during the warm months. (A Texas conservation passport is required for admittance to the WMA.) The overall area encompasses more than 60,000 acres, and its freshwater inflows are critical.

Sea Rim State Park is filled with mammalian life, including nutria, muskrat, mink, and river otter. You may encounter a fearless raccoon on the Gambusia Trail boardwalk, cleaning his catch of crayfish. The park reports infrequent sightings of the endangered red wolf, at one time thought to be extirpated in Texas. Open-water ponds are habitat for amphibians and reptiles: turtles, snakes, alligators, and aggressive water snakes, as well as the poisonous cottonmouth moccasins. Park rules forbid swimming in the freshwater ponds; the cottonmouths and alligators (up to fourteen feet long) are good reasons to obey.

Texas Point Refuge is another example of marshland meeting Gulf, and it has no sand beaches. The entire strip, starting at Sabine Pass, is called "sea rim" because of this. These sea-rim marshlands were formed when silt from the Sabine River delta was carried down the beach by the longshore currents. The marshlands are especially rich in plankton and decomposing organic matter. They provide a backdrop for the coast's food web, a fertile nursery for aquatic life. They are essential for the productivity of marine fisheries and support of migratory waterfowl.

HIGH ISLAND

According to Bob Thornton, a trustee of The Nature Conservancy of Texas, High Island is "revered in bird-watching circles worldwide, ranking in importance with Cape May, Point Pelee, and Hawk Mountain as one of the four most famous migratory traps in North America."

Some 250 species of songbirds winter in Mexico, Central America, and South America, visiting the United States only in the spring months to nest. The migration begins about mid-April when great numbers of orioles, tanagers, buntings, flycatchers, and warblers launch from the Yucatán Peninsula of Mexico and cross a 600-mile stretch of the Gulf to arrive on the mainland some twenty to twenty-four hours later.

I have sailed this course many times in my ketch, *La Scala,* following the course of the migrants across the Gulf, often with southeasterly trade winds of 20 to 25 miles per hour. The birds fly in waves, maintaining an airspeed of 15 miles per hour, so normally they can sail across the Gulf in twenty to twenty-four hours, typically landing 50 to 100 miles inland, in the Pineywoods and beyond. Should these small travelers encounter a norther with rain and head winds, their progress, like that of a sailboat, is slowed, and their energy consumption soars. They will land in the first suitable vegetation they see. Under these conditions, I've even had wing-weary songbirds mistake *La Scala,* at forty-four feet, for suitable vegetation and alight for a life-saving ride. They will seldom take nourishment; they seem totally exhausted. Invariably, my tiny, colorful stowaways awake with beak to sunrise, fidget on a boom perch as if they were getting their bearings, then circle the boat a few times before heading straight for the Texas coast. It's as if these birds had a GPS (Global Positioning System) on board.

The oak mottes at High Island beckon migrating songbirds; emerging evidence indicates that both oaks and birds benefit. In a study published in *Ecology* in November 1994, on the oak-laden Ozarks outside St. Louis, researchers documented for the first time how insect-loving songbirds contribute to tree health by eating insects harmful to bark and foliage. "The impact of birds on plant growth is something no one has ever really looked at before," says Dr. Robert J. Marquis, coauthor of the study and associate professor at the University of Missouri–St. Louis. He and Dr. Christopher J. Whelan, from the Morton Arboretum in Lisle, Illinois, plan to expand their study of migrant songbirds in Costa Rica. "We want to see whether or not these potentially same birds are having the same kinds of effects in tropical rain forests as well as through their long migration path, which flows through Texas."

A norther will cause a natural phenomenon called a fallout, which occurs once, perhaps twice, a season and represents one of the most magnificent of our Texas wildlife spectacles. When a fallout occurs, the birds spiral into the trees of a twenty-four-acre area, which includes the

Boy Scout Woods and the Smith Woods. Bushes and trees can be covered with an enormous number of different species of different colors, likened to Christmas tree ornaments adorning the foliage. As many as thirty species of warblers can be viewed during a single day, including Cape May, Cerulean, Blue-winged, Golden-winged, Blackpoll, and Black-throated Blue. The weather and time dictate numbers and combinations of birds seen, and the makeup can change hourly. They stoke up on insects and other foods, then disperse into the Pineywoods habitat to the north. The Audubon Woods, now named the Smith Woods, is a wonderful place to observe windblown migrants such as Hooded, Kentucky, Worm-eating, and Swainson's warblers, vireos, orioles, tanagers, flycatchers, grosbeaks, thrushes, and buntings.

High Island is located on a chenier plain that extends for 200 miles along the upper Texas and Louisiana coasts. Most of the land along these coasts is flat, low-lying, and marshy with a high water table. The cheniers provide enough high ground to support dark green hummocks, or oak mottes, with live oak, willow oak, hackberry, and Chinese tallow trees. A chenier plain is a long, sandy ridge usually well above the high-water line. The word "chenier" is derived from the French word "chene," for oak, and the sandy soil of the chenier grows tall oaks. The chenier plain was formed of silt, sand, and especially clay from the Mississippi River, borne westward by longshore currents. The cheniers are sandy ridges within compacted sediment mud. They are similar to barrier islands. A main point of difference is that cheniers stay put, while barrier islands are always migrating. The geographic limits of the chenier plain are the Bolivar Peninsula and Trinity Bay on the west, the Gulf of Mexico on the south, Vermilion Bay on the east, and the transition from plain to prairie and longleaf pine habitat on the north.

According to David Pashley of The Nature Conservancy of Louisiana, few cheniers support high-quality examples of the natural community, and very few of those are protected. To spearhead this effort The Nature Conservancy has formed the Chenier Plain Conservation Initiative, working in harmony with the Louisiana Nature Conservancy, various federal agencies, the Audubon Society of Houston, and major corporations such as Amoco to conserve this valuable natural resource around the Texas coast and into Louisiana.

The chenier plain ecosystem encompasses ten thousand square miles of rich and complexly mixed wetlands, uplands, and open water. Jeff Weigel, stewardship director of The Nature Conservancy of Texas, says the region "provides critically important habitat for millions of migratory songbirds and shorebirds. It also supports an extraordinarily valuable assemblage of resident wildlife and winter waterfowl." Weigel points out that state and federal conservation agencies have acquired nearly

400,000 acres of mostly wetland habitats in the chenier plain. Thousands of additional wetland acres are endangered and need conservation by private and corporate landowners.

Jim Bergan, of The Nature Conservancy, claims that the chenier plain of Texas and Louisiana is "more important to migratory birds than any other physiographic area in North America." Of most concern are the neotropical migratory landbirds that heavily utilize the few available patches of wooded habitat in the spring after their stressful journey over the Gulf from the Yucatán Peninsula and Central America. Other transient and wintering shorebirds also depend on the area. Bergan reports growing evidence that "other groups of migrants as diverse as Broad-winged Hawks in fall and monarch butterflies in spring make very heavy use of the chenier plain. Concentrations of most North American species of herons and egrets and incredibly productive shellfish and finfish fisheries are among the other wildlife features."

Coastal refuges strung down the Texas coast form a lifeline for North American waterfowl. They include Texas Point, McFaddin, Anahuac, Brazoria, San Bernard, and Big Boggy and are managed by the U.S. Fish and Wildlife Service. At the southern end of the Texas coast, the National Park Service stands guard at Padre Island, America's longest national seashore, and in the South Texas plains ecosystem, the USFWS starts its guardianship of the Lower Rio Grande Valley at the dramatic Laguna Atascosa National Wildlife Refuge (see Chapter 7). Although most of these refuges are accessible and visitors are welcome, they have little traffic since there are few public facilities. But in December and January they are treasure chests for bird watchers, and some eighty bird species are either abundant or common, which means that even you can spot these birds.

BRAZORIA NATIONAL WILDLIFE REFUGE

This 40,854-acre refuge is located in Brazoria County, ten miles east of Freeport. The refuge is bordered by Chocolate Bayou on the north; by Bastrop, Christmas, and Drum bays on the east; and FM 2004 on the west. The refuge habitat is a mixture of saline and freshwater prairies, salt or mud flats, fresh and salt marshes, even lakes and potholes, and a freshwater stream. Six miles of gravel roads lead through the refuge, but access is limited to most of the refuge.

More than 425 wildlife species including 270 bird species use the refuge during all or parts of their life cycle. Birders often identify 200 or more species during the annual Audubon Society Christmas Bird Count in mid-December. This area has one of the highest counts in the United States.

In addition to giant gaggles of Snow Geese and flights of Canada and White-fronted geese, 20,000 to 30,000 ducks of several species use the

Flocks of Sandhill Cranes, along with many other migratory birds and shorebirds, find winter nutrition at The Nature Conservancy's Mad Island Preserve. This crane seems oblivious to the Environmental Excellence Award that the Environmental Protection Agency gave to the preserve in 1994.

refuge from October through March. The refuge supports an abundance of coyotes, raccoons, and bobcats as well as more than a hundred alligators and reputable populations of rattlesnakes and cottonmouth moccasins. As on many of the other coastal refuges, management practices include cattle grazing, controlled burning, water controls, and some limited plantings in the wetland areas.

Brazoria National Wildlife Refuge has been significantly enhanced through the efforts of The Nature Conservancy working with Texaco. TNC approached Texaco in 1955 to purchase the surface rights to Hoskins Mound, while leaving intact Texaco's mineral rights, sine qua non for a conservation negotiation with an energy company. TNC finally consummated the transaction with Texaco in 1991, enabling the Fish and Wildlife Service to purchase the property from TNC with federal duck-stamp revenues. This addition nearly tripled the size of the refuge.

By 2000, the Hoskins Mound acquisition just might be the salvation of another endangered species, Attwater's prairie chicken. Attwater's, a race of the Greater Prairie-Chicken, is on a serious decline, and habitat within its ancestral grounds is critically needed. The first in-depth study of Attwater's prairie chicken, named for University of Texas professor H. P. Attwater, was in 1937. Populations once estimated at more than a million on the Texas and Tamaulipas Gulf coasts had dropped to under 9,000, and hunting was stopped. As recently as 1983, populations were near 1,600, but by 1994 they had plummeted below 500, or 6,500 less than the far more famous Spotted Owls of the Pacific Northwest. Perhaps chickens don't have the cachet of owls.

There is now a propagation project utilizing captive breeding. In May 1993, the TPWD announced that captive-raised Attwater's prairie chickens had successfully bred in captivity for the first time. When this population is exportable, Hoskins Mound will be one of the potential habitat sites. In mid-1994, Mobil Exploration and Production U.S. donated a 2,050-acre tract to The Nature Conservancy. This Texas City tract provides habitat for one of three remaining populations of Attwater's prairie chickens and the only stable population. Only about 150 prairie chickens exist at the Attwater Prairie Chicken National Wildlife Refuge, which is managed expressly for their protection and breeding efforts.

BRAZOS BEND STATE PARK

Just sixty minutes into my last late-winter visit to this park twenty miles south of Houston, I was able to check off forty-six species of birds on the park's professionally prepared bird list. (The trip had been quickly organized in response to yet another Masked Duck alert by the Audubon rare-bird hotline.) Of the species listed, more than sixty have been confirmed as nesting; another fifteen are suspects. The Masked Duck, as usual, had been "there yesterday" and remained aloof from my life list, but the birding was fabulous along the trail by the forty-acre lake to the observation tower overlooking Pilant Lake. Sightings included American Bittern, Tricolored Heron, Green-backed Heron, White Ibis, Fulvous Whistling-Duck, scores of Wood Ducks, Ring-necked Duck, Common Moorhen, and a King Rail who strolled nonchalantly up to a troop of Boy Scouts on the trail to another hotspot, Elm Lake. Various warblers were just beginning their migration, and Sandhill Cranes continued theirs. It's easy to imagine that this has been the site of human habitation since at least 300 B.C. Karankawa Indians probably camped out here, and we know that this area was a part of Stephen F. Austin's first colonial land grant from Mexico, later to become a landing for riverboats loaded with cotton from nearby plantations.

Park superintendent Dennis Jones makes a strong case for calling this the most diverse of our state-owned parks. Rivers, creeks, ponds, marshes, and lakes make this unquestionably one of the best places in Texas to see a wide variety of wildlife, including the alligators in nearly 4,900 acres of natural Brazos bottomlands habitat. Close-up views of white-tailed deer, nutria, bobcats, swamp rabbits, and raccoons are as common as the many varieties of songbirds. An observation tower provides a dramatic view of a large rookery of wading birds as well as waterfowl. Summer provides good viewing of Wood Ducks and Black-bellied Whistling-Ducks, although they are most abundant in winter. Rules for viewing the alligators are available from the office and must be followed.

Brazos Bend State Park is at the heart of an initiative to conserve bottomland forests known as the Columbia Bottomland Conservation Partnership. Organizations taking a role in the initiative include the USFWS, the TPWD, and TNC. Once there were 700,000 acres of bottomland forests in this area. Today fewer than 170,000 acres remain, threatened with urbanization, logging, clearing for agriculture, and chipping for the paper pulp industry. The Columbia partnership was formed in mid-1994, and acquisition of land will, as always, depend upon willing sellers, quality of habitat, and availability of funds.

CLIVE RUNNELS FAMILY MAD ISLAND PRESERVE

Mad Island Marsh is a 7,048-acre preserve located in Matagorda County. In addition to TNC, project partners include the American Wetlands Conservation Council, Dow Chemical, the National Fish and Wildlife Foundation, Ducks Unlimited, the Environmental Protection Agency, the Troll Foundation, and the Communities Foundation of Texas. This tidal wetland and coastal grassland area is of value as wintering grounds to a wide variety of migratory waterfowl, as a shell and finfish nursery area, and as a habitat for typical Gulf faunal species. Restorations of palustrine and estuarine wetlands and coastal prairies are important projects at this preserve, along with the incorporation of waterfowl and wading-bird habitat values in an innovative program of rice-field management. There is a research station on Mad Island.

Mad Island came into being through a $1.3 million gift of land from Clive Runnels, and The Nature Conservancy used the gift to garner matching funds for stewardship. Mad Island Marsh has suffered from the decrease in freshwater inflows over the last fifty years. It was once the premier freshwater ecosystem of the Texas midcoast. It provides habitat for sixteen species of ducks and four species of geese as well as Sandhill Cranes and many wading and shorebird species.

Another link in the chain of protection provided by TNC is on Lamar Peninsula, a 734-acre site for Whooping Cranes. At La Bahia, close to the historic site of Indianola with its statue of La Salle, in ancestral Whooping Crane habitat, TNC has acquired a 3,500-acre tract from the estate of Myrtle Whitmire, who wanted to preserve this land in her name for all time. It is particularly important as expansion area for the whoopers of Aransas, because these birds need large territories and the refuge itself doesn't contain enough land for the hoped-for increase in Whooping Cranes.

ARANSAS NATIONAL WILDLIFE REFUGE

This is the defensive base camp for most of North America's migratory birds, the core that must be defended if our continent is to have birdlife. Thanks to a tremendous public-private effort fueled by the decline of the Whooping Crane, the refuge is now more than 85,000 acres, with prospects of more additions and with a ring of defenses that is also steadily increasing. A recent major addition to Aransas was made possible by TNC when it acquired the 11,502-acre Wynne Ranch in 1986, transferring title to the U.S. Fish and Wildlife Service, thus allowing all of Matagorda Island to be managed as part of this key refuge.

Although this refuge is known to most Americans as the winter home of the Whooping Crane, more than 80 percent of the continent's migrating bird species funnel through it every year. The whooper may be the star, but it's far from a solo act.

According to the USFWS, Whooping Crane totals hit a low of 21 in the winter of 1944–1945. But the real challenge came in the thirties when hunters put serious pressure on these magnificent cranes. On December 31, 1937, Franklin D. Roosevelt signed the executive order that created the Aransas National Wildlife Refuge in Aransas, Calhoun, and Refugio counties. Had that not happened, there is no doubt that this species would be extinct today. In fact, recent Aransas populations ranging around 140 to 150 do not guarantee survival. In the 1992–1993 season, 16 whoopers failed to make it back from nesting areas, and the population plunged again to 124. The 1993–1994 season saw the number traveling to the refuge area in a self-sustaining flock rise to 143, but only 140 are expected in the 1994–1995 season.

Among the best early examples of cooperation were those spearheaded by Robert Porter Allen of the National Audubon Society and the U.S. Fish and Wildlife Service. Allen became one of the foremost students of the whoopers. Through his magical writing (*The Whooping Crane,* 1952) and other exposures he created a great interest in the birds.

The whoopers arrive at Aransas and Matagorda Island in November after a long and hazardous flight from their breeding grounds at Wood Buffalo National Park, south of Great Slave Lake in Canada's Northwest Territories. They make their return flight to Canada in early April.

Once safely landed at Aransas and Matagorda Island the flock quickly spreads out in pairs and families, which establish exclusive foraging territories where they feed on shrimp, crayfish, blue crabs, and other crustaceans. Protecting the low-lying ponds and marshes from erosion caused by the Gulf Intracoastal Waterway is a perpetual challenge for the U.S. Army Corps of Engineers, galvanized into action in 1993 to install 7,000 feet of concrete matting on the refuge's edge. Local residents chip in by placing sacks of cement along the GIW's banks, but erosion still occurs at the rate of one or two acres annually. Mitchell Energy Company of Houston is establishing new crane habitats away from the canal on barrier islands made from dredged material collected during construction of pipelines and gas wells.

The Aransas National Wildlife Refuge is located on Blackjack Peninsula, formed as a Pleistocene sandbar, which 100,000 years ago resembled a barrier island such as Matagorda. When the Wisconsin glaciers began their meltdown the seas rose, and about 10,000 years ago the outline of the coastal plain and bays began to shape into the landform we see today.

About 3,000 years ago the coastline reached its present level, and the Gulf wave action began the process of piling sand on sand until shoals broke the surface. Then, the wind began its shaping, piling the dry sand yet higher, and an island was born. Now Blackjack Peninsula and its surrounding estuaries, flats, and bays are protected by nature from nature but, of course, not from humans. The passes cut eons ago by the river mouths allow the blending of aquatic systems, and the resulting gradient of salinity—from fresh to brackish to hypersaline, even out to the marine systems of the Gulf—is essential to the marvelous diversity of life forms. The refuge takes advantage of other gradients as well. It occupies important transition zones in the east-west moisture gradient and in the north-south shift from a temperate climate to the Lower Valley's subtropical climate. Plants and animals stay active all year in this environment.

Because of this diversity of habitats and its coastal location, Aransas is the most-needed oasis along the Central Flyway, the ancient migration route for millions of birds. No matter the bird's dietary requirements or habitat preferences, the right avian motel and restaurant will be found at Aransas. About 400 species of birds have been identified at Aransas, with an average of 300 species recorded each year. Because of the songbird migration, April is the prime month to visit Aransas and Matagorda Island, when birders accumulate an average of 215 species. By contrast, June bird counts drop to an average in the eighties.

The savanna and live oak woodlands have large populations of Wild Turkey, javelina and feral hogs, coyotes, bobcats, cougar, and jaguarundi. This last cat is new or perhaps returning to the area; it is typically found along the South Texas border. It's a small, dark cat, very hard to spot. A tour road rims the bay past pools, then up through the woodlands. There are observation towers, the one at Mustang Lake being particularly popular for spotting the whoopers. Best of all, there are trails that lead along marshes and beside ponds through the live oak thickets. It's here you'll find your conservation ethic renewed.

I suggest you take time to poke along the Heron Flats Trail at Aransas; if your visit is in the spring, you'll receive a lovely wildflower bonus. Whatever the season, only the best mosquito repellent will do. Heron Flats allows you to learn much more about the plant diversity of the refuge. Vines abound, including dewberry, pepper vine, and snout bean. In another spot, you'll find common reeds. Another turn of the trail brings you into a grove of 200- to 300-year-old oaks. The understory shrubs you'll see include yaupon, an erect shrub with horizontal branches. Mustang grape, granjeno, sugar hackberry, and agarita are just a few of the other interesting plants to be found.

MATAGORDA ISLAND

In 1986, The Nature Conservancy purchased the Wynne Ranch on the south end of Matagorda Island. The north end was already held by the U.S. Fish and Wildlife Service, which now owns the island as part of the national wildlife refuge. Permitted hunting is allowed under the TPWD management of the north end.

I first walked down Matagorda Island beach on an Easter weekend birding trip, and by coincidence had with me the translation of a diary written in 1687 by the first Spanish explorer to actually enter and probe the shallow coastal bays from a sailboat he could row when necessary. Robert Weddle, a historian who has documented the Spanish explorations in the Gulf of Mexico, has given us a marvelous translation of the record of that voyage, "carried out by two piraguas, built for coasting and reconnoitering all the Mexican Gulf." This diary (*The Enriquez Barroto Diary: Voyage of the Piraguas,* 1987) began on Christmas Day 1686, and the piraguas reached present-day Cedar Bayou on Easter Sunday 1687.

As I first read this section of the diary on another Easter Sunday, some three hundred years later, I was stunned by the similarities and the differences. This was before The Nature Conservancy had completed its transfer to the U.S. Fish and Wildlife Service and before the island began its march back in time under the watchful eye of USFWS managers. As I read Barroto's diary, I had a premonition of what this restoration would accomplish; it was exciting to think of the contribution to conservation of one of the most important barrier islands in North America.

Thanks to the work of The Nature Conservancy and the Fish and Wildlife Service, both the flora and the fauna of this ecological area are gradually returning to a natural state. TNC and USFWS staffers and volunteers such as myself have now recorded more than three hundred species of birds on this island alone. The black-mustachioed Peregrine Falcon still crisscrosses the beaches, and I've had the thrill of watching a male (tiercel) rocket down in a 200 mph stoop to explode into a Blue-winged Teal who infelicitously shared the fall migration route over the island. I was able to observe the feeding falcon closely, as he took no note of me while he used his wicked, hooked beak to good advantage. The urge was to inch closer, but that would have been wrong. Enthusiastic birders, though their generous donations make them the birds'

best friends, often unwittingly stress them. During the Nature Conservancy survey prior to transferring ownership to the USFWS, we quickly learned to stay at least a thousand yards from Whooping Crane pairs, especially those with chicks. Good optics are a must here, first for your conservation ethic, second for your pleasure.

Matagorda Island is part of the fragile sand barrier that fringes the Coastal Bend of Texas. Conserved through private and public partnerships, it provides critical staging habitat for migratory birds.

To write in depth of Matagorda birding would be almost to replicate the National Geographic Society's *Field Guide to the Birds of North America,* my soiled, tattered copy of which is stuffed with notations from here. There are many special places and special times; for the birds, a fallout is the apex. But any time is marvelous, with natural migration peaks in April and September. The winter months bring many waterfowl, when the island ponds are awash with paddlings of ducks.

The study of migration is a study of nearly infinite breadth and complexity, striving for a complete understanding of the interconnectedness of nature that is, of course, beyond us. Those with a conservation ethic have accepted this interconnectedness as truth and know that a seemingly inconsequential event, like a persistent northwesterly wind, can have a profound effect on nature. Among other things at Matagorda, it can cause neotropicals from many different countries to rain down on the same day in the spring, or wintering birds to seek food elsewhere as the island's flats are blown dry.

Flashbacks and fragments of many trips to the island stick in the mind: the roost of a Great Horned Owl in an old rocket launch stand; the roost of Black-crowned Night-Herons that also harbors large numbers of White Ibises; the Black-shouldered Kites perched in scraggly mesquite trees like symbols of surrender; the Roseate Spoonbills' bright pink formation against a pearlescent sunrise; egrets and herons of all species stationed across the flats, harpoon beaks at the ready; American Avocets rushing about in ranks, giving new meaning to the phrase "feeding frenzy"; rounding a corner on a shell road to sight a gulp of cormorants perched on pilings, a split second later realizing they are actually Magnificent Frigatebirds; and slowly easing down a sunlit brushy lane flickering in brilliant shades of indigo and the rainbow effect of Painted Buntings.

Once, on an educational tour through the scrub on the island's western edge, I noticed a jackrabbit catapulting itself into the mosquito-laden air, resembling a scrambling cartoon character as it hit the ground running. Knowing what was coming, I stopped to let the students watch as two 5-foot rattlers slithered out of the weeds bordering the rabbit's former location. One of the students wanted a jackrabbit on a leash for the rest of his stay.

I have been tromping about in rattlesnake country for more than fifty years, and I have never seen so many rattlers as on this island. They'll join you for cocktails on the lodge's patio and on the roads during your evening constitutional. The TPWD ranger at the north end warns everyone of the danger, even citing a rattler swimming in the surf (new to me). True, with the grasses growing taller, they are more difficult to spot—but they are there and are a real danger, especially in the rodent-rich dunes. Massasaugas and cottonmouth moccasins like moist sites and are also common on the island. I have seen only one coral snake and no pygmy rattlesnakes, although they're said to be present.

Another island attraction is the American alligator, which should not be considered a pet, despite the human tendency to give them familiar names, such as "Jaws" and "Charlie Brown." Jaws lives in the man-made ponds near the Wynne lodge and in 1994 had grown to more than fourteen feet, thanks to having been fed by USFWS personnel, a dangerous practice since it causes alligators to lose their fear of humans. Jaws is quick enough to take the occasional unwary white-tailed deer fawn, and I saw him narrowly miss a golden retriever. Another alligator, Charlie Brown, would accost you from his favorite pond near the terminus of the hardtop road to the beach: do remember that alligators can outrun you over the short haul. Charlie Brown wasn't quick enough to avoid being eaten himself in 1994 by a yet more aggressive gator. Returning to the lodge after an educational tour, I was compelled to stop as an eight-footer slowly inched off the road. The next thing I knew, it lunged into the air, seeking my left elbow, thumping into the rusty Suburban hard enough to dent the door. The female can become downright feisty when guarding her nest and will attack sideways to bring her powerful tail into the fray. The idea is to knock you down with a powerful swipe, then chomp whatever extremity is nearest. By the way, they love dogs.

Farsighted businesses such as Houston-based Enron Corporation are major contributors to wetland preservation. Continuing its strong commitment to conservation, Enron funded a $2 million endowment for the Enron Matagorda Island Environmental Education and Research Center. The new facility at Matagorda, the last major undeveloped barrier island on the Texas coast, will offer unique educational and research opportunities for graduate and undergraduate field research. The new center will be managed jointly by the USFWS and The Nature Conservancy. Other major contributors to the effort at Matagorda Island include the Communities Foundation of Texas, with a $500,000 grant, and the Hoblitzelle Foundation, with a $50,000 grant.

When you are on Matagorda Island you have a sense of isolation, an otherworld feeling that will stir your conservation ethic. You'll sense, more than see, hear, and smell, that you have gone way back in time, maybe to 300 years ago, when this was Karankawa country. A walk on the island's remote beach is a wrenching experience; you are drawn to the inherent wildness but repelled by the litter from careless Gulf users. Still, beachcombing here is usually rewarding, with hundreds of species of mollusks leaving their shells for you to identify: clams, oysters, cockles, mussels, scallops, and arks.

Shell authority Jean Andrews, who describes and illustrates 279 mollusks in her *Texas Shells* (1981), estimates that there are about 50,000 species of mollusks (the word is from a root meaning soft bodied). This staggering diversity makes shell identification challenging. You'll occasionally find snails, with shells that coil and spiral and whorl to fashion a sculpture of exquisite loveliness.

Sargassum seaweeds often cover the beaches, a nuisance to swimmers but a boon to the beach itself; sargassum holds sand until other plants can grab hold. You'll amble by harmless cabbagehead jellyfish and poisonous Portuguese man-of-war, its purple, gas-filled float telling you to give it wide berth. Even after the man-of-war is seemingly dried out, the tentacles can wound, as the nematocysts will still fire their barbs into your tender hide if you touch them.

Part of the story of Matagorda Island represents the evolution of a sportsman's ethic into a conservation ethic. The ranch was owned by Toddie Lee Wynne, an avid sportsman. As the years passed, he became increasingly committed to the protection of wildlife. His developing conservation ethic led to his desire that the island would eventually be protected. His wishes were honored by Jackie Wynne, wife of Toddie Lee Wynne, Jr., at his death. Jackie Wynne fell in love with the island herself and thus welcomed the sale to The Nature Conservancy. As in the case of La Bahia, Matagorda Island affords excellent Whooping Crane habitat, enough room for twelve territories and twenty-four adult birds, some hopefully with chicks.

MATAGORDA ISLAND STATE PARK

A trip to this facility requires some advance planning, because the highlight of the Matagorda environmental, educational, and interpretive services is a guided tour in a state vehicle, available only by prior arrangement. Educational programs and tours can also be arranged for school groups. The TPWD booklet on Matagorda Island State Park suggests that visitors leave tape decks and radios at home and be quiet in campgrounds and on docks, great advice for allowing this magical island to work on your personal conservation ethic.

Obviously, visitors may expect to find the same proliferation of birds and wildlife described earlier. This is one of the premier experiences in Texas conservation education. Recreational activities include swimming, fishing, hiking, camping, individual nature study, picnicking, boating, canoeing, photography, collecting shells, and, by permit, hunting. One of the most enjoyable ways to see the island is by bicycling the beach and roads. Surf fishermen have been known to use nonmotorized trail bikes to prowl the surf line for redfish and trout.

The only way to get to Matagorda Island is by boat, an eleven-mile journey from Port O'Connor. A passenger ferry is available on Saturdays, Sundays, and holidays. Charter services are also available. Every weekend, weather permitting, a shuttle vehicle makes round-trips from the docks to the Gulf beaches, but the TPWD advises visitors to call ahead to check all schedules, as they are subject to change.

WELDER WILDLIFE FOUNDATION

The Rob and Bessie Welder Wildlife Foundation is a private, operating foundation funded by an endowment, oil royalties, and cattle income. Since its establishment in 1954 it has gained international recognition through its graduate student research programs.

The Welder Wildlife Foundation egg collection played a role in Rachel Carson's study for her book *Silent Spring*, published in 1962. This was the book that motivated me, and thousands like me, to acquire a deeper conservation ethic and more knowledge of ecology and ecosystem health. Carson worked with the original foundation director, Clarence Cottam, and used the bird shell collection as part of her benchmark research. These shells were from normal eggs, with thickness unaffected by DDT and other pesticides then under suspicion in the decline of raptors such

No twigs in sight, but the definition of "nest" is "a bed or receptacle" for bird eggs, and these Black Skimmers prove the point at their Padre Island home. They skim the surface of nearby Laguna Madre with their extended lower mandibles, scooping up fresh fish for themselves and junior.

as the American Bald Eagle, the Peregrine Falcon, the Brown Pelican, and numerous other birds.

The primary purpose of the foundation, according to its director James Teer, "is to conduct research and education in the field of wildlife management and conservation and other closely related fields." The foundation's 7,800-acre wildlife refuge is thirty-five miles north of Corpus Christi, in a transitional area between the Gulf Prairies and Marshes and the South Texas Plains ecological areas. Permanent facilities include offices, a 10,000-volume research library, dormitory, study, lecture hall, laboratories, museum collections, and rotunda.

Teer reports that each year fifteen to twenty carefully selected graduate students from universities across the nation are granted fellowships to conduct research and pursue advanced degrees in wildlife conservation and management. In a recent year, participating universities included Montana State, Oregon State, Purdue, Texas A&I, Texas A&M, Texas Tech, University of California, University of Idaho, University of Minnesota, University of Missouri, University of Oklahoma, University of Texas, University of Wisconsin, and Utah State.

The foundation is able to do its work "unhindered by outside political or institutional pressures," reports Teer. "No other organization has dedicated itself solely to conducting wildlife research in the midst of a ranching operation and an active oil field," he states.

PADRE ISLAND NATIONAL SEASHORE

Enriquez Barroto was one of the first Europeans to set foot on Padre Island, on March 13, 1687. His exact location can be calculated from his diary notes; the latitude he recorded was just a few minutes off from measurements made by today's scientific instruments, an impressive performance considering his equipment. The first European record of the island was made in 1519 by Alonso de Piñeda; he named it Isla Blanca, the White Island.

Barroto's notes describe a Padre Island much like the one we see today, thanks to its preservation as a national seashore by the National Park Service: "The large, long and barren dunes that I have mentioned extend this far, and there are some knolls among them at intervals. We got under way at daybreak and went north by northwest [Padre Island runs this direction] one league, where we saw three huts of Indians and not many breakers on the coast. Here, with the canoes, we finished watering, for which purpose we anchored near shore in a small lagoon not far from the huts. There were five Indians and they presently fled behind some large and extended dunes like those I have mentioned. The river that flows within is seen, but very far off." The river is Laguna Madre.

From Piñeda's Isla Blanca sighting to President John F. Kennedy's signature on the law authorizing an 80-mile-long national seashore on Padre Island (September 28, 1962), 443 years passed, plenty of time to figure out that this 113-mile-long island was a conservation treasure of inestimable value. It has value not just to wildlife but also to the millions of visitors who find this a special place, a place to hone a conservation ethic, a place to renew one's soul. Padre Island is the longest of America's 295 barrier islands, which stretch from the tip of Maine to the Mexican border at Boca Chica, 2,800 miles representing the best-developed (geographically and biologically speaking) system of barrier islands in the world. Padre Island is also the longest undeveloped coastal wilderness in the continental United States.

The Nature Conservancy has played a major part in preserving barrier islands, its most notable effort being the Virginia Coast Bioreserve, protecting the entire barrier chain off that state, the bays within, and even the mainland coast where it would threaten the barrier island's ecosystem.

Once protected doesn't mean always protected, as barrier islands are very fragile, dynamic ecosystems, naturally everchanging but even more susceptible to destruction by human actions.

There are multiple theories of barrier-island formation and undoubted multiple origins as well. Primary barrier islands are formed on land that would later be flooded by the sea; secondary islands develop seaward of the primary coast on the continental shelf. There are two types of secondary islands, breached spits of land and emergent offshore bars. From observation of the Texas coastline, with its alternating peninsulas and islands, one could argue that Padre Island represents a combination of breached spit and emergent offshore bar formed as the sea added sand to a submerged bar. Then wind action took over in the accretion stage, with stabilizing vegetation finally forming the barrier island we see today, or think we see today, because barrier islands continually change. Padre rolls over itself, migrating shoreward as sand eroded from the beaches is carried back into Laguna Madre. Hurricanes can blow out an entire section of the island and also create an overwash that can carry huge quantities of sand into Laguna Madre. Scientists arriving after Hurricane Carla in 1961 were astonished at the damage, noting that ten-foot-high cliffs had been carved away as if made of whipped cream. Other islands, most notably Galveston, prograde (advance toward the sea), as they have a large amount of sand piling in thanks to longshore currents. Galveston Island has moved seaward several miles in the last three thousand or four thousand years.

When driving on the seacoast, whatever you do, stay off the dunes. Don't drive on any vegetation. And be careful as you approach camps, since the surf and wind can mute the sound of your vehicle. By all means carry fishing gear, as the surf fishing can be outstanding for redfish, speckled sea trout, black drum, and whiting. Binoculars are a must too, for during spring and fall migrations, there's a good chance of seeing a Peregrine Falcon. Coyotes and their favorite meal, black-tailed jackrabbit, are common on the island, and so are western diamondback rattlesnakes and alligators.

Padre Island provides protection for a special habitat, Laguna Madre, a highly diverse hypersaline environment. Millions of marine creatures are sustained by this lagoon, marking the start of a food web extremely important to the marine life of the Gulf and therefore to humans. Critical to this web are the seagrass beds in Laguna Madre, some of the finest, most productive habitat for crustaceans and other wee creatures. Most hot, hypersaline environments are not nice places to live, but Laguna Madre's large seagrass beds are wonderful nurseries for finfish. A brown-tide bloom of plant plankton covered much of the surface by 1994, blocking life-giving sunlight from the grasses and shrinking their area. Adding to Laguna Madre's woes was a breach in the dam holding back sludge dredged to maintain the Gulf Intracoastal Waterway near Port Mansfield. The sludge spread to destroy another large area of seagrass.

Efforts to save Kemp's ridley sea turtles on Padre Island have not fared well. Despite massive efforts, it would appear the Kemp's ridley sea turtle is all but gone. In 1947, a film of the beach at Rancho Nuevo

Goatsfoot morning glory not only glorifies Texas coastal marshes, but its vines also help stabilize barrier-island dunes. Vegetation is essential to dune formation, trapping windblown sands and minimizing blowouts.

on the Mexican Gulf coast of Tamaulipas showed an estimated 40,000 Kemp's ridleys swimming ashore. Forty years later, the annual count for the same beach was 500. Most of the 39,500 missing turtles were eaten by poachers, along with their eggs. The last turtle I knew to come ashore was just south of my place on Mustang Island in 1990. Its 105 eggs were discovered by Tony Amos, with the University of Texas Marine Science Institute at Port Aransas, and excavated and incubated by Donna Shaver at the Padre Island National Seashore. After hatching, the baby turtles were set loose at the very point their mother buried the eggs. All of the hatchlings, guarded by volunteers, made it into the surf. They're not expected back for many years, but one would think a few of the 18,000 hatchlings that have been launched off Padre beaches in the past fifteen years would return. None have, except mine at Mustang, if in fact she was a Padre release.

Another disgrace of the Texas coast is the debris that washes ashore. Tony Amos has done exhaustive studies of this problem during the course of more than two thousand beach patrols of Mustang Island. His daily records are documented with his on-truck computer. The Marine Pollution Act Annex 5, known as Marpol 5, went into effect on December 31, 1988, and is designed to regulate shipboard garbage disposal with special emphasis on plastics. According to Amos's 1993 work, *Solid Waste*

Sea oats, vines, and salt-tolerant grasses intertwine on a large dune on Padre Island National Seashore. A relatively continuous dune ridge has been established on the island as a by-product of the onshore wind and sand-stabilizing vegetation.

Pollution on Texas Beaches: A Post–Marpol 5 Study, efforts such as Marpol 5 have cut down a little on the garbage, but the problem continues. Amos feels justified in pointing out that the merchant marine and shrimping fleets are contributors to the beach pollution. Amos says, "Waste from the ships' kitchens (galleys) has been traditionally chucked over the side. Despite some improvements since Marpol V, this practice has been continued by some, and readily identifiable 'galley waste' still washes ashore on our beaches. Even though some shrimp boats are at sea for only a few days, there are hundreds of them operating at any one time. They use standard galley supplies such as one-gallon milk jugs and egg cartons and bags, and chemicals. When hundreds of plastic milk jugs are found on a remote Texas beach, you know they weren't brought there by people going to the beach for a picnic. Likewise with plastic buckets containing sodium metabisulfite with labels stating 'For the treatment of black spot on shrimp.' Also, the multiplicity of containers bearing labels with foreign languages were borne to the beach from a tanker or cargo ship, not in a beachgoer's bag." Amos continues to monitor the condition of Texas beaches.

Padre Island is especially important to scientists, as they can study the island both in a stabilized state and in an eroding mode, to measure the impact of tide, strong currents, and sea-level changes. Helping such studies is the lack of development pressures, at least on the national seashore. Padre thus becomes a baseline study of this most important part of America's natural heritage.

That Padre Island is subject to change is brought home to visitors immediately upon entering the national seashore, on what is known as the Grasslands Nature Trail. The first exhibit on this trail is a blowout dune, where the wind has carved out a saucer-shaped depression in the side of the dune. This dune, if not stabilized, will move toward Laguna Madre at an average rate of thirty-five feet a year, perhaps as fast as seventy-five feet per year.

This is a safe place to study dune ecology, starting with the tall sea oats with their fluttering tassels. It's the initial colonizers that have the critical job of beginning the stabilization process. They are sand-hugging plants such as beach morning glory with its white blossom, the magenta-flowered goatsfoot morning glory, and yellow-flowered beach evening primrose. You'll need to get up early to enjoy those sun-shy blooms. The reason you'll see many doves over the dunes is the presence of goatweed, a variety of croton with distinctive, silvery leaves, a favorite dove food. There are several species of sunflowers, including the downy sunflower, and a profusion of flowers lumped together in a category we amateurs call daisies but only slightly more precisely classified by botanists as DYCs (damned yellow composites). The cordgrasses and saltgrasses (described earlier), bushy bluestem, and seventy other grasses are important to keeping the sands in place. Keep off the grass—all the grass. You will even see live oaks, hackberries, red bay, and yaupon holly in the areas behind the dunes, but they are rarities in a dune environment.

The encroachment of Padre Island into Laguna Madre's space is not the major threat to the habitat, however. This, as usual, will come from humans. South of the Mansfield Channel, Padre Island is privately owned, with some large corporate holdings. If full-scale development takes place, Laguna Madre will be at risk. The water is shallow, with no riverine input. The system is stable in that it doesn't fluctuate much from year to year, but that also makes it more fragile and more vulnerable to human impact. The effluence—nutrient flow—from major development on South Padre would eventually devastate Laguna Madre. Today, you can drive north toward Mansfield Channel from the town of South Padre and see where dirt bikes and dune buggies have torn up the dunes, stripping away the vegetation that holds them together. Many of the dunes are already blowouts headed right for Laguna Madre.

On the west side of Laguna Madre, the King Ranch has long provided environmental protection—it has a 100-year history of outstanding private conservation. But now the oil and gas reserves are depleting, and the ranch will be adjusting its revenues through increased agriculture. Already tens of thousands of acres have been planted in soybeans. Once again, nature faces the balance between economics and ecology, but I hope the King Ranch management will consider a conservation easement on the Laguna Madre borders. In 1994, the King Ranch, threatened with condemnation proceedings to provide a dump area for U.S. Army Corps of Engineers dredging in the Intracoastal Waterway, filed suit to force the Corps to produce an environmental impact plan for Laguna Madre.

RARE BIRD ALERT

Lone Star Rare Bird Alert, also known as the Texas Rare Bird Alert, 713-992-2757 (sponsored by the Houston Audubon Society). Texas Coastal Bend Bird Hotline, in Sinton, 512-364-3634 (sponsored by the Mangram Bird Club).

"THE WILD HORSE DESERT"
THE SOUTH TEXAS PLAINS

CHAPTER 7

Crossing the Mustang or Wild Horse Desert, either from the Nueces or the bay, the country is almost as level as the ocean, which it strikingly resembles when clothed with the tall grass, which is ever fanned by the bland southern breeze. Except a motte or small chaparral of bushes at long intervals, it is destitute of timber.

WILLIAM A. MCCLINTOCK
Journal of a Trip through Texas and Northern Mexico in 1846–1847

Driving south on Highway 77 through the country that mapmaker Thomas Bradford, in 1835, first labeled "Mustang or Wild Horse Desert," I couldn't help but recall a conversation with James Teer of the Welder Wildlife Foundation about how the South Texas Plains were not scenic in the sense that the Rockies are. Many people find this area uninteresting, monotonous, and desertlike. That perception was heightened for me on a recent trip when fog, mist, and drizzle shrouded the bleak landscape. What is really there, if only we could see it, is rich, abundant, diverse life.

There is a monotony to the landscape as the traveler pushes through miles of ranch country, heading into the Lower Rio Grande Valley through the biotic communities of coastal brushland and middelta thorn forest. This is big country, 20 million acres in the entire ecological area, big enough for one of the world's largest private ranches, the celebrated King Ranch, established in 1851 by Richard King and his friend Mifflin Kenedy, with more than 800,000 acres in four huge divisions.

Mapmaker Bradford was cheating when he labeled the area a desert. He had a large, blank space on his map that had to be called something, an area avoided, apparently not even thoroughly explored, by the

OPPOSITE PAGE
Cha-cha-lac *grates the cacophonous chorus, much to the enjoyment of visitors to Bentsen–Rio Grande Valley State Park. Chachalaca choruses are larger and louder today along the Rio Grande, thanks to the ban on DDT.*

Spanish in the 1600s and 1700s. About two miles south of this so-called desert lies Sal del Rey (King's Salt). This historic lake, a source of salt for the early Spanish settlements, is now protected by the U.S. Fish and Wildlife Service via efforts of The Nature Conservancy.

The open grassland of 200 years ago—with scattered shrubs, a few low trees, and wooded floodplains—has been transformed by overgrazing and fire suppression into a thorn forest. The Bordas Scarp, described by the Texas Natural Heritage Program as "a long, curving outcrop of caliche once covered with a savanna-like carpet of shrubs and grasses," is now cloaked with solid thickets of thorny brush.

To someone developing a conservation ethic, the plant and animal diversity here makes these plains one of the most important areas in the nation. In the Lower Rio Grande Valley we find another ecotone, where some temperate-zone species reach the outermost limits of their range, as do the species working their way north from the tropics just 100 miles to the south.

Rainfall varies widely in the area, from sixteen inches in the west to thirty-five inches on the coast. Adding to the diversity are the Mississippi and Central flyways, which both funnel into the Valley. Swainson's and Broad-winged hawks migrate by the thousands through a fifty-mile section of the Lower Rio Grande Valley, right over Santa Ana National Wildlife Refuge, and the Laguna Atascosa National Wildlife Refuge on Laguna Madre is a magnet for migratory waterfowl. The remnant subtropical ecosystems such as those at the Sabal Palm Sanctuary and Santa Ana are filled with fascinating, colorful birdlife found nowhere else in North America.

The Rio Grande Plain remains a haven for many rare species of plants and animals. The vegetation is a unique mixture of plants with western desert, northern, coastal, and tropical affinities. The total number of native plants found in this area is unknown, but an astonishing number of plants occur here and nowhere else. Rarities include Johnston's frankenia, Runyon's cory cactus, and the famous black lace cactus. This cactus is so rare that its few locations are zealously guarded by conservationists and landowners, protecting it from the increasing plague of cacti rustlers. Ocelots, jaguarundi, and black-spotted newts still skulk through the remnant sabal palm and riparian woodlands.

The Tamaulipan brushland of the Lower Rio Grande Valley is a unique ecosystem, found only in Texas and northeastern Mexico, with eleven interrelated plant and animal communities. Ecosystems there host some 700 vertebrates and 1,200 plants, an international biological crossroads.

According to USFWS Biological Report 8836 (November 1988), 95 percent of native Tamaulipan brushland has been cleared in this century for agriculture, urban development, and recreation. In the lush riparian forest areas along the rivers, 99 percent of native plant life has been destroyed, and in the process, we have lost much biodiversity through extinction of many species.

Rachel Carson's *Silent Spring* goaded our federal government into taking action against certain pesticides years before it would have normally reacted. Today, more benign pesticides are used on Valley crops. Hard pesticides, the chlorinated hydrocarbon pesticides, are magnified as they pass up through the food web. By "magnified," scientists mean that chemicals become more concentrated in living tissue and therefore more dangerous. What Carson accomplished was far more than the saving of some birds—she saved life on this planet, which someday will be recognized.

As mentioned in the previous chapter, pesticides such as DDT so weakened eggshells as to lower populations of Brown Pelicans. Green Jays, Groove-billed Anis, Black-bellied Whistling-Ducks, and chachalacas were especially affected in the Valley, and out on the coast the stately Brown Pelicans were almost lost.

David Blankinship, a National Audubon Society biologist now with the U.S. Fish and Wildlife Service, began in 1971 to restore the Texas Brown Pelican population from an estimated low of thirty-five birds. Blankinship, along with Emilie Payne of the Audubon Outdoor Club of Corpus Christi, provided concentrated protection for the remaining pelican nesting sites near Rockport and Corpus Christi. Additional nesting islands were leased from the state of Texas. The work has paid off. Coastal visitors now frequently enjoy the spectacular headfirst dive-to-feed antics of these homely surf riders as they fold their seven-foot wingspans for impact.

In the mid-nineties, the Environmental Protection Agency has begun to modernize its policies, updating pesticide laws to help farmers use valuable chemical tools that would give us more protection, not less. The EPA has been hamstrung by conflicting standards in pesticide laws since the mid-eighties. Increasing populations of Groove-billed Anis, Black-bellied Whistling-Ducks, and chachalacas in the Valley and Brown Pelicans on the coast are good indicators of progress. Partnerships between the agricultural community and regulatory agencies are a vital component of saving the best of Texas.

Also affecting the Valley ecology has been the construction of extensive flood-control levee systems and upstream dams such as the Falcon Dam on the Rio Grande. Economically, these levees and dams have worked as planned by the U.S. Army Corps of Engineers, but without seasonal flooding, the patches of remnant riparian forest are slowly becoming less diverse. Honey mesquite has consequently displaced original species such as Texas ebony, sugarberry, anacua, and Mexican ash.

An Altamira Oriole puts the finishing touch on a nest at Bentsen–Rio Grande Valley State Park. Formerly known as Lichtenstein's oriole and formerly rare, the Altamira is now, according to Audubon authorities, the most common resident Valley oriole.

THE WILDLIFE CORRIDOR

The real story of the South Texas Plains and especially the Lower Rio Grande Valley is in the massive conservation effort going full tilt, not only to conserve the remnants that are left of a wildlife-rich ecosystem but also to restore and even link these remnants in a way that helps wildlife utilize the natural environment. The heart of this conservation effort is called the Lower Rio Grande Valley National Wildlife Refuge, or the Wildlife Corridor, led by the U.S. Fish and Wildlife Service, again in partnership with Texas Parks and Wildlife, The Nature Conservancy, the Audubon Society, local groups such as the Valley Land Fund, and, in a departure from other areas of the nation, even the Cameron County Agriculture and Wildlife Coexistence Committee.

In fact, the success of this project, with the core USFWS refuge now pegged at 132,500 acres, is really in private hands. To the credit of the people of the Lower Rio Grande Valley, a strong conservation ethic is building, and people are pulling together to arrest the decline of the Valley's fragile ecosystem. The project sweeps from the tidal flats of the beach at Boca Chica to the Chihuahuan Thorn Forest below Falcon State Park at Falcon Lake. Here are found scraps of one of only two subtropical biotas in the continental United States, the other being in Florida.

In the early sixties, the White-winged Dove population in northeastern Mexico, according to David Blankinship of the USFWS, was around six million. Grain-field expansion in this area increased the population to more than eighteen million in just a few years, but now the elimination of nesting habitat for yet more grain fields is again reducing the dove population. Hunters toting TPWD licenses and White-winged Dove stamps contributed millions of dollars to the local economy, and hunting is still a significant source of revenue for Valley businesses. The TPWD is attempting to provide more nesting areas for this bird, so important to the local economy.

Gary Waggerman of the TPWD recently showed me one of the units of Las Palomas Wildlife Management Area, explaining how he had managed the effort to restore nesting habitat for many years. The first efforts, at the Longoria Unit, emphasized establishment of five native woody species: huisache, Texas ebony, anacua, granjeno, and brasil. The Palomas WMA–Rio Grande units are composed of eight tracts located in Cameron, Hidalgo, Starr, and Willacy counties. They are all important as nesting habitat for the White-winged Dove, but the restoration process relied on hand labor and proved far too costly. The most significant problem was that the area lacked the necessary diversity.

Today, much more efficient techniques of brush restoration are in use. Large quantities of seeds, representing a wide diversity of plants, are collected, stored, and germinated under optimum conditions. Greenhouse seedlings are then planted by mechanical means. Waggerman and his TPWD team established a basic restoration strategy: "We established islands or patches of native shrub land on previously cropped lands to provide seed sources for subsequent colonization." An optimum placement pattern was then determined.

Dave Blankinship explains that the USFWS "plants an area with numerous native species, as close as possible to the native mix, because of the complex web of organisms involved." Blankinship adds that the microorganisms in the soil are a point of vulnerability because pesticides destroy or weaken them. Many of the sources to replenish them, such as the wind, water flow, and birds, could take quite a while to spread, but thanks to land conservation of the remnant patches, at least we have a rootstock to work with.

TNC has launched a private land initiative in South Texas with a beginning target of restoring 300 acres of native habitat. One of the challenges is to link habitat across tracts of land owned by people who do not wish to sell. The TPWD and TNC work together to restore selected portions of privately owned tracts. The many landowners who volunteered are expressing a personal commitment to preserving things wild and free for the future. Landowners have been frustrated in their own restoration efforts by the lack of availability of native species of trees and shrubs. As a TNC staff member points out, you can't get granjeno, amargoso, or guajillo at your local Wal-Mart garden center.

Today, both the USFWS and the TPWD are using cooperative farm agreements as a means of managing the land during the transition phase from newly acquired cropland to restored woodland, and local volunteer citizen groups such as the Valley Land Fund are making a big difference. This group, formed by Steve Bentsen and John Martin, describes itself: "The Valley Land Fund is not political and takes no stand on the issues affecting the 95 percent of Valley land that is already cleared. We are a group of Valley citizens who feel we owe it to our children and their children to save something of the tremendous bounty that was, and is, the Rio Grande Valley." This local, nonprofit organization of volunteers is dedicated exclusively to preserving the remaining 5 percent of the natural environment. In 1994, the Valley Land Fund sponsored "The Richest Wildlife Photo Contest in History" to recognize the role private landowners play in habitat conservation. Prizes totaled more than $75,000.

The Valley Land Fund has acquired, among other tracts, the 220-acre Chihuahuan Woods in Hidalgo County. This tract has been identified by TNC and USFWS scientists as having unequaled natural value. Dr. Bob Lonard, professor at the University of Texas–Pan American, has said of Chihuahuan Woods, "I have never seen such species richness or diversity anywhere else in Texas."

To link existing habitat remnants and form viable wildlife corridors, the USFWS, the TPWD, and TNC are purchasing land from willing sellers, which will be revegetated with native species. The South Texas Private Land Initiative of The Nature Conservancy is helping to restore native habitat on hundreds of acres of corridors linking wildlife preserves.

For the record, USFWS purchase offers made to landowners are based on appraisals that consider recent sales prices of comparable land. The price offered cannot be less than fair market value. Although the lands acquired are taken off the respective counties' tax rolls, the Federal Refuge Revenue Sharing Tax Act provides for annual payments to the counties in lieu of taxes, usually equal to or even greater than previous tax revenues, and always on time. Each acquisition, each small or large parcel of land conserved as wildlife habitat, is essential in ensuring that this national treasure survives.

Other projects farther north in the ecological area seek to protect native brushland, such as the 683-acre TNC preserve of native brush at the Albert Mesquite Brushlands. This land was donated by Richard Albert, who bought the land solely to conserve it, then willed it to TNC so future generations could study the native brush, which once covered that entire area of Texas.

Another fine example of native brush is found at the 15,200-acre TPWD Chaparral Wildlife Management Area, near Artesia Wells, one of

the areas you may visit with your conservation passport. Almost two hundred bird species have been recorded here, and three endangered species of reptiles found here are the Texas tortoise, Texas indigo snake, and Texas horned lizard. In addition to the usual South Texas deer and javelina, a badger or bobcat may surprise you around the water tanks.

Sal del Rey Lake in Hidalgo County, just north of Highway 186, represents another great private-public partnership. The Nature Conservancy acquired the lake, situated within a 5,436-acre parcel, in 1991, and today the USFWS owns Sal del Rey.

The history of Sal del Rey is fascinating. No doubt Indians valued the area, as it attracts many species of wildlife, and Spaniards were using the springs heavily in the mid-eighteenth century. You can still see traces of ancient trails leading to the springs. In addition to providing high-quality salt for meat preservation and seasoning, the springs were also valued for therapeutic reasons. It was believed that salt water cured skin diseases. The salt is of extraordinary quality, although it is not completely understood how it works its way to the surface. Commercial extraction continues to this day. Sal del Rey is also an important stopover for migratory waterfowl. Thousands of grebes, ducks, and shorebirds dine on a fine entrée of tasty, tiny brine shrimp, which thrive there. Sandhill Cranes, raptors, and a variety of other waterfowl also use the area.

This lake has been valued for centuries by humans for the quality of its salt and by migratory waterfowl and shorebirds for the proliferation of its tiny brine shrimp. Sal del Rey, or King's Salt, is today protected by the USFWS, with an assist from The Nature Conservancy.

To the east of Sal del Rey are La Sal Vieja lakes, which the USFWS lists in fourth place nationally as unique and threatened ecosystems. They are now partially owned by the USFWS, and work is going forward to link this area with the river corridor via an existing canal system.

The local Valley economy is benefiting from USFWS's Wildlife Corridor efforts. The biggest boost to the Valley comes from the hundreds of thousands of visitors who are attracted to the area each year specifically by wildlife. Santa Ana and Laguna Atascosa national wildlife refuges and Falcon and Bentsen state parks check in more than 500,000 visitors annually, and the figure is increasing. This is an economic windfall to Valley businesses. I'm certain that many of the winter Texans who keep this economy robust in the colder months are also attracted by the wildlife in their quest for warmth.

The USFWS recognizes eleven biotic communities within the Lower Rio Grande Valley NWR, which represents great diversity. This diversity provides the food chains within the web of life that support 115 vertebrate species of wildlike management concern.

Dave Blankinship urges patience: "While insects, birds, and mammals can move back and forth, snails and plants don't find the corridors too conducive to travel. . . . They move by generations." We know there is a large degree of organization in the connections between species, but we still have a lot to learn. Edward O. Wilson, in *The Diversity of Life* (1992), explains, "Most species of birds, ants and other plants and animals are linked to multiple chains in the food web. It is very difficult to assess which survivors will fill in for the extinguished species and how competently they will perform in that role." Wilson adds, "Keep in mind that ecology is a far more complex subject than physics."

LAGUNA ATASCOSA NATIONAL WILDLIFE REFUGE

This 45,190-acre refuge is the southernmost of the coastal national wildlife refuges that The Nature Conservancy helped to increase in size. TNC acquired 2,028 acres from the Armstrong family and added it to the Laguna Atascosa Refuge, which gave the refuge more than 8,000 acres of brushland. The TNC land was a pothole area, a good prairie freshwater source where there isn't much, a natural attraction for the rare and beautiful ocelot. The USFWS has a program to place radiocollars on some of these ocelots to learn more about their patterns, habitat use, and life-styles.

Other cats include the rare and endangered jaguarundi, a small, weasellike cat with a long tail, and the cougar, rare here but not in other parts of Texas. The bobcat thrives here, as it does across the state. Rats and mice abound to augment the cats' diets should they miss out on the raccoons, opossums, hares, rabbits, squirrels, and pocket gophers.

Feral hogs and collared peccary (javelina), even coyotes and gray foxes, occasionally dash across the trail, and white-tailed deer are common. Badgers find the sandy soil to their liking. They can outdig any predator or prey and stand their own in any battle.

The refuge was established in 1946 to preserve salt- and freshwater marsh, coastal prairie, savanna, and thornbush habitat not only for native wildlife but also for migrating waterfowl. It is home to the largest population of Redhead ducks, and more than 390 species of birds have been recorded, the largest variety of birds of any refuge in the nation.

If you are a first-time birder from anywhere north of South Texas, this is the place to see birds you've not seen before, such as the chachalaca, Green Jay, Great Kiskadee, Couch's Kingbird, Olive Sparrow, and Groove-billed Ani, and perhaps hundreds more. Self-guided automobile tours make it easy to see the huge array of shorebirds and waterfowl. A spotting scope is worthwhile for bird-watching from places like the Redhead Ridge overlook. A scope can settle disputes over sightings of the uncommonly seen Common Loon and the very common Double-crested Cormorant feeding on the sheltered lagoon.

Each season of the year is special at Laguna Atascosa. As noted in the last chapter, fall and spring are great for bird migrations, with the spring's top billing being the same spectacular fallouts that occur all along the coast to High Island. At Laguna Atascosa the presence of a gusty north wind up the coast will keep the birds anchored for your viewing pleasure. Special stars include warblers, Brown-crested Flycatchers, Blue Grosbeaks, and the polychromatic Indigo and Painted buntings. In the winter, migrations of 250,000 or more ducks, 10,000 geese, and thousands of Sandhill Cranes make this refuge extra special.

One of the bird species that has eluded me over the years is the Aplomado Falcon, reputed to be the fastest bird on earth, even faster than the Peregrine. The steel-gray speedster can be found here on occasion, although some bird reference books list the Aplomado as extirpated in Texas. Aplomado releases have been made here since 1985. Black-helmeted Peregrines target the area during fall migration for their favorite menu selections of duck and shorebird. Endangered Piping Plovers are common most of the year, southern Bald Eagles are seen on occasion in the winter, and Brown Pelicans are seen throughout the year now.

The refuge is also home to a goodly selection of reptiles and amphibians, including the Texas coral snake, with venom eight times more lethal than the western diamondback's. At Laguna Atascosa this snake is very common in thornbush areas with heavy leaf litter. The snake isn't aggressive, and people who have been bitten usually picked the snake up to admire it, ignoring the old adage "red and yellow kills a fellow."

Only a relative handful of Sabal texana *palms still survive where once there were thousands. One of the remnant populations is here at the Audubon Society's Sabal Palm Grove Sanctuary, six miles southeast of Brownsville; a few other palm patches in the area are protected by the USFWS, TPWD, and TNC.*

Many interesting nonpoisonous snakes live here; some will bite, such as the bull snake and the Texas indigo snake, which can grow longer than eight feet and take a hunk out of your hide. This beautiful blue-black creature is my favorite snake. I consider the one on my ranch a friend of the family. At Laguna Atascosa or on any state or federal land, to disturb in any way or to possess any reptile or other animal without proper authorization is a violation of both state and federal laws. Don't pick up a coral snake: you may be jailed as you're dying.

Salamanders, turtles, lizards, and alligators are found at Laguna Atascosa, including the famed horny toad, which is really a lizard. The horned lizard is threatened, mainly by loss of habitat and the use of pesticides. Texas Parks and Wildlife zoologist Andrew Price explains that the favorite food of the Texas horned lizard is the harvester ant, known to most of us as "the red ant." Price says that the introduced fire ant "comes in and takes over and wipes out native invertebrates, including especially the harvester ant, through predation and competition for habitat." That and wide use of pesticides to kill off the fire ants are the probable causes of the decline in our horny toad populations. Price reminds us, "We should take this as a warning to respect the integrity of nature. If you do things to the natural environment that are detrimental to a particular organism, it's going to disappear, regardless of the best intentions."

A mighty Texas tortoise stalks along a loma at Boca Chica beach, ready to attack its preferred winter prey—a cactus. At maturity, these handsome tortoises reach a length of six to eight inches; they are threatened by rustlers supplying the pet trade.

The Texas tortoise is another threatened species. This land-based reptile is most active in early morning and late afternoon. Look for him near his favorite food, prickly pear cactus. A lizard common to the area is the four-lined skink, indigenous to South Texas.

BOCA CHICA BEACH

The Reddish Egret, obviously wandering about in a postbreeding dispersal mode, stood out in the bright sunlight on the tidal mud flats, his breast feathers a beacon—no binoculars needed as I drove by. I was on my way, the only way (Highway 4), to Boca Chica Beach, the first place going west where the United States and Mexico abut. I took the Reddish as a good omen. It was not; warm air wrapped the beach, causing heavy fog over the last hundred feet of sandy land, making birding impossible. No matter, my real reason for being at Boca Chica Beach was to get a feel for the coming conservation effort on this fragile and pivotal stretch of remote barrier beach. The TPWD would like to establish a state seashore here, and the USFWS would like to see the area become the eastern anchor of the Wildlife Corridor. TNC is helping with sensitive land acquisitions, including a significant area called the Barnes Tract. So, if I missed seeing a Peregrine, I could take solace in the hope that maybe, someday, this vital place might be protected.

On this trip, at least, I was consoled by the Reddish Egret's appearance on the Texas side of the Rio Grande. These egrets are threatened because their nesting and feeding grounds in Mexico are polluted.

Boca Chica Beach is uncrowded during the fall raptor migrations, giving birders a better than average chance of seeing a Peregrine over the dunes, and it's a cinch to spot Broad-winged, Swainson's, and other hawks. Near the river's mouth is the Loma Ecological Preserve. Lomas are geological structures that provide a little altitude in this flat terrain. They are created from the silt and clay particles deposited in the surrounding tidal flats by a flooding Rio Grande. When the flats are dry, the constant trade winds pick up tiny bits of silt and clay and dust the dunes with them. These special, clay-based dunes may grow up to thirty feet above the surrounding tidal flats, forming a separate habitat of wooded islands in the flats. They are like miniature Galápagos islands, complete with their own tortoise, the also miniature Texas tortoise. Fiddlewood, Texas ebony, and black mangrove on South Bay are characteristic of the area. Lomas create habitat for ocelots and jaguarundi. The Nature Conservancy gave the conservation of this area a boost in 1990 through the acquisition of Vista del Mar, a 1,673-acre area now managed by the USFWS.

South Bay is one of the most unusual areas on the coast, harboring the combative snook, sought by combative sportsfishers. It also supports a unique oyster that can tolerate hypersalinity. This species of oyster may well be of great importance to a world whose oyster production is threatened. In 1993 scientists noted that this oyster was migrating up the coast into the increasingly hypersaline Laguna Madre. Oysters are in serious trouble everywhere in North America; the once huge haul in the Chesapeake Bay estuary dropped from 15 million bushels a year to about 350,000 in 1993 after a century of fishery mismanagement, pollution, overfishing, and disease. During the early nineties, selected estuaries along the Texas coast were closed because of pollution or oyster disease. The tough little guy from South Bay may well turn out to be the salvation of this industry and much more. Studies at Chesapeake Bay indicate that oysters play an important part in water quality. Each oyster filters about two gallons of water per hour, removing sediment and plankton. The nutrient-rich oyster feces then provide the base of a food web that ultimately supports crabs and finfish.

SABAL PALM GROVE SANCTUARY

The Black-throated Blue Warbler darted in and out of the rustling fronds, at home as he could be in the tall sabal palm in the midst of what could only be described as a tropical jungle. Somehow, this colorful wandering warbler, seeking sanctuary from Castro's Cuba, had located the only habitat to its liking in all of the western United States. Since only 32 acres of the 172-acre Sabal Palm Grove Sanctuary consist of native palms, the little warbler can be commended for its survival instincts. The Black-throated Blue Warbler's normal habitat is Cuba, and it was badly off course, much to the birders' delight. The warbler owed his life to the National Audubon Society, which bought the sanctuary in 1971. It is now managed by Rose Farmer, one of the Lower Rio Grande Valley's expert conservationists.

When the blackthroat alert sounded, the birders rushed into the jungle, where an Audubon Society professional had the rare bird on hold. While pursuing the blackthroat, we spotted the uncommon Yellow-throated Warbler, and chachalacas sounded nearby. Later, I was buzzed by a Buff-bellied Hummingbird, a tropical fellow who goes no farther north than the Valley. The sanctuary's logbook listed recent sightings of pauraques, Groove-billed Anis, Great Kiskadees, Green Jays, Olive Sparrows, and Altamira Orioles.

Some of the early maps in the Sid Richardson Collection of the Cartographic History Library at the University of Texas, such as the Cornelius Wytfliet map of 1597, refer to an "R. de Palmas" in the vicinity of the present Rio Grande. Spanish records tell of an impenetrable palm jungle along the river, and some even named it El Río de las Palmas. Spanish overland search parties, set in motion by word that La Salle had penetrated the Gulf of Mexico, had to divert a great distance around this jungle. Arthur Schott of the First Boundary Survey in the 1850s is quoted in E. U. Clover's 1937 *Vegetational Survey of the Lower Rio Grande Valley, Texas* as reporting that the sabal palms grew some eighty miles up the river, maybe occupying as much as 40,000 acres.

Today, because the records are so incomplete, Dave Blankinship cannot verify this, although the USFWS has identified what appear to be isolated remnants, not transplants, of sabal palms well up the Rio Grande. Blankinship recalls that when the freezes of 1983 and 1989 killed many of the exotic palms that had been brought in as ornamentals, the sabal survived. Now Florida sabal palms are being brought in, but they are not as hardy as the *Sabal texana*, and there is now fear of hybridization, which could weaken the indigenous plants.

In 1980, The Nature Conservancy acquired 367 acres in the vicinity of the sanctuary that still have some of the remnant sabal palms. TNC entered into a partnership with the Brownsville public utility company, enabling it to build a cooling pond on half the tract while preserving the other half for conservation. This is another example of the economy and the environment both winning through private conservation efforts. The USFWS now manages this tract, located at the southernmost bend of the Rio Grande near Brownsville and known as the Boscaje de la Palma. Characteristic fauna include ocelot, jaguarundi, lesser yellow bat, Hooded Orioles, northern cat-eyed snake, and the speckled racer, one of the rarest snakes in Texas.

SANTA ANA NATIONAL WILDLIFE REFUGE

This 2,080-acre national wildlife refuge is one of the oldest and most fascinating in the system. Like Laguna Atascosa, it was acquired by the USFWS in the forties. More than 370 species of birds have been sighted here, and 31 are found nowhere else in the United States. This is basically a bottomland hardwood site with tropical overtones, and it contains stands of cedar elm, Berlandier ash, ebony, anacua, soapberry, brasil, and tasty sugarberry mixed with mesquite and granjeno.

The winter visit is consistently rewarding, as visitors can enjoy an incredible variety of birdlife while strolling through the densely canopied subtropical woodlands and around the resacas, which provide aquatic habitat for unfamiliar plants and animals. Although you will be looking aloft for Golden-fronted Woodpeckers, Green Jays, Audubon's Orioles, and Olive Sparrows, you should glance at the trail frequently, on guard to step over ocelot or bobcat scat.

A resaca is a channel that has been cut off from the main stream of a river. It is usually still marshy and often receives enough rain or flooding from the river to contain standing water. At Santa Ana, three wildlife trails take hikers around Willow Lake and Pintail Lake, an enchanting, magical promenade on an early winter's morning, where you may spot some of Santa Ana's rarities such as the Hook-billed Kite, Couch's Kingbird, Clay-colored Robin, and Gray Hawk. A dozen or so warblers winter in the region.

After Hurricane Gilbert, which entered Mexico south of Santa Ana, I saw Cattail Lake filled with both water and waterfowl. In fact, there was a danger that flooding of the Rio Grande would reopen a resaca and thereby transfer part of Santa Ana to Mexican federal control by diverting the river north around the refuge.

BENTSEN–RIO GRANDE VALLEY STATE PARK

Visitors to this unusual park are asked to report sightings of rare jaguarundi and ocelots, and about five ocelot sightings are made weekly, an encouragement to cat lovers. Incredibly, the even more shy jaguarundi is spotted, on average, once a week. This park is most popular during the winter, and with 500,000 visitors a year, I guess rare feline sightings are to be expected. February and March are the prime months for birding, and more than 280 species have been identified, including the colorful Green Jay, Groove-billed Ani, Red-billed Pigeon, Altamira Oriole, and Common Pauraque.

Africanized bees have swept through the Valley, and as at several other locations, visitors are warned as they enter. The bottom line on the warning is to leave bees alone. Don't swat them, just walk or, if necessary, run away. These bees are another example of what can happen when humans interfere with nature. Introduced just a few years ago in Argentina, they have marched up the Americas and invaded much of Texas,

especially this area. So it was no surprise that my picnic, foolishly complete with a bouquet and sweet pickles, eventually attracted enough bees to cause me to move—a first. If you use a little common sense, avoiding bright colors or flowers on your table and sugary foods, the odds are you won't be bothered. The first death attributed to Africanized bee stings since the bees' migration into Texas in 1990 was near here on a ranch north of Rio Grande City. Lino Lopez, 82, had attempted to burn out a hive containing an estimated 60,000 bees, later determined to be mainly the African strain. Africanized bees, which look very much like their European cousins, only a tiny bit smaller, are much more likely to attack in swarms, especially when their nests are invaded.

What was absolutely delightful about this particular picnic was a fully orchestrated chachalaca concert. The large birds seemed to be everywhere in the woods around the picnic area and kept up their "cha-cha-laca-cha-cha-laca" refrain all during the picnic. Cardinals and bluebirds, predictors of the future in many American Indian cultures, added color to our picnic but no prognostications.

The parents of former Secretary of the Treasury Lloyd Bentsen donated the 587 acres of this exquisite park in 1944, and thankfully, much of the original vegetation remains intact. In the forty years between the arrival of rail lines in Brownsville in 1904 and the acquisition of the park, land companies were successful in their efforts to sell off the fertile land of the Valley. Millions of acres, especially rich lands near the river,

ABOVE LEFT
A Black-bellied Whistling-Duck sails into a favored habitat at Santa Ana National Wildlife Refuge. Tree-lined ponds appeal to these tree-roosting ducks, which are easy to find in the Valley summers.

ABOVE RIGHT
This Elf Owl couldn't resist Leroy Williamson's screech-owl call, and so came to this pose at Bentsen–Rio Grande Valley State Park, standing tall at 5 3/4 inches. They winter in the Valley and in Mexico.

were bulldozed for crops. The four counties of the Lower Rio Grande produce all the citrus and 84 percent of the vegetables grown in Texas, and the Valley population is now approaching one million. The Bentsen family's contribution has proved to be of critical importance. This state park will be the seed stock for much restoration work of the future in the Wildlife Corridor.

The variety of bird and other wildlife species at Bentsen is on a par with that of Santa Ana, which obviously ranks this park near the top in North America for birders. This is the place in North America to spot Hook-billed Kites. Also of special interest here are night birds, including North America's smallest owl, the Elf, very rare and seen only in the winter, usually just at sundown. According to naturalist Frederick R. Gehlbach, the Elf Owl "reappeared in 1960 after sixty-six years of absence." Eastern Screech-Owls, the Great Horned Owl, Barn Owls, and even the Ferruginous Pygmy-Owl are here. Bentsen State Park is one of the only places in North America where you have a hope of seeing the Ferruginous Pygmy. Look for the bright orange eyes of pauraques on the roads at night.

The park provides excellent camping facilities, even a boat ramp into a resaca. The river may also be accessed by a 1.8-mile Rio Grande hiking trail, which touches upon another large resaca lake. The Singing Chaparral Trail takes the visitor into an entirely different habitat, where you might spot a roadrunner or perhaps an indigo snake.

FALCON STATE PARK AND DAM

The Chihuahuan Thorn Forest, a 24,000-acre area just below Falcon Dam, is ranked fifth nationally as a unique and threatened ecosystem by the USFWS. This area is the starting point for the Wildlife Corridor. Falcon Dam, completed in 1953, has had a major effect on the ecosystems downstream. Like all dams, Falcon represents a huge tradeoff in loss of diversity versus economic gain.

The Chihuahuan Thorn Forest is a desert shrub community that includes a riparian zone all along the Rio Grande south of the dam. The unique feature of this community is the edge formed at the juncture of the riparian zone and the desert scrub. You'll find black willow, Montezuma bald cypress that survived the flooding caused by the dam, and Texas ebony. The upland has sotol, catclaw mimosa, and blackbrush acacia. The area is known for its nesting Brown Jays, Green Kingfishers, Ringed Kingfishers, Belted Kingfishers, and Ferruginous Pygmy-Owls.

Frederick Gehlbach reports in *Mountain Islands and Desert Seas* (1981), "In the 1950s, the Ringed Kingfisher was only casual in these borderlands. By the late 1960s, it was seen regularly here, and in April 1970, it nested." Gehlbach speculates that the control of the Rio Grande allowed the Ringed Kingfisher to shift its habitat northward.

Falcon State Park, with 573 acres overlooking giant Falcon Lake, is not heavily vegetated. Despite this, the park is rich in birds, reptiles, and wildlife such as white-tailed deer, javelina, bobcat, and raccoon. Your conservation passport will allow you use of good campgrounds with all the amenities. Amenities here include a goodly collection of snakes, well fed thanks to frogs and toads, whose populations increased with the flooding of the lake.

The brushlands around the park feature Golden-fronted Woodpeckers, Bewick's and Cactus wrens, Curve-billed Thrashers, Altamira and Hooded orioles, Crested Caracaras, Harris' Hawks, Vermilion Flycatchers, and many of the other birds common to the Valley farther downriver.

Further conservation work in this area is vastly complicated by the pattern of land ownership dating back centuries to the Spanish settlements. The system is called porciones, which is the automatic creation of undivided interest. Unless otherwise specified, heirs received fractional interests at the death of a landowner, with everyone getting a piece of the action. Over the decades, virtually every parcel of this land accumulated hundreds of owners, each with a small percentage, and no one can obtain clear title unless everyone else signs off. Many relatives don't even know they own a fraction of land. In other cases, relatives have long since ceased speaking to each other, let alone agreeing on a land sale. So, conservation here is blocked by ancient custom.

RARE BIRD ALERT
Rio Grande Valley Audubon Alert, 210-565-6773 (sponsored by the Frontera Valley Audubon Society of South Texas and Valley chambers of commerce).

"HORIZONTAL LAYERS OF LIMESTONE" THE EDWARDS PLATEAU

CHAPTER 8

We crossed the depth of valleys inhabited by multitudes of deer. The narrow passages are quite steep and reveal horizontal layers of limestone. We encountered black bears after entering the withered shrubbery in which movement was very difficult. . . . On some formidable hills covered with shrubbery, we saw buffalo tracks in all directions.

JEAN LOUIS BERLANDIER

"Hunting in Texas in 1828" (unpublished report on a hunting trip on the Guadalupe River near Kerrville, edited and translated by Richard G. Santos)

It's surprising how quickly a modern traveler can begin to enjoy the special beauty of this ecological area. Just minutes from either Austin or San Antonio, and you are climbing the limestone surface of the Edwards Plateau, encountering vistas of rugged cedar- and oak-covered hills. Although there is a lot less timber than there was 150 years ago, and very few black bears or buffalo, the Edwards Plateau still looks much as it did millions of years ago. The occasional wild black bear still wanders up from Mexico into the shrubbery of the "formidable hills."

By global landscape standards, this rocky, thin-soiled, sometimes scruffy land can't be described as beautiful. But it is scenic in its own captivating way. Comanches and 1840s European settlers alike had a hard-scrabble existence; the land provided enough for subsistence and a healthy climate, but nothing that would allow a sumptuous life-style just for the plucking. Settlers earned most of their livelihood from sheep and goats, and hardworking communities prospered modestly. Perhaps fortunately for what we can preserve today, the land would not support large-scale agriculture, did not yield great mineral wealth, and, thanks to the Comanche, was passed over for early major settlements. Now the

OPPOSITE PAGE
The author's Granada Springs ranch southwest of Kerrville is part of The Nature Conservancy's Texas Land Stewards Society, to help protect headwater springs of the Guadalupe River as well as the endangered Golden-cheeked Warbler.

people are coming, and for the first time in history, the Edwards Plateau's steady quality of life is challenged.

In 1992, The Nature Conservancy designated a portion of the heart of this ecological area, known as the Hill Country, as one of its original seven bioreserves in North America. Well known to most Texans for its scenic beauty, the Hill Country comprises some 18,650 square miles within the Edwards Plateau's total of 31,000 square miles. The area is a critical habitat for a wide assemblage of rare and endangered plants and birds, including the only bird that nests exclusively in Texas, the Golden-cheeked Warbler, as well as the Black-capped Vireo, basin bellflower, Texas snowbells, rock quillwort, Edwards Plateau cornsalad, bracted twistflower, Edge Falls anemone, and Texas wild rice. Seventeen major plant communities have been identified within the Hill Country Bioreserve, each with its own admixture of microorganisms and animals.

In addition to the Hill Country, the Edwards Plateau encompasses two other striking geological features, the Balcones Escarpment and the Llano Uplift. The Balcones Escarpment is the canyonland southern border to the Hill Country, running in a curve from north of Austin down above San Antonio, then west by southwest almost to Del Rio. It is a geological fault line, where the limestone cap of the Edwards Plateau meets the geological formations of the South Texas Plains. Over millions of years the coastal plain sank, leaving a cliff (the Spanish explorers called it a balcony) between the differing geological formations. Over time the cliff itself began to crumble and rivers eroded to form the canyons that are the hallmark of this area. Between Austin and San Antonio the Balcones Escarpment meets the Blackland Prairie, and the demarcation is clear. From San Antonio on to Del Rio, the limestone ridges of the Edwards Plateau feather into the South Texas Plains.

The Edwards Plateau was formed as ocean bottom about 100 million years ago in the Cretaceous period when Central Texas lay under a shallow tropical sea. The Edwards Plateau is therefore primarily a limestone karst formation made up of layers upon layers of the skeletons and shells of dead sea creatures, which formed sedimentary layers up to 10,000 feet thick, honeycombed with thousands of caves underneath, except for the Llano granite uplift. Thousands of clear springs seep or gush through the limestone into a landscape etched by lovely wooded canyons. These pure-water springs, with their constant temperature, are ideal habitat for rare fish such as Clear Creek, San Marcos, and Large Spring gambusia, for fountain darters, and for the San Marcos salamander.

Although the area is relatively dry, with fifteen to thirty-three inches of annual rainfall, the limestone formations are marvelous water collectors. Enchanting rivers with wildlife-rich corridors flow through the area. The Devils, Frio, Llano, Guadalupe, Nueces, Sabinal, and, on the north edge, the Colorado provide fertile banks for trees such as maple, cottonwood, pecan, hackberry, and sycamore. There is even cypress, looking a bit out of place along rivers such as the Guadalupe. The Guadalupe bass and Cagle's map turtle are found in some of these rivers. The rivers are not the most significant hydrological feature of this ecological area. That is hidden—the Edwards Aquifer, the largest aquifer within Texas borders.

My ranch southwest of Kerrville provides a good example of what is occurring, where the threat is not just to rare and endangered plants and animals but to humans as well. Part of the original Granada Spring Ranch, this land sits over the Edwards Aquifer and has numerous springs that feed Turtle Creek, a tributary of the Guadalupe River. The open pastures of area ranches are an essential element in maintaining the aquifer's recharge capability. The aquifer under my ranch will never be overly affected by human activities; building will be restricted, and we have installed a special septic system that will keep pollution from the springs and Turtle Creek itself. But as you wander through the rugged, rock strewn, heavily wooded canyons, through oak and Ashe juniper thickets, and along the ridge tops, you'll stumble across many suspicious, geometrically formed clearings. Only humans would cut a perfect circle in the woods, and only to human ends. This ranch was to be the site of scores of ranchettes and, therefore, would have had to cope with the water diversion and, more serious, the water pollution from use by hundreds of people, instead of the handful who will now have private access. Several pairs of nesting Golden-cheeked Warblers have been sighted in the old-growth cedar thickets, so today, this ranch is part of The Nature Conservancy's Texas Land Stewards Society.

The ranch is somewhat of a bird sanctuary, and a partial list of spring birds recorded there includes, in addition to the Golden-cheeked Warbler, Bewick's Wren, Bobwhite Quail, Painted Bunting, Lark Sparrow, Carolina Chickadee, Tufted Titmouse, Northern Cardinal, Yellow-billed Cuckoo, Blue Grosbeak, Black-chinned Hummingbird, Common Raven, Chipping Sparrow, Scrub Jay, Ladder-backed Woodpecker, Black-and-white Warbler, Ruby-crowned Kinglet, Ash-throated Flycatcher, Mourning Dove, White-eyed Vireo, Yellow-throated Vireo, Great Crested Flycatcher, Eastern Wood-Pewee, Eastern Phoebe, Cliff Swallow, Summer Tanager, Golden-fronted Woodpecker, Louisiana Waterthrush, and many other species.

The Llano Uplift was formed millions of years ago as a mass of molten rock, or magma, roughly seventy miles across and a thousand feet deep pushed, or uplifted, from the earth's crust. Several more million years went by, and the surface rocks eroded to expose granite, a variety of minerals including iron ore, gold, and silver in small amounts, and the oldest of rock formations, those from the Precambrian period. There is a rock named for the area, Llanite, and in Mason County can be found the blue topaz that is the state gem. Enchanted Rock State Natural Area is in the Llano Uplift. This striking granite dome rises 450 feet above surrounding ranchland.

Early accounts tell us of carpets of bluebonnets in the spring, grasses that grew to five feet, and thick oak forests. The bluebonnets are still here, along with Indian paintbrushes, phlox, daisies, and winecups, and roadsides are enhanced by wildflower seedings. But now there is competition from mesquite and bee brush. The tall grasses are gone, and oak wilt has struck the Hill Country with a vengeance. The Nature Conservancy is conducting oak-wilt symposiums to involve experts from government, businesses, private landowners, and academics concerned about reversing the loss of oak trees, especially the lovely, hundred-year-old live oaks gracing this area.

The area's grasses, forbs, and browse support the largest white-tailed deer herd in the world, some 400,000 in Llano County alone. The city of Llano modestly claims to be the deer capital of Texas. With more than 1.5 million white-tailed deer, the Edwards Plateau can lay claim to global preeminence in numbers of these graceful herbivores. However, overpopulation of white-tailed deer is a serious problem in the Hill Country, as is the propensity of hunters to shoot only bucks; only one in five hunters ever uses a doe tag. Killing bucks does not balance the deer herd, since almost 90 percent of the does breed each year, assuring that the entire herd well exceeds the carrying capacity of the typical ranch range.

Private landowners in the Hill Country have several opportunities for conservation partnerships. The Nature Conservancy provides them, as does the Texas Parks and Wildlife Department. The National Fish and Wildlife Foundation has awarded grants to the TPWD that will help private landowners protect wildlife through voluntary partnerships. "Our goal is to show landowners that it's a win-win situation for them, for us and Texas wildlife. We can offer them new ways to enhance wildlife habitat on their land," says Andrew Sansom, TPWD executive director. The TPWD has been expanding its existing Private Lands Enhancement Program for several years. By the early nineties, this program had reached more than 22,000 private landowners and resulted in direct habitat enhancement of four million acres.

Any conservation effort, however, is threatened by the potential inundation by people. In 1994, Texas overtook New York to become the second most populous state. And the secret is out on the Hill Country. It has been discovered by national magazines, by experts who declare it to be the "healthiest climate in the United States," by retirees, and by corporations seeking a better quality of life for their employees. Popula-

OPPOSITE PAGE
Rare lichens, plants that have a symbiotic association between algae and fungi, were one of the reasons The Nature Conservancy purchased Enchanted Rock, later transferred to Texas Parks and Wildlife as a state natural area.

tions of the twenty-six counties that comprise the Hill Country Bioreserve grew by 27 percent between 1980 and 1990, and increases are predicted for the rest of this century. Ranchers of the Edwards Plateau and Trans-Pecos have good reason to be worried that their quality of life will be affected. It already has been, and it's going to get worse as the Texas population continues to grow faster than the United States as a whole.

I view the Hill Country as a lovely mosaic, interspersed with settlements large and small, with economically productive agriculture and ranching, and still almost as rich in biodiversity as when the Comanche held it in thrall. To keep the mosaic as economically and biologically healthy as possible, The Nature Conservancy is proceeding on three fronts in the Hill Country, establishing a bionetwork of zones of varying ecological importance.

The first priority is to create ecologically healthy islands of habitat on the outskirts of cities, which will ultimately be surrounded by development. Perhaps the best example of this in all the world's conservation efforts has now taken place in the Hill Country, near Austin. The landscape north and west of Austin is scenic and logical for development. But seven protected species gave environmental groups the impetus to challenge further development, creating a highly charged, emotional, and confrontational atmosphere. The Nature Conservancy was asked to mediate.

David Braun, state vice president for The Nature Conservancy, entered the picture in 1988, when environmentalists were challenging development in the Balcones Canyonlands on the basis of protecting the endangered Golden-cheeked Warbler, Black-capped Vireo, four cave-dwelling invertebrates, and Texas wild rice. The Nature Conservancy and the city of Austin's Department of Environmental and Conservation Services jointly proposed developing a regional habitat conservation plan called the Balcones Canyonlands Conservation Plan (BCCP). The BCCP would get all the cards on the table at once, to help developers focus on sites that would do the least harm and keep as much habitat intact for endangered species as practical.

Economic and ecological goals can be compatible, and the BCCP proved this to many people. Public and private interests can be protected to the benefit of both. An independent study by the Bureau of Business Research in the Graduate School of Business at the University of Texas indicates that the BCCP will generate between $244 million and $439 million in additional property tax revenues for Travis County and the city of Austin. Without the BCCP, the study forecasts a twenty-year loss of between 9,763 and 39,050 jobs.

In late 1992, the citizens of Austin passed a $22 million bond issue to fund a major part of the BCCP, putting our state capital on its way to establishing a healthful environment, valuable for humans and wild creatures alike. Demonstrating the diverse support for the BCCP, this bond initiative was endorsed by the Austin Interfaith Council, Austin Sierra Club, Citizens for Open Space, Clean Water Action, East Austin Strategy Team, Greater Austin Chamber of Commerce, League of Women Voters, Real Estate Council of Austin, and Travis Audubon Society.

In mid-1994, TNC and FM Properties announced an agreement to donate two tracts, the Uplands and Sweetwater Ranch, to the city of Austin as protected green space. The Conservancy acquired the nearly 4,300 acres from the Resolution Trust Corporation with $7.3 million provided by FM Properties. The 4,000 acres of wooded canyon along Barton Creek would become a nature preserve at almost no cost to taxpayers.

Other communities across the country are looking to Austin as a model for their own conservation plans. Austin's big message is that environmental problems need not result in conflict and deadlock. Many other communities that have faced less difficult problems than Austin's have bogged down in bitter and seemingly unresolvable debates over the balance between the environment and the economy. Even with seven endangered species and the rapid loss of its scenic surroundings, Austin sought to find a pragmatic solution to environmental problems that would prove beneficial to the economy. Austin has assumed national leadership, on the cutting edge of what will increasingly become one of our most important international issues, economically sound environmental protection. In November 1993, when a county bond election failed, the city of Austin, ever optimistic and forward thinking, initiated its own conservation plan.

The next step in saving the best of the Hill Country involves setting aside a few protected, carefully managed core reserves for native fauna and flora. These core reserves could be owned and managed privately, or could be state or federally owned and managed. Ownership is not the issue; good stewardship of large natural areas is, no matter the steward.

Great examples of this core-reserve development are the Conservancy's purchase of Dolan Falls Ranch and the conservation easement at the Chandler Family Ranch on the western edge of the Edwards Plateau. The Dolan Falls and Independence Creek preserves are described later in this chapter.

Once cores are established, the work lies in surrounding them with ecologically friendly buffer zones. Good buffers would be ranches that maintain wild habitat, which may support hunting and attract tourists, such as the Prade Ranch in the Hill Country.

Dr. Lawrence E. Gilbert, a professor at the University of Texas Department of Zoology, stated in a 1993 memo to me,

The increasing public awareness of the global loss of natural habitat ecological systems, and decreasing per capita availability of recreation areas has magnified the political pressures on the few who "own" environment. The increasing urban many who consider natural products and processes of the environment to be common property are and will be a serious threat to the landowner's way of life. . . . In Texas, it is in the interest of large landowners to ally with conservationists who are politically to the right of center. . . . As one travels from West Texas and its splendid isolation to San Antonio, the control of large chunks of habitat shifts from few to many, and the political reality of insuring that parts of Texas' natural heritage survive changes dramatically. Demand for recreation and outdoor experiences is high in urban populations. This demand provides both a challenge and an opportunity for landowners and practical environmentalists alike. The economic opportunities for private landowners require a change in vision and goals.

Conservationists must deal with balancing the needs of ecosystems and the wants of people. In most cases, city, county, and state governmental coordination and leadership become more important as habitat conservation comes into conflict with other competing agendas of the urban population. One concern of free-market environmentalists is that any involvement of private conservation groups such as The Nature Conservancy or of government in developing parks and reserves reduces the economic potential of their land. This viewpoint ignores or underestimates the growing demand of an expanding population for a shrinking resource called wilderness. Those wishing to hunt on the state's wildlife management areas outnumber those chosen by lottery by as much as sixty to one. Moreover, no matter how extensive, public lands near urban areas will never provide the religious wilderness experience that everyone needs from time to time. Six-dollar-a-day quail hunts with 600 other people at Chaparral Wildlife Management Area will not cut into the San Pedro Ranch's $450-a-day hunts for the very few.

The Prade Ranch, west of San Antonio, has blended economics and ecology quite profitably. Ecotourists have spotted some 160 species of birds on the ranch, including the endangered Golden-cheeked Warbler and Black-capped Vireo. The majestic Golden Eagle puts in frequent appearances, causing tourist binoculars to come up and the ranch's cash register to ring. This wedding of economics and ecology will come to many other ranches as landowners fight a tough battle to maintain profitability with livestock and hunting operations alone.

Another ranch that typifies great private conservation efforts is that of J. David Bamberger near Blanco. I first met Bamberger on an outing to the Honey Creek Preserve, where we discovered we were both alumni

OPPOSITE PAGE
The unique plant communities of Honey Creek Ranch make this a special Hill Country preserve. Golden-cheeked Warblers begin to nest here in late March, as males sing lustily from the tops of old-growth trees. They are headed to Central America by August.

of the Kirby Company; we had worked some four decades back as door-to-door sellers of vacuum cleaners. Bamberger went on to help Bill Church found Church's Fried Chicken, and it was that business success that enabled him to buy 5,500 acres of Hill Country in 1969. Bamberger says that the ranch was very poor in those days, completely without water. Now that all but the old-growth Ashe juniper has been cleared and grazing is carefully controlled, aquifers under the ranch have been replenished and many springs are again flowing. Signs on his ranch reading "Selah" sum up his philosophy. In Hebrew, the word exhorts the reader to slow down and smell the sage blossoms, to meditate upon the natural world. Bamberger thinks of himself as the steward, not the owner, of this land, which is the essence of the conservation ethic.

Rancher James L. Powell, former president of the Texas and Southwestern Cattle Raisers' Association, reminded me, during a visit to his ranch, of the different challenges the early ranch settlers faced: "Our forefathers, to settle this country and build a life, had to be concerned about predators killing their livestock. They had to determine where the water was and how to get water to their livestock. Their main interest was in survival and educating their families rather than good range management. Today, that has changed, and the modern rancher has to be concerned about how to project a good range into the future so that livestock can graze on it and it can be a renewable natural resource. If a rancher destroys that capability, of course the livestock can't survive. And neither can he, so ranchers are learning to be very good stewards of the land."

Powell's ranch is about six miles from Fort McKavett, where westering settlers would set out in the early 1850s, watering up at a ciénaga on what is known now as Six-Mile Ranch. Ranald Mackenzie, of Indian fighter fame, commanded Fort McKavett, and undoubtedly spent time both watering at and defending this same ciénaga after the Civil War. It was here, in 1871, that General William Sherman was inspired to declare war on the Comanche.

Powell recalls growing up on the ranch and seeing this watercourse almost dry, all the grass apparently dead in terrible droughts. When he returned from army service in 1974, no grass was left on the land. He determined that since his ancestors had settled the land, protected it, and fenced it, it was his turn to make it productive. He now employs a high-intensity, low-frequency grazing system based on fencing each half section (320 acres) and supplying water to each area.

Powell rotates his livestock through eighteen pastures during the growing season. Cattle feed for two weeks, then that pasture rests for about six weeks. "That allows the roots to penetrate to the subsurface of the soil," says Powell. "You never want to suppress the growth of grass and forbs to where they cannot develop a root system." The result is rich pasture land, and the undamaged roots penetrate deeper and deeper during the year. Wildlife such as white-tailed deer thrive on the forbs and greater variety of grass that Powell's pastures provide. All the living things are winning. Land in such fine stewardship should remain as a sustainable natural resource for all time.

Powell also voluntarily participates in U.S. Department of Agriculture studies of unique grass varieties growing on his land. He hopes that new knowledge will be gained of hardier grasses genetically structured to provide more nourishment to livestock.

Powell has also implemented innovative ways to conserve this land's most precious resource, water, by rooting out the invader mesquite trees. But he always keeps the beautiful native live oaks, pecans, other hardwoods, and other indigenous plants so important to wildlife. On a visit to his ranch Powell showed me the lovely, burbling headwaters of the San Saba River, which have backed way up on his land since his mesquite battle, proof to him of the water saved by removing the mesquite cover.

Powell's efforts, like those of many ranchers like him, certainly demonstrate the all-important role that private landowners can perform in conservation work.

GUADALUPE RIVER STATE PARK AND HONEY CREEK RANCH

Here is another example of private-public cooperation. The Nature Conservancy acquired the old Doppenschmidt Ranch, known as the Honey Creek Ranch. This hauntingly beautiful locale, blessed with a clear creek running into the Guadalupe River, harbors two native fish species found only on the Edwards Plateau. The Nature Conservancy allocated $1 million to protect 1,825 acres of this juniper and live oak savanna. An unusual feature of Honey Creek is the preserve's grasses, which are found only in this area on the Edwards Plateau. The Nature Conservancy has transferred the preserve to the TPWD, and Honey Creek is open only for guided tours. (Texas Parks and Wildlife acquired the 1,239 acres on the south side of the Guadalupe in 1975.)

The one and a half miles of limestone cliffs, huge bald cypress trees, and clear-flowing water—including four natural rapids—give the hiker a feeling for the rugged Hill Country. In addition to pecan, sycamore, hackberry, persimmon, and willow, the park features old-growth Ashe juniper that when combined with oak makes it prime habitat for endangered Golden-cheeked Warblers. Their migration from Central America to the Hill Country for nesting begins in March, and the birds stay until late summer.

Close by is the 5,370-acre Hill Country State Natural Area. It is being allowed to revert to its natural condition, so only a few people are admitted by permit only.

LOST MAPLES STATE NATURAL AREA

The big attraction in this lovely 2,208-acre natural area is the bigtooth maples, which obviously makes early fall the prime time for visiting. Unfortunately, it seems most of the population of the Hill Country and beyond knows this, so your conservation education experience will be blunted somewhat by bumper-to-bumper crowds on crisp fall weekends. Weekdays offer a sight-seeing trip. The maples can be showy in late October and early November if they have received just the right amount of rain and sunshine. Too much rain causes the maple leaves to turn muddy brown prematurely. Too little rain mutes the normally brilliant red, yellow, and orange colors.

I find it intriguing that the maple trees are a tip-off that in an earlier period the Edwards Plateau was significantly more moist. Botanists tell us these trees grew in more parts of the Hill Country when the climate was probably cooler and more moisture was available.

My favorite experience in Lost Maples is a weekday hike along the ten miles of trails back into Hale's Hollow and Can Creek. Here you'll find the really lost maples, those that 99 percent of the park's visitors never see. Hiking here can be especially rewarding for birders. The Golden-cheeked Warbler frequents the area from March to September, and so does the endangered Black-capped Vireo. Canyon Wrens and Green Kingfishers nest in the natural area. There's a chance to see a Golden Eagle, and in the winter, even a Bald Eagle.

ENCHANTED ROCK STATE NATURAL AREA

Here again, the private conservation efforts of The Nature Conservancy partnered with Texas Parks and Wildlife to preserve a landmark chunk of the environment. The landmark is literally a chunk of granite, the largest in Texas and one of the largest stone mountains, or batholiths, in America, second only to Georgia's Stone Mountain.

The seventy-acre Enchanted Rock heaved up with the rest of a huge mass of magma a billion years ago. It now sits 1,824 feet above sea level. From an ecological point of view, the delicate green and blue lichens and other plants that struggle to grow in such a stolid, forbidding granite environment are also important to study and preserve.

Just a few miles north of Fredericksburg, our Texas batholith was in private hands from the formation of the Texas Republic in 1836 until 1978, when it was purchased by The Nature Conservancy. Even though it was on private property, Enchanted Rock has always been a natural attraction. Uncontrolled foot traffic threatened the plant communities of Enchanted Rock, which was the motivation for TNC investment. Later, the site was transferred to the TPWD, with the understanding that it would be managed as a state natural area. As a consequence, the threatened plant communities of the batholith are protected and visitors can still enjoy an invigorating hike to the top, with the reward of

Lost Maples State Natural Area is one of the favored destinations of late October Hill Country explorers.

a stunning view of the Llano Uplift. Even today, that panoramic view is not impeded by much in the way of commercial development. You can renew your conviction that we really can conserve much of our Texas natural heritage simply by looking out from the peak of Enchanted Rock.

ECKERT JAMES RIVER BAT CAVE

Richard Philip Eckert and Virginia Eckert Garrett, concerned that their family could no longer protect some six million bats that use this Mason County cave as a nursery roost, donated the cave to The Nature Conservancy in memory of their grandfather W. Philip Eckert. TNC maintains ownership and jointly manages the cave with Bat Conservation International.

TNC volunteers built a walkway around the cave entrance to minimize disturbance when the Mexican free-tailed bats are exiting and entering the cave. The cave entrance is relatively small, yet five million to six million female bats must squeeze out and back in, and any interference with the process causes a huge bat traffic jam. Continual disturbances can seriously harm the colony of pregnant and nursing mothers; entire colonies can easily be destroyed by a single vandalous act.

You can recognize the Mexican free-tailed bat by her tail: one-third of it protrudes beyond the membrane that connects the legs and tail. Most other bat tails in North America are enclosed in the tail membrane.

According to Bat Conservation International's Merlin Tuttle, in his fascinating book *America's Neighborhood Bats* (1988), most Mexican free-tailed bats in the United States live in only a dozen caves, several of which are in Texas. In fact, Bracken Cave near San Antonio contains some 20 million bats, which consume about 250,000 pounds of insects each night, and Frio Cave is home to another 10 million.

The Eckert James River Bat Cave has only about 25 percent as many bats as Bracken, but the dusky evening exodus is one of the most spectacular sights in nature. The eerie flow of millions of these mammals into the red-lit evening sky is riveting. A Red-tailed Hawk usually shows up at sunset, cruising patiently until its evening meal gets airborne. Watching a raptor at work is a part of the fascination of this experience, especially when the hawk makes a mistake and a tiny target escapes. Part of developing your conservation ethic involves understanding the web of life and the critical role of predators at the top of that web.

The real show, however, is just before daylight when the insect-stuffed mother bats come home to their babies. After ranging out fifty miles or more in search of insects, at speeds clocked at sixty miles per hour and altitudes near 11,000 feet, they return and begin a free-fall from 2,000 feet. You can hear the whistle of wind over their folded wings as they funnel down into the small cave opening.

Now one of nature's great miracles occurs. Each female bears but a single young, which must be cared for. The young are plastered to the cave walls in densities up to 500 per square foot. Each mother remembers the location of her young within a few inches. Tuttle explains, "As the mothers return from feeding, each baby recognizes its mother's voice, rears up and calls to aid in its location." Tuttle adds that the identification that assures the mother she has located her baby has to do with a special smell. Female freetails will also suckle any young within their colony, like wet nurses for the millions of young in their roost. This contrasts with most other bat species, in which mothers nurse only their own progeny and a stronger mother-child bond supposedly exists. At night, while their mothers forage, the baby bats form an active cluster on the cave walls. This is believed to help maintain warmer body temperatures.

The estimated nightly insect take by free-tailed bats alone in Texas is one million pounds. (Red bats and brown bats are also fairly common.) I've leased a ranch within twenty miles of the Eckert Cave for more than twenty years, and bats are common visitors on a summer's eve. Our flying insect population there is nil. Besides eating mosquitoes, these bats provide critical damage control over cutworm and corn borer moths that could explode exponentially into a severe danger to crops.

Since this is a small site with potential crowding problems, The Nature Conservancy asks that you call its San Antonio office for further information. As a Texas conservation passport holder, however, you can witness the bat extravaganza at two other great sites: Kickapoo Cavern near Brackettville and Old Tunnel Wildlife Management Area near Fredericksburg.

DOLAN FALLS RANCH AND DEVILS RIVER STATE NATURAL AREA

When James King, The Nature Conservancy's Texas director of land protection, arranged for me to visit Dolan Falls Ranch in 1991, I took him up on his offer instantly. The Nature Conservancy had inventoried this tumultuous landscape for several years, measuring its great potential for conservation, but because of its size we had small hope of being able to afford it, even if it did come on the market.

Coveted for abundant water by Native Americans for at least twelve thousand years, the site was first grazed by Erasmus Keyes Faucett in July 1883. Faucett managed his sheep and goat herd from a rock overhang shelter near the falls for the first four years, and from that bare-boned start eventually controlled some 60,000 acres in the Dolan Falls area. The TPWD acquired 20,500 acres from Faucett's descendants in 1988, forming the Devils River State Natural Area in spectacular canyon country, which with The Nature Conservancy's preserve supplies more than 75 percent of the Devils River live water.

Dolan Falls Ranch is on the western edge of the Central Texas Hill Country, north of Del Rio on the Devils River, at the biological epicenter of the United States where East meets West. It therefore forms the extreme western border of the Hill Country Bioreserve. This 18,552-acre ranch is the first of four to six core preserves planned for the Hill Country over the decades ahead.

Dolan Falls Ranch lies on the transitional zone between three biologically distinct ecosystems: the Edwards Plateau to the east, the dry Chihuahuan Desert to the west, and the subtropical Tamaulipan brushlands to the south.

In the July-August rainy season, moisture from the Pacific Ocean and the Sea of Cortez flows over the Sierra Madre Occidental and can dump eight-inch frog chokers. This water, which cannot soak into the rocky land, can form a twenty- to fifty-foot wall of rushing water, like a tsunami in the middle of the canyonlands, pushing before it house-sized boulders. These floods wreak havoc with the ranch roads, sometimes making them impassable even with a four-wheel drive. In the summer of 1993 a Nature Conservancy land steward was trapped for days, finally forced into swimming the raging Devils River when supplies ran out.

Mexican free-tailed bats swarm at the mouth of The Nature Conservancy's Eckert James River Bat Cave, first in a procession of six million females on their way out for the evening's insect hunt.

"This is a mixing bowl of Texas ecology," says TNC biologist John Karges. Researchers interested in flora and fauna evolution will find Dolan Falls Ranch a rich source of data, from the falls themselves to the rugged limestone cliffs and mesas to pleasant sycamore and live oak forests in the canyon bottoms. Endangered Black-capped Vireos and other rare terrestrial species such as the endangered gopher tortoise occur on the preserve, adding to its biologic quality. Then there's the most unusual barking frog, noted not only for its vocal ability but also for the way it develops. After this frog lays its eggs, not in one of the pools of water but in a moist place, like under a rock, the tadpoles actually metamorphose into froglets entirely inside the egg.

Visiting Dolan Falls with Dr. Clark Hubbs, professor emeritus of zoology at the University of Texas, helped me understand the importance of the living waters of Dolan Spring, Dolan Creek, and the spring-fed Devils River. These waters harbor an endemic fish fauna of the Rio Grande system, with an assemblage of minnows and other species found only in the Chihuahuan Desert.

In *An Annotated Checklist of the Freshwater Fishes of Texas* (1991) Hubbs reports that of the native fishes originally found in Texas, five taxa—phantom shiner, Rio Grande bluntnose shiner, Maravillas red shiner, Amistad gambusia, and San Marcos gambusia—are apparently extinct, and three—Rio Grande cutthroat trout, Rio Grande silvery min-

now, and blotched gambusia—appear to be extinct. Hubbs says, "More than twenty percent of the remaining primary freshwater species appear to be in some need of protection."

Dolan Creek, which flows from the TPWD Devils River State Natural Area through The Nature Conservancy's Dolan Falls Ranch, is home to minnows and other species of fish found only in the Chihuahuan Desert. This view is from the Conservancy's preserve toward Yellow Bluff, located on TPWD land.

Like the birds of Rachel Carson's prescient *Silent Spring,* these fish are early indicators of ecosystem health and certainly of water quality. Hubbs has recorded twenty-one species of fish at the Dolan Falls Ranch preserve, as well as three amphibian species and thirty-four species of reptiles, including the rare Texas tortoise.

The Devils River is one of the last unpolluted streams in Texas. Springs percolate up from the Edwards Aquifer into Dolan Creek and directly into the river above the falls. Although vital, the hydrological aspect of Dolan Falls is just part of the protection story. The variety of plant communities is reflected in a wide variety of wildlife. Already recorded, with more being added regularly, are 29 mammal species and 208 species of vascular plants (many endemic to the Edwards Plateau), and as of mid-1994, more than 200 species of birds had been listed on TNC's camp bird list (I even added one myself, a surprising Greater Yellowlegs). The bird species count is expected to rise because the ranch is on an important corridor for migratory birds, as I found to my joy during a recent spring trip. My group was treated to sightings of many neotropicals, including an array of colorful buntings and warblers. Natural habitat has been pretty much destroyed to the south of Dolan Falls Ranch, so the ranch is the first natural refueling stop that spring migrating birds will come to on their way north.

On my first visit to the ranch, I picnicked right on the falls, to be overflown by a curious osprey; to see an osprey in desert country is a rarity. This one was drawn to the falls from Amistad Reservoir by the abundance of fish, which are blocked from going farther upriver by an impassable twelve-foot limestone barrier. Golden Eagles and Green Kingfishers also adorn the skies of Dolan Falls, and rare Texas horned lizards and the Trans-Pecos ratsnake grace the ground.

At Dolan Creek you can sit where Indians carved out arrowheads and see them on the surface of a nearby midden. Most striking are the pictographs, one of which reminds me of a mission. While building a new road to access an isolated pasture in late 1993, road crews discovered a cave shelter that Solveig Turpin, of the Texas Archeological Research Laboratory at the University of Texas, has estimated to be five thousand years old. Winged shamans, which according to Turpin are among the rarest of religious depictions, decorate the walls of this shelter. Archeologists believe that these shamans acted as the medium between the world of creation and the spirit realm and that many ceremonies featured shamans.

E. K. Faucett's grandson, H. K. Faucett, Jr., is a supporter of The Nature Conservancy and has been helpful in suggesting good stewardship practices, especially in range management. As my group reminisced around a campfire above the falls, H. K. regaled us with descriptions of the 1880s Devils River as told to him by his father. One story was of riding horseback along the Devils River and never leaving the shade of live oaks, pecans, and sycamores, and through grass so high that sheep avoided walking through it. Where there is scoured rock today, then there were grassy banks. The contrast between the heavily grazed pastures surrounding the state natural area and Dolan Falls Ranch is most remarkable in the spring—one notices not only the tallness of grass but also the proliferation of wildflowers, such as the mealy sage carpeting the pastures in a lovely violet-blue. Botanists studying the ranch in 1994 were startled to come across a large population of the extremely rare Texas snowbells, once thought by Jackie Poole of the TPWD to be almost extirpated in West Texas, with only one reported location. This lovely shrub, with its clusters of delicate white flowers that hang down like bells, has been federally listed as endangered since 1984. We found them clinging to a limestone bluff above the Devils River, protected by both humans (a barbed wire fence installed to keep stock from entering the river) and nature (the rugged terrain and bluffs). As botanical and biological inventories continue, many more rare and endangered plants and critters are expected to be found, sometimes in numbers great enough to argue for removing them from certain lists. The stewardship plans call for scientific research, such as discovering how to maximize the sustainable yield while increasing grass cover to protect the quality of runoff, taking inventory and monitoring of rare species and natural communities, and protecting the all-important aquifer features that support Dolan Falls Ranch's springs.

Texas Parks and Wildlife's natural area abuts the Dolan Falls Ranch, so the two ranches provide a valuable conservation resource. The state natural area will be under careful study for years to come, but limited numbers of Texas conservation passport holders will be welcome, conditions permitting. Access is limited while a sound stewardship program is being established. The Conservancy is eager to showcase the preserve and is conducting limited, guided tours for members and scientists.

CHANDLER FAMILY RANCH AND INDEPENDENCE CREEK PRESERVE

Just after receiving an award for conservation work at Independence Creek, Jo Beth Holub, a member of the Texas Land Stewards Society of The Nature Conservancy, invited me to the ranch owned by her mother, Mildred Chandler. It is west of the Pecos and south of Sheffield but still in the Edwards Plateau.

The endemic wildlife and the Indians who inhabited this land thousands of years ago were on my mind as I drove through the familiar Pecos desert terrain en route to the ranch on Independence Creek. The secret of life here is one of water, the water of the springs along the Pecos, where one can find red-eared turtles, mottled rock rattlers, and any number of birds. The springs are home to many rare or endangered fish. The key to these sources of water is a recharge area seventy miles to the northwest, where drainage from Sixshooter and Escondido draws flows into the porous limestone, which is capped by Grayson shale until the life-giving water reaches the Edwards limestone outcrop near the Pecos. There, the water bubbles to the surface and forms oases such as the one Charlie Chandler stumbled upon in 1900 while looking for a place to start a ranch operation. Chandler was not the first to find the springs, as ancient cave artifacts, mortars, and rock middens testify. The ranch does exhibit many characteristics of the Chihuahuan Desert ecosystem, although it is fair to say it's in a transition zone from the Edwards Plateau to the desert ecosystem farther west.

Twenty years ago, I used to walk the barren canyons south of Independence Creek, and based on that experience, I couldn't argue with anyone who described this country as "the Pecos Desert." It's what we call header-draw country, a Texan's way of describing lots of steep arroyos and stony mesas that nevertheless boast a surprising variety of vegetation on the thin but fertile, fragile topsoil. As one of the first people allowed into this area after a decade in which that particular 55,000-acre ranch was not hunted, I had the rare privilege of wandering through what at first appeared to be desolate landscape. To a creature such as myself, reared in lowlands and swamps, it was formidable country. The quiet solitude and grand, uninhabited vistas were intimidating at first, but gradually, if I took care not to scuff the rocks, to walk softly and be still, the land began to reveal much wildlife beyond its plenitude of whitetail, those recent invaders from across the Pecos River. The white-tailed deer migration chased the native mule deer into the more remote, wilder canyons of the ranch. The smaller, more aggressive whitetails pose a breeding threat to the mule deer.

This land abounds in collared peccary, or javelina, herds of which flow like gray-brown ghosts through the cedar-wooded canyons. Social animals, javelinas are really not a threat to humans despite folklore to the contrary. They will attack and kill rattlesnakes and can do serious damage to a coyote or your dog, however. Their rapid tooth-chattering when they are threatened is certainly unnerving, no doubt giving rise to the "dangerous" label. They will also appear to charge as a pack, seemingly directly at an intruder. Usually, they're frightened themselves and are just trying to get out of the way; their eyesight is so poor that they probably can't see what they are running from. Use common sense to stay out of accidental harm's way if this happens. If you are patient and can tolerate the aroma emitted from the scent glands on their backs, it's fun to watch their reciprocal grooming. They will stand head to tail beside one another and take turns rubbing each other's hind legs, rump and scent gland. When they are finished, there is no doubt javelinas are nearby, because this nuzzling action releases more of their pungent, skunklike scent. Biologists agree that javelinas are exceptionally well adapted to arid country and can maintain full hydration without free water. They drink prickly pear cactus! This unhandsome creature is often called a little pig, but it is only distantly related to the domestic pig. Both are scientifically classified with the ungulates, which include elk, white-tailed deer, and mule deer. It's definitely not a hog, as the only feral swine in Texas is the exotic *Sus scrofa,* which probably made its way to Texas via the Spaniards, as escapees from Columbus's livestock stores.

I saw my first ringtail in this country, a catlike, pointy-faced, nocturnal cousin of the raccoon with a bushy, ringed tail as long as its body. I counted eight rings on its tail, but I've since learned that they can have from six to nine rings. Their white-ringed eyes give them a feline appearance, thus the common appellation "ring-tailed cat."

Here, too, was my first brush with *Felis concolor,* a.k.a. cougar, mountain lion, puma, león, panther—all the same cat. Our boy Kernon, age thirteen, had permission to climb from our camp to atop a nearby ridge line. A short while later he rushed into camp, breathless. Quite flustered, he told us of a large cat he'd encountered under a rock outcrop of the mesa above camp. Wandering about with his camera, he had spotted

large paws over the rock ledge. When he looked up, his predicament became clear: he was staring wide-eyed into the equally spooked, amber-green eyes of an adult cougar. Then Kernon made an understandable but potentially fatal mistake; he dropped the camera, turned his back to the cat, and ran. Don't ever do that, despite the urge. It's better by far to stand tall and still and speak calmly to the big cat in a "nice kitty" tone of voice, all the while backing slowly away. Professional wildlife managers add that if a cougar behaves aggressively, throw a rock at it and speak louder and firmly. If a cougar attacks, you are supposed to fight back. I suspect that advice is easier to give than to take.

The spring-fed waters of the Devils River cascade over Dolan Falls at the heart of this Nature Conservancy preserve. Rich in rare, threatened, and endangered plants and animals, Dolan Falls Ranch is also a critical migratory-bird waystation.

Ranchers hereabouts are not fans of the cougar, which can kill a white-tailed or mule deer every week or so, nibble javelina and Rio Grande Wild Turkey as appetizers, decimate a herd of Mexican goats, and make life difficult for sheep and their sheep herder. On the positive side, they also thin out the skunks and porcupines. The day before I visited Independence Creek, a cougar had slaughtered some fifty goats in a nearby canyon, and twenty others just up the road from the Chandler Family Ranch. This is called surplus killing by the cat specialists. The cougar's urge to kill prey outweighs the need to eat it, and when domestic livestock cannot or will not escape, the cougar's urge to kill takes over. To a cougar, multiple kills are an efficient way to procure a lot of food in a short period of time. Cougars with injuries or other impairments also often become livestock predators. Leases for deer and turkey hunting are money in the bank to ranchers, therefore ranchers have reason for concern. Game biologists have not demonstrated that cougars kill only the halt and the lame: more often it is the unwary. Cougars are not protected in Texas; there is no closed season or bag limit, and ranchers will usually shoot them on sight.

Still, ranchers seem to be split on the subject of extirpating cougars, although they agree that ranchers should have the right to kill predators of their livestock. Killing off resident cougars can make matters worse, because younger, transient cougars more willing to kill livestock may move in. Cougars are serious about protecting their territories—there cannot be an overpopulation of cougars. To some ranchers, having the big cats around is a part of their natural heritage, and some like to hunt them for sport. The cougar controversy will continue to pad through Texas for many years. Enlightened private landowners who willingly shoulder both a land and conservation ethic know cougars are part of the natural ecosystem.

For more than forty years this ranch has provided a scenic and refreshing environment for West Texans, to whom fishing and swimming are real treats. Today the ranch is managed by Joe and Mildred Chandler's daughter Jo Beth Holub. She lives on the ranch with her sister Charlena Vargas-Prada. The ranch now has a conservation easement on 701 acres of ecologically sensitive land along Independence Creek. This arrangement leaves ranch ownership in the family yet protects the biological diversity of this special place. The conservation easement was purchased by The Nature Conservancy, allowing the Chandlers to retain the ranch. Developers had been circling like the Turkey Vultures common to this rugged landscape, offering attractive financial inducements at a time when ranch fortunes were at an ebb. By partnering with TNC, the Chandlers were able to preserve their heritage.

The aquatic life of Independence Creek, like that of Dolan Creek, is one of the reasons the area is ecologically so important. The creek is one of only a few perennial streams in the Trans-Pecos, and it is the largest spring-fed creek in this part of Texas, with 18 million to 21 million gallons a day of surface flow. The groves of old-growth live oaks are beautiful testimony to the creek's constant flow. The creek provides a temporary refuge for fish to migrate into when deadly golden-algae conditions exist in the Pecos River. These golden-algae blooms are found in brackish water. One bloom killed about 30,000 fish in November 1993, which was considered a minor kill. Blooms usually affect the sixty to seventy miles of river in the stretch from Sheffield to Pandale. In the past, despite major fish kills, some fish populations have been saved by swimming upstream away from the killing river until the bloom subsides. These fish then flow back into the Pecos and repopulate it.

Independence Creek is home to seventeen species of fish, including the rare proserpina shiner and Pecos pupfish. Many raptors, including Red-shouldered, Swainson's, Zone-tailed, Red-tailed, and Ferruginous hawks, provide air cover, and the creek provides habitat for an unusual assemblage of plants—ocotillo and sotol growing side by side with live oaks.

Spring and summer bring a rainbow variety of birds, from the endangered Black-capped Vireos to Yellow-billed Cuckoos and Black-chinned Hummingbirds. Green Kingfishers speckle the creek along with seven varieties of wrens, adding new tints of color to the brush. For more brilliance, Vermilion Flycatchers, Golden-fronted Woodpeckers, Eastern Bluebirds, Yellow Warblers, Summer Tanagers, and Painted Buntings are among the migrating favorites.

Downstream from Independence Creek, the Pecos River Canyon and the canyons that once carried the flow of other mighty rivers continue to gash the earth's crust, creating an unusual world that with the beginning of human incursions at least twelve thousand years ago became a trap for buffalo. This was the final winter-range destination for the huge herds that moved ahead of the blue northers of the Great Plains, more final for some than others after people arrived. There were megafauna of all sorts: mammoths, ground sloths, horses, and more.

Solveig Turpin, of the Texas Archeological Research Laboratory, describes an ancient buffalo slaughterhouse called Bonfire Shelter in *Ancient Texans* (1986), by Harry J. Shafer. These early-day hunters conducted their big-game hunts in a choreographed dance of death, using piles of stones to form a V-shaped funnel path to the cliff's edge and perhaps even a decoy (an Indian hidden under a buffalo robe wearing a horned hat). This kill site, near present-day Langtry in Val Verde County, is west of the Pecos near its confluence with the Rio Grande. Here, as elsewhere through the Great Plains, Paleo-Indian hunters of eleven thousand or more years ago stampeded herds of giant bison (now extinct) over the cliff. Turpin reports that artifacts here, such as projectile points, are similar to those found over a wide area of the Great Plains from the same era.

The earth warming period of ten thousand years ago, with its increased aridity, apparently drove away what remained of the prey of these ancient native predators; after a lapse of eight thousand years, increased moisture produced enough grass to attract herds of buffalo once again, about the time of the Grecian Golden Age of Pericles in 460 B.C. This is known from carbon dating of burned bones and charcoal from the butchering process.

RARE BIRD ALERT

Austin Area Audubon Alert, 512-483-0952 (sponsored by the Travis Audubon Society). San Antonio, 210-733-8306 (sponsored by the San Antonio Audubon Society).

"A PICTURE OF BARRENNESS AND DESOLATION" THE TRANS-PECOS

CHAPTER 9

No one can imagine the feelings of a thirsty man till he sees one. I would not describe it by a vain attempt, as vain almost as that would be which I might use in describing the region of country just passed over which made them so; a region in its original chaotic state, as if the progress of civilization was too rapid for the arrangement of chaos; a picture of barrenness and desolation, when the scathing fire of destruction has swept with its rapid flame mountains, canyons, ravines, precipices, cactus, soap weed, intense reflections from the limestone cliffs, and almost every barrier that one can conceive of to make an impossibility to progress.

LT. WILLIAM H. ECHOLS
aboard a camel, Dog Canyon, 1859, *Report to U.S. Senate,* 1861

What a difference an air-conditioned auto, ice chest, and interstate highway can make to one's perspective of the Trans-Pecos. Still, motorists whizzing through the high, dry Chihuahuan Desert at open-road velocities may soon be jaded by endless creosote bushes and cacti, bunchgrass interspersed by green-barbed lechuguilla, itself not a natural wonder to observe, and the occasional spiny, spidery ocotillo. Little does this high-speed viewer know, or perhaps care, that the creosote bush has a thirty-foot taproot that produces toxins to keep roots of competitive plants away; that the ocotillo, which is not a cactus, conserves water by eschewing leaves until rain comes, and it may develop and drop leaves several times a year; that spiny armor and a waxy water seal enable cacti to survive; or that lechuguilla lives only here, and some say it was once a source for cortisone. It is the merest trace of water—the ten inches of rain a year falling on the flat lands—that supports the vast diversity of desert-floor flora and fauna, the latter an eclectic assemblage of amphibians, reptiles, lizards, geckos, skinks, mammals, and relict fish. There are

OPPOSITE PAGE
Six species of Spanish dagger appear in the Big Bend area of Texas; this specimen of Yucca torreyi *is in The Nature Conservancy's 10,000-acre Brushy Canyon Preserve. The isolated preserve parallels the eastern slope of the Dead Horse Mountains and supports many rare plants and animals.*

toads (Couch's spadefoot) that spend most of their time underground, covered in a gelatinous coat that seals in body liquids, and dimorphic spotted whiptail lizards that produce offspring without breeding.

There are hundreds of springs in the Big Bend, 180 within Big Bend National Park itself, and they are easy to find because of the rarity of their vegetation. Tinajas are natural basins that collect water; some are so deep that they contain water most of the time, such as Ernst Tinaja, and trap unwary cougars in dry times. The highest peaks, such as Livermore in the Davis Mountains, the Guadalupes on the New Mexico border, and the Chisos in the Big Bend, catch more rain, sometimes as much as twenty inches a year, and feature pinyon-oak-juniper woodlands.

Lieutenant Echols, a topographical engineer cum camel tester, was most observant, seeing the Trans-Pecos as geologically young, its ragged landforms ungroomed by the erosive passage of time. The Trans-Pecos is filled with the life-on-the-edge zones that produce a wide diversity of plants and animals. Brilliant white sand dunes (under which lie the bones of mammoths, sloths, and extinct camels), brightly painted cliff faces, petrified trees, chimney-stack hoodoos teetering above waterless flats, moist and lush 8,000-foot mountain highlands—all manner of improbable contrasts can be found here. Echols's comments echoed the legends sung by Indians who lived here: After the Great Spirit had made the earth and had finished placing the stars in the sky, the birds in the air, and the fish in the sea, there was a large pile of rejected stony materials left over. Finished with his job, he threw them into one heap and made the Trans-Pecos.

Despite the Hades-like heat, the bone-chilling wintry cold, and the dryness, a vast variety of life thrives in the Trans-Pecos. In fact, the Trans-Pecos contains the greatest variety of plants, animals, and natural communities in Texas, many of which are unprotected. The American Peregrine Falcon is making a comeback here. Park rangers told me about zealously guarding nesting pairs in aeries high on isolated cliffs, both in Big Bend National Park and in Guadalupe Mountains National Park. Black bears, long on the state endangered list, have been reported in the Guadalupe Mountains and have sneaked back north of the Rio Grande into Big Bend Park, where bear-crossing signs are posted on the drive up to the Chisos Basin. Unique species of pupfish, mosquito fish, and shiners are here. In the Chisos Mountains, the Colima Warbler attracts its share of birders to Boot Springs. Birders can find more than four hundred candidate species for their life lists in the Big Bend area alone.

Mountain ranges such as the Franklin, Guadalupe, Davis, Glass, Chinati, Christmas, Rosillos, Dead Horse, Sierra Diablo, Chisos, and others rise up from the desert floor creating their own special habitats.

The Davis Mountains are the highest entirely within Texas, with the Baldy Peak of Mount Livermore reaching 8,378 feet. These are true sky islands formed of igneous rock. The Guadalupe and Glass mountains are formed of an ancient fossil reef, one of the largest in the world. Guadalupe Peak at 8,749 feet is the highest point in Texas. The ecosystems that form over igneous rock are entirely different from those associated with the more alkaline reef formations.

The Davis Mountains are the only home of the Livermore sandwort, little ajuga pondweed, and Shinners tickle-tongue, and several other rare plants are sheltered here. In the Guadalupes, golden columbine, McKittrick pennyroyal, McKittrick snowberry, and Guadalupe valerian are endemic. The Guadalupe and Franklin ranges harbor some of the flora and fauna endemic to the Rocky Mountains, as do the Davis, Chinati, Glass, Chisos, Dead Horse, and Diablo ranges to a lesser extent. The Chisos Mountains are the sole refuge for Big Bend bluegrass, slender oak, robust oak, and Chisos Mountain oak. The canyons of Capote Falls, with the highest falls in Texas, contain the only recorded stand of the rare Hinckley's columbine. Hinckley oak is yet another relict, existing in only a few locations.

Cattle ranching in the Trans-Pecos began in the 1860s, and Mexican ranchers allowed their herds to roam up across the Rio Grande. There were no regulations to control the free range of cattle. By the 1880s, graze was already thinning out east of the Pecos, and more cattle stomped their way into the Big Bend country. Much of the grassland was irrevocably lost because of overgrazing. Roland H. Wauer, former chief park naturalist for Big Bend National Park, addresses this critical issue in his work *Naturalist's Big Bend* (1973). Wauer recalls the park's two-year free-graze period between 1942, when the state of Texas purchased the land, and the park's opening in 1944. In 1942, there were 3,880 cattle and 310 horses in the area; by 1944 19,000 to 25,000 cattle and 1,000 horses were removed. The overgrazing devastated the ecology. Some areas have never recovered in the fifty years that have elapsed. Once there was good graze in the park, as noted by Lieutenant Echols during his camel expeditions of 1859–1860.

Today, however, many ranchers have brought their pieces of the Trans-Pecos back to a healthy biodiversity. I visited the Iron Mountain Ranch of Bill Blakemore, now a treasure for botanical research. Dr. Barton Warnock has studied the ranch since 1940 when, in his words, "It was heavily stocked with goats several years previously, and I did not feel it was worth the time [to study the vegetation]." But by 1969, Blakemore had managed the ranch back to health and invited Dr. Warnock to study it. Since then, Dr. Warnock has established a center for Trans-Pecos plant study on the ranch.

Some of the last wilderness in North America is preserved by Texas Parks and Wildlife at the Big Bend Ranch State Natural Area west of Big Bend National Park. Truly a land of contrasts, the ranch encompasses many natural wonders, such as the austerely awesome Solitario Basin, used as a landmark by astronauts, and surprisingly bountiful waterfalls such as Madrid Falls, the second highest falls in Texas. Big Bend Park and the Big Bend Ranch together protect more than a million acres of the fragile Chihuahuan Desert ecosystem.

What is incredible to me is the widespread lack of understanding, or even appreciation, for the value of protecting these million-plus acres. Some people are vitriolic about the very existence of these protected areas, and I hear complaints from those who deeply resent that they can no longer carom their souped up four-wheelers through the vastness of Big Bend Ranch. In fact, what these off-roaders remember as free access was actually trespassing. The only real difference now is that the state has the resources to protect and preserve the land.

The atmosphere of cooperation that The Nature Conservancy has cultivated among ranchers, farmers, and the petroleum industry puts it in a pivotal position to reduce the threats to the natural riches of this area. The major threat is from a human population explosion in the area, as wide-open ranchlands are converted to smaller parcels more intensely used, with subdivisions encroaching upon the special places where water and mountain views are found. TNC vice president David Braun is concerned about a backlash from the activities of other environmental organizations, which have created some resentment among ranchers, farmers, and oilfield workers who believe their industries are misunderstood. There *is* misunderstanding, but not among TNC members. Says Braun, "The Nature Conservancy has been hurt as the bad feelings make it more difficult to work with local people, even though our approach is to work cooperatively with all groups to reach common goals. Broad accusations of overzealous action on the part of other environmental groups have been carelessly leveled at The Nature Conservancy despite our history of conservative, market- and science-driven action." The Nature Conservancy recognizes the efforts being made by private landowners to improve range management, oilfield practices, and water conservation in the rare habitats of the Trans-Pecos.

I believe most local landowners—ranchers as well as others who make a living there—and those who simply enjoy the remoteness and the special beauty of the desert do understand the treasure that has been conserved. Certainly, former gubernatorial candidate Clayton Williams does, for he is a major supporter of the Chihuahuan Desert Research Institute, with headquarters at Sul Ross State University in Alpine and a research center just south of Fort Davis.

The Chihuahuan Desert Research Institute has conducted several

One of the most famous features of the Big Bend Ranch State Natural Area is the Solitario, formed by two geological events. First, magma muscled its way up through the earth's crust, then millions of years later a volcano blew through the formation, killing every living thing for miles around.

symposiums on the region's resources, which has at least drawn scientific attention to the area. There is some concern about the declining access to ranches for scientific study in the Trans-Pecos. This is caused in part by an unfounded fear that some endangered plant will be found that will allow the federal government to take over and condemn ranchlands. Continuing scientific study of this area is seriously hindered by a closing of the gates to scientists by ranchers who needlessly fear loss of their private property—a fear fueled by radical wise-use activists.

Another problem is the air quality and visibility in the Chihuahuan Desert, further threatened by Carbón II, a large coal-burning power plant in Mexico, 125 miles southeast, typically upwind. Air pollution and visibility are monitored by the Park Service Air Quality Program and showed a degradation of visibility during "episodes of severe magnitude" in 1986. These episodes are now more frequent. Pollution could cut visibility by 60 percent, reducing the normal view of 100 miles to just 40. Those of us who have been visiting Big Bend National Park for many years can easily see the degradation. While no one can put a dollar value on it, there are those who believe that the night sky in this remote area is one of its most valuable assets. The air and light pollution now building up in the Davis Mountains already adversely affects the aesthetic experience, not to mention the scientific work of the McDonald Observatory north of Fort Davis.

Yet other issues that will heat up the Trans-Pecos in the nineties will be water rights and waste disposal. For example, the city of El Paso has bought the water rights under a large ranch and when, not if, the time comes would suck the underground reservoir dry to accommodate the city's urban sprawl. One of the questions is, what would be the impact on all the other ranches in the area? Another issue involves the search in Hudspeth County for a low-level radioactive waste disposal site, to the grave concern of local ranchers. This could also be a conservation issue, although not quite so evident as the water problem. In all likelihood such a facility could be located in this area with complete safety and maybe even contribute to the tax base and other revenues of this sparsely populated county. If there were any contamination danger, however, the ranchers could find no better partners than environmental activists. What was that about strange bedfellows?

DIAMOND Y SPRINGS PRESERVE

The infamous Comanche War Trail snaked across the Pecos River out of the Llano Estacado just north and east of Diamond Draw, at a place fabled in western literature as the Horsehead Crossing. When early westward-bound explorers crossed here, they had entered the Trans-Pecos. For hundreds of years Comanches drove stolen horses and mules through the desert up from Mexico. Uncontrollably gulping the first water they had seen in days, many of these animals died in convulsions. Their skulls littered the Pecos banks, grim warning to settlers and the forty-niners headed for California gold. Frances T. Bryan, writing a report to the U.S. Senate in December 1849, described the crossing: "[The Pecos] is not visible until you come directly upon it, its banks not being marked by trees and anything different from the surrounding plains. . . . The crossing which we used is known as the 'horse-head' crossing—the soil here is very light, like ashes, and a camp soon becomes intolerable. . . . Grass here is coarse and hard, and appears to have but little nourishment. There is no wood at all to be had."

The Comanches who prowled their war trail would be saddened to learn the legacy of Comanche Springs in Fort Stockton, which once flowed, at the turn of the century, at 65 million gallons daily. As you'd guess, these springs were rich in aquatic fauna, including the rare Comanche Springs pupfish. By 1950 irrigation wells were being drilled southwest of the spring in increasing numbers, and as more wells were drilled, the spring flow declined dramatically. By 1956 Comanche Springs had ceased to flow.

Just ten miles to the north of Comanche Springs, The Nature Conservancy's Diamond Y Springs is an uncommon West Texas natural area that provides critically important habitat for two species of rare fish, a rare plant, and three species of rare snails. The spring is actually a ciénaga, a desert spring system, which during the Gold Rush days was not such a rare watering hole but now has joined the ranks of vanishing natural phenomena. These stream courses are remnants of powerful ancient river systems, making them places where rare flora and fauna may still survive.

According to Gunnar Brune, who studied Texas springs beginning in 1971 and published some of his work in 1981 in the book *Springs of Texas,* Diamond Y Springs was also known as Deep Springs and is the largest of the surviving springs in Pecos County. Brune states, "Diamond Y Springs issue from a deep hole into Comanchean limestone about eighteen meters in diameter. The upstream Leon Springs probably looked like this at one time although they were much larger. . . . This is one of the last footholds of the Leon Springs pupfish."

That pupfish is, of course, one of the reasons The Nature Conservancy acquired the 1,502 acres that encompass the springs and its perennial spring run. Diamond Y Springs also harbors the rare Pecos gambusia and is the only known locality for a rare wildflower, the puzzle sunflower.

A conservation-minded Texan, M. R. Gonzalez, Jr., whose family purchased the springs in 1969, can be credited with a major save of these endangered creatures. Gonzalez found the springwater to be high in dissolved salts, foul tasting, and unhealthy for livestock. He built windmills in the highlands away from Diamond Y for fresh water and instituted a rotational grazing system to protect plants from overuse. Gonzalez will continue to lease grazing rights from The Nature Conservancy as part of the acquisition agreement, another case of rancher-conservation partnership with a win-win solution.

Grazing wasn't the only challenge to the springs. The preserve is located in the middle of an oil and gas production field, with mineral rights beneath the property owned by Exxon and British Petroleum, and Enron Corporation runs a large gas plant adjacent to the preserve. Not all Conservancy acquisitions are scenically stunning; Diamond Y certainly proves this. The energy companies have been extremely cooperative in helping the Conservancy protect the fragile spring system. A side benefit has been the experimental work done on restoration of nearby abandoned drilling-site pads, and reseeding of these areas is under way. The site has enormous potential for nature education, and proximity to Fort Stockton makes it ideal for study by local students. Since the land is privately grazed and is a producing field, access is by permission only.

BIG BEND NATIONAL PARK

After an inevitable and regretted absence, when I ease through the ancient stream bed now called Persimmon Gap that cuts the Santiago Mountains, I am invariably overcome with a sense of unimaginable geological time. I envision long-departed Amerinds who first crossed the gap, wonder at nature's grandeur, and feel grateful for those farsighted people who helped preserve what lies before me. Here, your conservation ethic will touch the past in a way unlike any other Texas experience. I am grateful, too, that the park's isolation keeps it on the National Park Service's "ten least visited" lists year after year.

If you come into the park from Marathon, as most visitors do, you'll see a marker at a rest stop south of the Persimmon Gap Ranger Station that declares this is the place where the Appalachian and Rocky Mountains meet. The Big Bend is in the Ouachita Trough, through which the Appalachians formed during the Permian period 250 million years ago. Mexico's Sierra Nevadas were formed in the Jurassic, 181 million years ago, followed 50 million years later in the Cretaceous period by the Rocky Mountains. So three mountain systems come together here.

Persimmon Gap is special to me in another way. In 1989, I stood on this now paved segment of the Comanche Trail with a small group of conservationists while the Park Service officially acknowledged the addition of the 67,214-acre Harte Ranch to Big Bend, a gift via The Nature Conservancy from the Harte family. This gift added the Rosillos Mountains to the park. The mountains can be seen on the horizon to the southwest as you cross through Persimmon Gap. Forever enhancing the park, the mountains increased its size to 801,163 acres. Like the park itself, the Rosillos Mountains were a gift from Texans to all the people of the United States and the world. However, a handful of local ranchers affiliated with Wise Use objected to this donation. Even though Big Bend National Park pays $330,000 a year to Brewster County in lieu of property taxes, relations with some large ranches have been cool.

Several pastures on the original Harte Ranch that were not designated as part of the national park were sold to a local rancher. TNC used the funds from that sale to buy a 10,000-acre preserve in the Dead Horse Mountains. Brushy Canyon Preserve is nestled between TPWD's Black Gap Wildlife Management Area and the eastern edge of Big Bend National Park. Giant dagger yuccas are plenteous here, and with spring rains the slopes and headers are awash in their creamy blossoms. According to John Karges, this diminished and sensitive ecological community, isolated as it is, supports many rare plants and animals. The highest diversity of bat species is found here, as are the rare reticulated gecko and endangered Black-capped Vireo.

Early Big Bend settler J. O. Langford built his home on a bluff over Tornillo Creek's juncture with the Rio Grande and established the famous Hot Springs spa, where the flow rate today is only a little less than in 1936, about 250,000 gallons of water a day at 105 degrees Fahrenheit. The hot water emerges from a pocket of water heated geothermally. This area used to be good fishing for blue, channel, and flathead catfish, but now signs warn of pollution.

Clark Hubbs can be credited with saving the Big Bend gambusia from extinction. He and Roland Wauer studied the fish along the lower Tornillo Creek for three years, finding the creek to be a breeding ground for many Rio Grande fish species, such as the Mexican tetra, Chihuahuan shiners, and plains killifish.

During the Cretaceous period of the Mesozoic era, a sea covered the much older Paleozoic rocks of the Ouachita system, a sea teeming with life: clams, oysters, snails, corals, and ammonites. Ammonites are the handsome coiled mollusks that resemble today's chambered nautilus. Marine reptiles left their bones at the bottom of this sea; when it withdrew, these bones provided the fertile soil for dense vegetation—ferns, mosses, canes, and plants that exist today, 135 million years later. Dinosaurs that evolved to feed on this vegetation didn't fare as well, perhaps because oxygen levels declined sharply in the Cenozoic era. They survived for only 100 million years or so, becoming extinct in the Cenozoic era as mammals continued to evolve: horses, saber-toothed cats, and, in the Quaternary, woolly mammoths, and eventually man. Modern research, however, indicates that one branch of the dinosaurs did make it through evolutionary time—birds. The fossil record of the Big Bend is fascinating, and there are important implications to naturalists and conservationists.

The Big Bend has edges that slice back into primordial time, and plants can be found here that are typical not only of the southwestern United States but also of Canada, Mexico, even Central America. Many of the animals here are not found elsewhere north of Mexico, such as the dainty Carmen Mountains white-tailed deer and the Colima Warbler. The former hides itself in the wooded mountains above five thousand feet, and the tiny yellow and gray warbler likewise prefers the cooler uplands for nesting in spring and summer. A sighting of this bird usually requires a strenuous nine-mile round-trip hike almost two thousand feet from the basin up toward the south rim of the Chisos Mountains, diverting down a bit to Boot Canyon and its springs. This canyon also features a tree found nowhere else in the United States, the drooping or weeping juniper. Yet another bird unknown to the rest of the country is the Lucifer Hummingbird, which hums its pretty way through the century plant's blooms. A rare south-of-the-border visitor is the female long-nosed bat, always in search of agave flowers from which to sip nectar as they pollinate. Roland Wauer has stated that these bats "roost in a cave high on the north side of Emory Peak." Bats make up about 25 percent of the park's mammal list.

According to Wauer and Midge Erskine of the Eos Bird Rehabilitation Center at Midland, there are five distinct ecological zones in the park, each with its own flora and fauna. Of the park's more than 1,000 identified plants, 430 are woody plants, but most are wildflowers, and in the spring this area can rival the Hill Country for variety of floral displays, given just a hint of rainfall at the right time. Adding to the potential for color are the cacti, which really bloom as the park receives spring and summer rainfall. Knowing the common ecological categories can help locate the more common flowering plants. Wauer's *Naturalist's Big Bend* is a good guide. Experienced birders challenge you to spot more than 100 species in just one day by ranging through these biological zones in April or May. On one lazy day in early May I was able to identify 78 species of the 434 currently listed in the bird checklist of Big Bend National Park, the largest checklist for any national park. Fall migration patterns add a host of waterfowl sightings.

The area close to the Rio Grande has fast-growing plants that thrive in moist soil, such as Texas virgin's bower, morning glory, and globe mallow. At Hot Springs, the yellow blooms of acacias are common in April and May. You'll also find the purple-flowered silverleaf nightshade, the poisonous berries of which are sometimes used by Mexicans to curdle milk for cheese, according to TPWD's David Alloway of the Warnock Environmental Center at Lajitas. Alloway has his cheese made by a Mexican lady, who says she uses four berries per gallon of milk. There is a safety valve built in, because if you use too many berries, the cheese turns green and you know not to eat it.

Although the area is not aesthetically pleasing because of debris, you may want to explore the brush around Boquillas Canyon, where I found a Northern Parula, the minute, lemon-lime tinted warbler. A Green-tailed Towhee flitted about bright-red cardinals and Indigo Buntings. You are also apt to see Mexican vaqueros herding cattle illegally across the border to feed. Upriver is the village of San Vicente, not an authorized border crossing but a well-used smuggling point.

At Rio Grande Village campground a Ladder-backed Woodpecker watched me gas up, and Blue Grosbeaks belied their secretive nature by feeding next to the entrance of the nature trail. Yellow-billed Cuckoos also nest here, as do innumerable doves, their coos echoing through the park. Look for Inca, White-winged, and Common Ground doves as a change of pace from the ubiquitous Mourning Doves. Roadrunners running, Black-chinned Hummingbirds hovering, and flycatchers, vireos, buntings, and finches fluttering add to your sightings, especially the Mondrian-style buntings and Vermilion Flycatchers. Eye-catching are the Hooded, Northern, and Orchard orioles, their orangy plumage standing out against the dense green of the subtropical foliage. And then there are the Turkey Vulture crowds massed upon the picnic tables. Climbing up the nature trail from the Rio Grande, you quickly enter open desert, with a likelihood of seeing White-throated Swift, a Peregrine, or even the rare Aplomado Falcon. Instead of a Peregrine, I settled for a Lesser Nighthawk, uncommon for most of the United States.

In the dry shrub of which deserts are made, rainfall is less than ten inches annually. Half the park can be so described. In early April head for Dagger Flats; with luck you'll look out over a sea of yuccas in bloom, especially the Spanish dagger. As you drive the unpaved road into the flats, you're apt to see yellow huisache blooms. Elsewhere in the lowlands look for Chisos bluebonnets, similar but different from the state flower that covers the spring Hill Country. Desert verbena blooms in the desert in the winter and spring and in the mountains the rest of the year. Chisos prickly poppy, white to pink, is easy to spot. The yellow swatches seen early in the spring are probably caliche bahia and parralena, which are sunflowers. Other yellow flowers include those of the creosote bush. Lechuguilla, the sure identifier of Chihuahuan desert, is found here. Its leaves curve up; those of the false agave curve down. Candelilla, once raw material for a thriving wax-rendering industry, is also found down here. The taper-thin stems were yanked from the ground, bundled up, and transported to processing plants close to water. There was so much candelilla harvested that special efforts had to be taken to guard the remnant plants. They are still not nearly as plentiful as they were before the century-long wax raids.

This is good, open raptor-spotting country, with kestrels, Prairie Falcons, Zone-tailed Hawks, and Red-tailed Hawks often seeking their hapless rodent prey. Look closely at the ravens; they are most often the Common Raven, not the Chihuahuan species one might expect. The wee gray bird scudding through the huisache is surely a Verdin if you see a yellow head and a tiny spot of red. Hard to miss are the Pyrrhuloxia and mockingbirds. Male Summer Tanagers provide rubescent relief to the gray desert, their mates a spatter of saffron.

The grassland just above the desert is where you begin to see more low-growing shrubs and even tall shrubs. This is the other big chunk of the state and federal parklands. Some of the desert flowers will bloom up here a little later in the summer. You'll also find red flowers such as bracted paintbrush and, in a wet July, scarlet morning glories. A personal favorite is the fragrant purple New Mexico verbena, and I love the plains fleabane, a tiny white daisy with a yellow center. Settlers thought the daisy was, like Avon's body lotion, an insect repellent, especially of fleas. It didn't work with the last bird dogs I hunted over.

Both the Sage Thrasher and Crissal Thrasher frequent this area. The Crissal is common but careful; look for the spot of red under his tail as

The Chisos Mountains are the focal point of Big Bend National Park, and hikers are rewarded with this view from the Lost Mine Trail into the southern Chisos and Mexico. The Chisos are mainly volcanic in origin, but dikes of harder igneous rock fill fissures in the lava.

he hides in dense brush. Scaled Quail will hotfoot it in and out of the brushy areas, and you'll see a lot of sparrows, such as the Rufous-crowned and Black-throated. As you climb higher in this zone, Gray-breasted Jays dart about importantly, and the Hepatic Tanager takes over from the Summer. Look for the grayish cheek patch to distinguish the male and female Hepatic from the Summer Tanager. Our most diminutive owl may be seen here, roosted in a yucca during daylight. Otherwise, the Elf Owl is hard to glimpse since he is nocturnal. Look upward often, since this zone produces more cover and food for rodents and thus attracts more raptors. Then look down for black-tailed rattlesnakes.

The higher woodland formations feature broad-leaved and coniferous plants, beginning where the grasslands leave off and going right to the top of the Chisos—only 2 percent of the park can be so categorized. Bright pink phlox are usually the earliest bloomers up here. Wildflower aficionados will seek out the red Chisos paintbrush, found only here. Milkweeds add white relief to the green backdrop.

My favorite bird in this hospitable Big Bend zone is the friendly Brown Towhee who welcomes most hikers just up from the Basin headquarters. It's now called a Canyon Towhee, with a tiny bronze medallion on its breast. Acorn Woodpeckers hammer away, and the petite Black-crested Titmouse, the White-breasted Nuthatch, and bushtits flit about. Pine Siskins are common on the trails to Boot Canyon and Laguna Meadow.

According to Wauer, only about eight hundred acres of the park is in the moist Chisos woodland formation, mainly forest edge vegetation within Boot and Pine canyons, much of it shaded and cool. It's to these rare and beautiful places that hikers flock, perhaps to admire longspur columbine. This pretty flowering plant likes the wet of the upper canyons such as Dripping Springs, where it grows in the summer. Cardinal flowers bloom later in the summer and fall. A yellow flower up here is the evening primrose, which, as its name implies, doesn't open until late afternoon. The yellow primrose is a hummingbird's treat. Lucifer Hummingbirds attend blooming century plants sometimes seen along the trail, and Broad-tailed and Blue-throated hummingbirds like it up here, too, as do the Canyon Wren, Black-headed Grosbeak, and Rufous-sided Towhee. A specialty of this zone, although difficult to spot, is the Flammulated Owl. It is nocturnal, but it may sometimes be seen at first or last light. This means packing in, for it's a nine-mile round-trip to Boot Canyon.

The winter bird population features many migratory waterfowl species down by the river. Stimulating strolls through the brush will yield lots of varieties of sparrows, such as the Clay-colored, Brewer's, Baird's, Cassin's, White-crowned, and Lincoln's.

There are hundreds more birds and wildflowers to be found in the Big Bend, and if you're like me, you'll need other references (beyond Wauer's guide) and a lot of time. At least the wildflowers, given any rain at all, will tend to cooperate as to when and where they bloom. The birds tend to show up seasonally and where expected, with many delightful surprises, of course.

Cacti are highly adaptive latecomers to the desert bloom display. Their indomitable, thorny character no doubt explains some names, such as heart twister, pincushion, pest, horse crippler, dagger, club, fishhook, cat claw, and eagle claw. Despite the thorns and name-calling, cactus blooms are some of the most resplendent in nature. They are obviously doing their dead-level best to attract birds, insects, and bats—whichever special creature nature has nominated to aid in pollination. Cacti are the most patient of plants, waiting for a dash of water to bloom. If it doesn't rain, their germination inhibitors will keep the seeds safe, to wait out another year for the right amount of water. When the seed does germinate, things happen fast, with flower and fruit following much faster than in temperate annuals. My favorites include the pale yellow rainbow, pink magenta star rock (which looks just like a rock), rosy-red Turk's head, and strawberry, widely distributed in the park. The Turk's head was once the source of cactus candy. The strawberry cactus fruit is delicious and may be eaten just as one would the domestic fruit. Claret-cup blooms are a vivid scarlet red that rivets eyes in a brown desert. The purple prickly pear is named so because of the streaks on its pads, which may even turn completely purple in the winter. Its flowers are warm yellow, with reddish orange centers. Other prickly pears display incandescent yellow and fire-orange blooms, and I have made gallons of jelly from tunas picked in late summer (not in the park!). My most favorite, not so much for its color as for its smell, is the Texas night-blooming cereus, which does just that. As I sat outside a cabin at Lajitas one early May evening, just kicking back and star-gazing after watching Mexican free-tailed bats emerge for their evening insect *comida,* a powerful, sweet aroma swept down the Rio Grande canyon, washing its heady perfume across my campsite. You'll not forget this wild scent, which rivals in complexity and sensuousness any I've professionally sampled from the world's leading perfumers. This rarest of essences is created for only one or two nights at most. The plant's root can be two feet in diameter and weigh up to 250 pounds. If you ever do track one down in the night desert, you'll see large, distinctive white blossoms.

Of course, the park is better known for things that stick and scratch and bite and poison. The reptile and amphibian inventory is one of the largest in the nation, capped by five poisonous snakes. Black-tailed rattlers are found most everywhere, while the ever-popular western diamondback is a desert dweller, with his less well-known relative, the Mojave. The handsome mottled rock rattler, sometimes seen in pink and green finery, is aptly named and may be found from foothills to mountaintops. The Trans-Pecos copperhead, although sometimes found on high, is most often encountered down along the river where you'd expect.

Other watch-outs include the park's eleven species of scorpions, enough to remind you to shake out your sleeping bag each evening. None will kill (unless you are allergic to their venom), all will hurt. The six-inch-long, mean-looking Big Bend vinegaroon is a whip scorpion, with no stinger—no threat to you unless you don't like the smell of vinegar. Three other bad-looking dudes are the giant desert centipede, the millipede, and the tarantula. Of this threesome, only the centipede will hurt, but its poison shouldn't kill you. Some say tarantulas make good pets. Some of us prefer dogs.

While you are looking out for scorpions, centipedes, cacti, and snakes, remember to heed the park's signs about bear crossings and cougar presences. One sign says "Pick up small children." Cougars are camouflage experts of the first rank, and they know you are around long before you detect them—if you ever do. There have been two cougar attacks in Big Bend Park in recent years (1984–1986), right on the trails. Both victims turned and ran, but a cougar sprints at forty miles an hour and can launch itself like a surface-to-surface missile, seeming to sail through the air to a victim's back, forelegs extended to an improbable length. What you should keep in mind is that an adult, eight-foot-long cougar can break a mule deer's neck with one twist.

Unfortunately, although this is not regarded as an unsafe park, more people have been killed by people than by cougars since 1988 (three), and burglaries have been on the upswing, with forty in 1993.

Although the Rio Grande itself was referenced in an earlier chapter, I would be remiss not to mention the river canyons before exploring the Big Bend Ranch State Natural Area. From a perch at Lajitas, you can look north by northwest up the Colorado Canyon of the Rio Grande, the first of five canyons favored by canoers, rafters, and kayakers. While the best way (sometimes the only way) to view the flora and fauna of the riverine ecosystem is unquestionably to get into it, this is not an exercise for the amateur. River running for classes 1 through 4 is available through these canyon troughs, but the water is unpredictable. Depths can vary daily because of unannounced and sometimes unscheduled releases from the Río Conchos dam in Mexico. Contact the park at 915-477-2251 to obtain permit information and to check river depth and safety. I strongly urge you to join up with a professional river raft team, typically located in the Lajitas area.

After the Colorado Canyon run, which borders much of the Big Bend Ranch, there are three spectacular canyon runs and one gentler one possible as the river forms a 100-mile border for the national park. The first is dramatic Santa Elena Canyon, where the river rushes through the 1,500-foot-high (from the river surface) cliffs of Mesa de Anguila. About 450 yards inside the canyon, rafters come quickly upon one of the barriers feared by early explorers, the infamous rock slide, caused by rocks shearing off into the river from the Mexican side. There are two small channels through the rock slide; they're not for the faint of heart, and not even for the professional in high water. Once you are committed to Santa Elena, she owns you—you must go on through.

The next challenging canyon run is through the middle of another mountain, Mariscal, formed at the end of the Cretaceous. (The mountain on the right bank is Sierra San Vicente.) Like Santa Elena, there is a rock slide just inside Mariscal Canyon. Not quite as intimidating, it is best passed on the Texas side. A mile farther on brings the rafter to another place that proved fearsome to early explorers, the Tight Squeeze. Again, the Texas side is the safest way to go.

The San Vicente and Hot Springs canyons are the easy ones with few hazards and good bird-watching in the fall, a preferred time for me on the river. You're apt to see a Texas spiny softshell turtle, and others such as the yellow mud. In October, expect Blue-winged Teal, and you'll soon come upon sandbars formed by seep willows, a sunflower plant that builds sandbars for your enjoyment and that of various sandpipers. Along here are canebrakes that provide an insect buffet and rest stop for some of the migrating songbirds, such as warblers in the spring, headed back from their wintering grounds in Central America. In these canyons, time is transparent, and you can easily visualize that this area offered both a river and floodplain far from the sea. Some 80 million years ago, the pterosaur flew this area in search of food, although we don't know what food. This reptile had a wingspread up to thirty-six feet. A good take-out spot for this trip is Rio Grande Village—and as you now know, a fine migratory bird-watching spot and campsite.

The last canyon within Big Bend National Park is Boquillas Canyon, which you can run from Rio Grande Village to access points just outside the national park at Stillwell Crossing, a private spot requiring permission from the U. J. Adams Ranch, or at La Linda Crossing, which transects the TPWD Black Gap Wildlife Management Area. This is the largest WMA in Texas, a ruggedly beautiful destination for Texas conservation passport holders. Boquillas Canyon is scenic and not too hazardous, a favorite because its limited access narrows the float-tripper competition.

We now come to a place marked on your state road map "Rio Grande Wild and Scenic River." This is not just the rhetoric of a government public relations writer but rather an official designation indicating that a permit is also required to float the 83.5-mile stretch from La Linda to Dryden Crossing. Call park headquarters (915-477-2251) well before your trip to obtain the permit. "Wild and scenic" is also an accurate description of this rugged desert experience itself. If you are hardy enough, and by this I mean able to paddle twenty miles each day for a week if required, this is an unforgettable way to put the finishing touches on the conservation ethic you have been building since your first Pineywoods adventure 900 miles to the northeast.

By this time, I hope your appreciation for conservation has been sharpened with regard to this desolate-appearing landscape. The closer you look, feel, taste, and smell, the more life and interest you discover. Adaptation is the name of survival here, and it seems every plant and animal has its special story. This is a good place to find out how *you* adapt. Big Bend is, after all, a wilderness park with miles of primitive trails across jumbled, disorienting terrain. As extraordinary as it appears, early explorers could live off this dry, seemingly barren land. You can't do that, even if you dared, because park rules specifically prohibit "collecting any natural feature."

OPPOSITE PAGE
Rock-strewn Big Bend Ranch State Natural Area appears impervious to harm by puny human hands, but in reality the natural area protects many fragile ecosystems. One of the most delicate and beautiful is Mexicano Falls, third highest in the state.

BLACK GAP WILDLIFE MANAGEMENT AREA

A four-wheel-drive vehicle is suggested for driving the backroads on this 106,000 acres, the largest of the wildlife management areas in Texas. Your efforts could be rewarded with the sighting of a variety of seldom-seen wildlife, such as coyote, bobcat, or even black bear. More than 260 species of birds have been recorded in this rugged wilderness, including Peregrine Falcons, Bald and Golden eagles, hawks, warblers, ducks, geese, and hummingbirds. The management area and surrounding mountains have many aeries suitable for the endangered Peregrine Falcon, but in 1994 only twelve could be determined to be in use by nesting birds, according to nongame specialist Bonnie McKinney. Reptiles are also abundant, with lizards, whiptails, and rattlesnakes being common. In addition to the arid mountains, there is a diverse habitat of desert plants thriving in the lowlands. A Texas conservation passport is required.

BIG BEND RANCH STATE NATURAL AREA

As wild as the national park is, Big Bend Ranch State Natural Area will see its wild and raise it one better. It is truly *despoblado,* uninhabited. On a recent trip, I was greeted by that wildest of nature's free spirits, a Golden Eagle perched motionless as a bronze icon on a rock ledge. I thought at first it was a TPWD marker of some sort. Suddenly, the seven-foot wings spread, the bronzed head flared in the noonday glare, and this largest of Big Bend's raptors soared gracefully aloft, only to plummet into the desert almost at our feet. He was airborne immediately, kangaroo rat dangling from a huge claw. Other than the occasional failure to look up, kangaroo rats are wonderfully adapted to the desert. They metabolize water from carbohydrates in the seeds they eat, thus they never need a live water source.

The natural area's superintendent, Luis Armendariz, talks about how all the knowledge we have now has been learned from "traditions," and "we should follow the teachings of these traditions if we are to safeguard the environment; that is what Mother Nature has given us." Armendariz has the responsibility to balance the environment with human use and conservation education in a fashion that attempts to satisfy widely disparate points of view. The extremes of "no human use at all" and "no use restrictions at all" are both touted as wise use of the 264,000-acre Big Bend Ranch. Armendariz will, of course, be avoiding extremes as the management plan is drawn and redrawn during the balance of this century. In the process, he must also conserve irreplaceable and fragile ecosystems and natural features that just can't stand a lot of human intrusion. One key involves utilizing the existing natural and human-made routes through the area for hiking trails. Thus, creek beds and old jeep trails can be used for low-impact wilderness camping access. The main ranch roads allow groups to tour and obtain at least a feel for the land's grandeur. Other human-use opportunities will be carefully studied and implemented over time, always designed both to conserve and to educate.

One special challenge will be dealing with the exotic animals that have been released on the ranch, especially the aoudads, which are now a real problem throughout the Trans-Pecos. Aoudads compete with native deer and actually run them off shared range, according to TPWD ethnobotanist David Alloway. There is no doubt that the aoudad must be removed from the ranch; the only question is how. The most practical approach is by hunting, but animal activist groups oppose this and want the animals removed by nonlethal methods and put somewhere else. The problem is there is no somewhere else—no one wants them, and this is an expensive proposition. Once again, the ranch management is in the middle.

As you head into the ranch on the county-maintained road from Fort Leaton at about 2,200 feet, one of the first landmarks you cross on the property is Alamito Creek, with its source in the Davis Mountains and drainage in excess of 1,400 miles. During rainy seasons the creek can run bank to bank. The road parallels Terneros Creek. This was a route taken by Lieutenant Echols when he was exploring in 1860 with the Camel Corps, following the Chihuahua Trail into Presidio in search of an overland route between Presidio and San Carlos Crossing, the old name for Lajitas, a well-used ford across the Rio Grande. Echols skirted the Bofecillos Mountains in the heart of Big Bend Ranch, eventually finding Terlingua Creek; he explored down the creek to San Carlos. He determined that this was not the ideal place to build a fort because it lacked wood and, perhaps, because it was on the Comanche war trail. In honor of Lieutenant Echols, the Witte Museum of Natural History in San Antonio has formed its own Camel Corps, which tours sites of conservation and historic interest in Texas, but not on camels.

Although Echols's camels were from the Middle East, they were not the first to travel these stony paths. At one time there were ancient species of camels as well as four-horn and pronghorn antelopes, bison, zebras, mammoths, giant ground sloths, llamas, and horses in this area, hunted by the nomadic tribes, often called Clovis people. The megafauna and people were pushed south at the end of the last glaciation of the ice ages twelve thousand years ago, during the Pleistocene. Camels would appear to be as logical a choice for the Chihuahuan Desert as they were for the Silk Road through Asia. Only the pronghorn antelope made it through time and stayed here. The prehistoric horses (which evolved in this area), camels, and several other species migrated at the end of the Wisconsin glaciation across the Bering land bridge into Asia, the horses to return thousands of years later with the European explorers. Several

Black sand from ancient lava flows marks the course of Arroyo Segundo in the Big Bend Ranch State Natural Area. The arroyo, often dry, leads down to Mexicano Falls.

species of horses appear to have survived the Pleistocene, but all of them are now extinct. As the glaciers receded, the climate here changed drastically, and the Chihuahuan Desert expanded out of its central core in Mexico. "Chihuahua" is an Indian word that means hot, dry place, which even in late spring I find appropriate. The people who lived here had to go from a society of big-game hunters to a life-style of desert hunter-gatherers. They foraged for wild desert plants and learned how to hunt smaller game—anything they could get their nets, spears, or hands on, including rodents and insects. They developed the atlatl, ably demonstrated to us by Alloway, who launched a homemade spear from a homemade atlatl with remarkable distance and accuracy.

The hunter-gatherer subsistence went on for eight thousand to nine thousand years, up to about one thousand years ago. Then three new technologies were introduced into the Big Bend: agriculture, ceramics, and archery. People affiliated with the upper Rio Grande civilizations, the Pueblo, drifted down the Rio Grande at least as far as Redford. They built pit houses and erected frame houses plastered with mud along the river. They farmed the river floodplain much like the ancient Egyptians.

The route into ranch headquarters takes you past Cuevas Amarillas, an ancient campsite. Here, a beautiful stream course emerges as a spring called Agua Dentra (hidden water) surrounded by deer grass, seep willows, Gooding's willows, desert willows, cottonwoods, and other trees. Alloway uses the wood of seep willows as a fire stick, which when rubbed into sotol sticks quickly creates burning embers. The beautiful blossoms of the desert willows are boiled with honey to make a cough syrup. There are several such spring areas on Big Bend Ranch, signals that a full one-third of all the surface water of the entire Trans-Pecos is on this property.

The origin of all the springs is volcanic action that took place 14 million to 40 million years ago. The Bofecillos volcano that erupted 36 million years ago created many lava flows. The lava that cools on top first is crumbly. The lava below that top layer cools more slowly, is harder, and is permeable. So there is a hard layer of rock alternating with crumbly layers, and the water collects and flows through the permeable layers, being replenished by rainfall and cropping up on the surface as springs. The whole area bubbles with them.

On my trip in early May, this lush oasis was filled with neotropical migrants that, as it turned out later, were pausing in their northward migration because of a front moving in from the northwest. The wee creatures knew better than to fly into bad weather, preferring the hospitality of the springs.

Some of the edible plants and fruits pointed out by Alloway included desert hackberry, or granjeno. These yellow-red fruits may be eaten right off the shrub and are delicious. The small, reddish purple agarita is another tasty fruit, which makes a great game sauce and jelly. Texas persimmon produces a large, deep purple fruit, ripe in late July and, if they aren't appropriated by all manner of wildlife, still available come November. Persimmon Gap in Big Bend Park is named for this plant.

The century plant, or maguey (of the genus *Agave*), was used for food by Apaches and later by Mexicans who baked the plant's pulpy heart in midden ovens. Alloway showed me a huge burned rock midden at Agua Dentra where obviously many sotol hearts and magueys had been baked over the centuries. Sotol hearts wrapped in fleshy sotol or agave leaves were baked deep in the midden for forty-eight hours. They taste like sweetened cabbage and are very nourishing and high in carbohydrates.

After sending its stalk skyward fifteen to twenty feet, the century plant blooms with a shower of yellow blossoms, then dies. These blossoms are a food source for many animals, as are those of other desert plants. (Look carefully at the ground as you explore, not just for snakes but also for patterns of bright blossoms gathered and carried by ants to their hills.) The century plant's heart is tastiest when it is in full bloom. It was used the same way as sotol, baked like an oversized potato, usually for two days.

Tequila is made from a commercially grown maguey not found in the park, but you could create a fermented beverage from the heart of either the century plant or the sotol. The fresh root, ground up into a bowl of hot water, makes an acceptable shampoo. The Mexican fruit bat pollinates the century plant and thus shares credit for the margaritas of the civilized southwestern world. Even the ever-present lechuguilla's heart is edible, like the other agaves, and after hours of cooking can be made into slaw with appropriate condiments. Do not eat this raw. Apaches used the long agave leaves to make rope, and to this day professional ropers favor maguey ropes fashioned from refined fibers. Beargrass was also used by Indians for baskets, sandals, and mats. Flour can be made from dried mesquite beans, and you can nibble on the green bean pods. You can also cut hunks from barrel cacti as a source of water.

As you approach ranch headquarters at Sauceda, you have climbed to 4,200 feet. The highest spot in the natural area is Oso Peak at 5,135 feet. Alloway says the terrain of the ranch, especially the water, will eventually lend itself to more hiking trails than Big Bend Park has, though the ranch is only one-third the size. There is a bunkhouse at the headquarters used for study groups such as Texas Adventures and other organizations.

From the headquarters, another ranch road leads east into the Solitario, a formation Alloway describes as a geological "window, a giant hole in the world through which to look into its past." The outside measurements of the Solitario are eight miles east to west and nine miles north to south, and its sheer size makes it difficult to tell when you've entered it. This is confusing to some, who perhaps have seen pictures taken from high altitude that show a dramatic, craterlike, many-ringed structure. We entered from the north, through a contact zone, where we moved out of the volcanic rock into the limestone. The outside ring, only 65 million years old, is the youngest rock, and as you go deeper, each layer of rock is older than the preceding one. The Solitario was formed by two geological phenomena. The first was the upward thrust of a laccolith when magma forced its way up to bulge through the crust at that point. Usually the central magma chamber will cool and leave a feature like that of Enchanted Rock south of Llano. But at the Solitario, a massive volcanic explosion 35 million years ago blew the top off, sending 100 cubic kilometers of material skyward. After the pressure release, the dome collapsed to form a caldera, a bowl-shaped depression. The explosion had the effect of slicing an onion across the top, exposing ring after ring of rock. Let your imagination take you back to that tumultuous time, when all around you fire belched skyward, the land thrust and bulged, shifted and heaved, cracked wide open and, with a roar beyond human comprehension, detonated to vaporize life for thirty miles around. The truth is likely to have been far more awesome than science fiction.

There are three canyons in the Solitario, called shut-ups, which were used to pen livestock. The canyons cut through rock layers that are at a vertical tilt. You can idle through the shut-ups and put your hand on each separate rock formation as you take an easy stroll through geological time. Your walk starts at sedimentary rock 65 million years old and reaches Dagger Flat sandstone, which is 520 million years old; you've traversed a 455 million-year time tunnel through the earth's crust, which should make you feel a lot younger. It's here that you will find three of the only known sites of the rare and endangered Hinckley oak (*Quercus hinckleyi*), named for Leon C. Hinckley, who surveyed the plants of the area in the thirties. The oak could be an embarrassment to those Texans who insist on claiming the biggest of everything for the state—it's one of the smallest species of oak ever recorded, reaching only about three feet in height and often forming thickets. According to Michael Powell in *Trees and Shrubs of Trans-Pecos Texas* (1988), leaves and acorns of this endemic tree were found in a 15,000-year-old fossil packrat midden near Shafter, and fossil leaves were found in another midden in the Dead Horse Mountains, an area little explored by botanists.

DAVIS MOUNTAINS STATE PARK AND SCENIC LOOP

The cold wind swept down from the high reaches of the Sierra Diablo, Delaware, Apache, and Davis mountains into our early May campsite at Davis Mountains State Park, chilling enough so that later a fire was necessary. But for hours, the chill went unnoticed, as the brisk wind from the northwest gave pause to the neotropical birds making their way to breeding ranges and impetus to feed and nest to those who called this lovely park home. Birds fluttered through the oaks and shrubs of the camp like bright confetti. A Curve-billed Thrasher, handsome in gray-mottled waistcoat, pecked for insects in dry Keesey Creek, as did a Green-tailed Towhee, both oblivious to the Scrub Jay that whizzed close by and the rarely seen Blue Grosbeak sharing a tree canopy with a Black-headed Grosbeak and Ruby-crowned Kinglet. An Acorn Woodpecker worked over a nearby tree. Yellow-throated, Yellow, Hooded, and Wilson's warblers flitted about, causing binoculars to bobble. The shiny black crest of a phainopepla caught my attention nearby; they are rare in Texas outside the desert. But just then, an obtrusive member of the urban many burst into camp, on a beeline from the lovely adobe lodge just up the hill, demanding to know if we were bird watchers and "where that bird was." Taken aback, I couldn't imagine what he meant, as just a moment ago I had been surrounded by at least ten species of birds. I would have thought the binoculars around my neck, my National Geographic Society *Field Guide to the Birds of North America*, and the park

Montezuma Quail at Ranger Station, Davis Mountains State Park.

bird list in my lap might be clues that I was, indeed, watching birds. Then his meaning became clear when he bellowed, "Where's that quail?" The "Apache-masked" quail, with its bold black-on-white striped face (male), recorded in the late 1800s as a "fool's quail" near here by Col. Edgar Mearns, is the symbol of this park, even appearing on the cover of the bird list. It's difficult to see elsewhere in its range without some effort such as mountain climbing. The huffing executive clearly wanted to record this secretive, strikingly marked quail in his new, leather-bound bird list, and right now. Flustered myself, I explained that I had seen two pair of *Harlequin* Quail just minutes earlier down the dry creek near the park ranger's residence. He didn't seem satisfied until I remembered that the bird is now called Montezuma Quail and humbly corrected myself. At that, the nature lover said not a word of thanks but burst on through the middle of my campsite, loudly stomping through the dry creek bed, scattering dust upon my dinner and songbirds from the trees. That is not what I mean by developing a conservation ethic. I wondered aloud who was the fool, plump man or plump bird?

Kelly Bryan, regional resource specialist with the Texas Parks and Wildlife Department, is a proponent of the Texas Partners in Flight Program, part of a national program that focuses on the steady decline of neotropical birds. It was started by the National Fish and Wildlife

A diversity of plant life thrives atop one of the "mountain islands" of the Davis Mountains, looking south across the arid "desert sea." This is a view from the Davis Mountains State Park.

Foundation and includes the TPWD, the USFWS, the U.S. Forest Service, TNC, and the Audubon Society. One thing is sure, especially in the Davis Mountains: private landowners are essential to halting the decline not only of the birds but of wildlife in general.

The Texas list of neotropicals includes more than three hundred species that either nest or migrate through the state, including species of kites, hawks, falcons, owls, cuckoos, nightjars, hummingbirds, flycatchers, swallows, thrushes, vireos, warblers, tanagers, grosbeaks, buntings, sparrows, orioles, and blackbirds. These birds earn the neotropical designation because they breed mainly in the temperate zone and winter primarily in the tropics. A major cause of decline is loss of wintering habitats in Central and South America, but much of the problem is right in our own backyard. Many representatives of these species were either nesting or migrating through the park during this early May experience. A treat was spotting, from afar, a Black-chinned Hummingbird's tiny gray nest, complete with hungry young, in the fork of a tree, safe from intruders.

That the 2,350-acre park is an indispensable haven for birds and other wildlife is obvious, and it provides another example of partnerships. The park got its start when ranchers J. W. Espy, J. W. Merrill, and R. K. Merrill donated 500 acres to the state of Texas in the thirties. More land was purchased by the state, and the Civilian Conservation Corps built a pueblo-style adobe lodge, still one of the finest public lodge facilities in all of West Texas.

Nearby Limpia Creek has its headwaters up close to the Baldy Peak of Mount Livermore, near Madera Tank and near the quaking aspens at the head of Madera Canyon, on the U-up, U-down Ranch owned by Don McIvor and his sisters. Their generational-minded parents contributed the land for McDonald Observatory. Botanist Leon Hinckley clambered up the more than eight thousand feet of Mount Livermore and spent much time there between 1934 and 1939 studying the remnants of a forest of ponderosa pine and Gambel oak reminiscent of the Rocky Mountains. At least one of the forbs found there is named after him, Hinckley's Jacob's ladder. Jeff Weigel, of The Nature Conservancy of Texas, has spent much time in the vicinity and has identified twelve species of rare and endangered plants, including bush rock spires, birchleaf buckthorn, trumpet currant, mountain snowberry, American spikenard, Fendler's sandwort, bluebell, Bigelow's gentian, Powell's blue-eyed grass, and Wright's meadow rue. Most of the endangered plants are clustered around the peak and can be protected through conservation easements and rancher partnerships.

Flying over the ranch in a helicopter, it is easy to spot the old government sawmill site, which furnished lumber for Fort Davis, located in upper Limpia Canyon. The ponderosas that were cut for construction have been replaced with whiteleaf oaks. Each of the several canyons that cut down from the peaks seems to contain something else that should be conserved.

GUADALUPE MOUNTAINS NATIONAL PARK

"A reef? You must be kidding!" As you hike up bonny McKittrick Canyon toward the Pratt Cabin for the first time, you are compelled to look up at towering El Capitan, Guadalupe, Hunter, Shumard, and Bartlett peaks when you aren't absorbing the sheer glory of the lush canyon and its tumbling trout stream—the only place in Texas where trout reproduce. The last place you look is at your feet, which should be the first place in warm weather, for there will often be a rattler of one of five varieties sunning itself underfoot.

The banded rock rattlesnake responded with a soft, disgusted buzz and disdainfully slithered away from my clumsy boot. I had plenty of time to admire the gleaming, unblemished Mercedes-silver background color and the distinct, black, sawtooth-edged cross bands before he left the trail to me. A few minutes later I overtook a pair of hikers, one in National Park Service uniform. The park ranger turned out to be a descendant of Apaches, the people who occupied these mountains for centuries. When I mentioned stepping upon a snake, the ranger imme-

diately wanted to know if I'd hurt it, the implication being a serious federal charge for harming wildlife. He then began an inquisition on the exact color and band patterns of the snake, finally being satisfied that I had, indeed, stepped upon but not hurt a banded rock rattler. What I didn't know then is that the banded is a subspecies of rock rattlesnake and that there is another subspecies, mottled rock, common in the Big Bend. It was rare to see a pure banded specimen on the east slope of the Guadalupes, which explained the ranger's close questioning.

I had some questions of my own, to do with human traffic, rainbow trout, elk, cougar, black bear, Peregrine Falcons, and the fragile ecosystem of the Guadalupes, especially the very canyon in which we three found ourselves. To my joy, the ranger's answers were all positive, with elk and cougar populations in good balance, black bears moving in, Peregrines nesting, and humans (except for snake stompers) behaving themselves, treating the delicate environment with care. I did determine that the trout were not native, having been released by rancher J. C. Hunter in the forties. In case you're tempted, "no fishing allowed."

The Guadalupe Mountains, once a reef in an ancient sea, sheer off abruptly to form a palisade across the Chihuahuan Desert of Texas. One of the most scenic of our national parks spans the southern Guadalupes.

It *was* a reef, by the way, part of the 400-mile Capitan Reef, which pops up here and in the Apache and Glass mountains. A vast assemblage of marine animals, much later to become petroleum, deposited their skeletons, which formed the reef mass. Simultaneously, lime precipitated from the seawater, in a process similar to that used to make concrete, creating the basic composition of Capitan Reef. After 200 million years the sea dried up, covered by layer after layer of sediment. Then, only 10 million years ago, the uplift common to our western states from here to Nevada occurred, popping the reef back up, subjecting it to the erosion of the sedimentary coating, and voilà, the reef stood again, much as it had, only now above a desert sea.

That these mountains are preserved is yet another tribute to rancher conservationists in partnership with the National Park Service. Pioneer petroleum geologist Wallace E. Pratt was the catalyst, contributing almost 6,000 acres to the Park Service. J. C. Hunter, Jr. (son of the trout fan, who was an early proponent of preserving the Guadalupes), also cooperated in the land acquisitions of the late sixties that eventually resulted in the 86,415-acre park. Guadalupe Mountains National Park was dedicated to public use in 1972.

Spring can be rewarding to birders, as more than 40 species are known to nest in the canyon, out of about 230 that have been noted in the park since records have been kept. The one time of the year that this canyon is crowded is the time you'd expect, for it is the most resplendent place in Texas in the fall, when oaks and stands of maples go into their deciduous red and gold act. The National Park Service often limits the number of people allowed into the canyon in the fall, so it's best to plan ahead. The trail is interspersed with ponderosa pine, alligator juniper, gray-leaf oaks, ash, and Texas madrone. From McKittrick Ridge, 3,000 feet above the mouth of the canyon, your eyes can benchmark the term "scenic" at a level not soon to be surpassed. Guadalupe Peak, the highest point in Texas at 8,749 feet, can be a ten-mile round-trip day hike for the tough, but is better enjoyed on an overnight itinerary. There is no water along the trail, and you will need a lot—a gallon a day per person in the hotter months. The hikes include treks up to El Capitan and Bush Mountain, at 8,631 feet the second highest peak in Texas and a two- to three-day adventure. Up here, you can even find aspens, mountain mahogany, limber pine, and Douglas fir, along with stands of ponderosa.

Guadalupe mountain laurel and Texas madrone to thirty feet tall are found at lower elevations. The madrone, a tree with smooth red bark, is related to blueberries and cranberries. It sheds its bark in the summer, flowers in late spring through late summer, and produces delicious dark red berries in the fall. The berries make a terrific tart jelly that's perfect with roast venison, if you can beat the birds to them. Early settlers fashioned the madrone's hard wood into tool handles, and Mexican curanderos used the bark for yet another medicine. The Texas madrone is at the extreme northern part of its range here, Douglas fir is at its extreme southern range, and the chinquapin oak is as far west as it grows.

At least a dozen of the plants found here are rare for this area, and the relict forest is habitat for neotropicals and other birds you'd expect to see in the spring much farther north. Bird-watching can have its hazards; experienced hikers warn of spring winds over 100 mph, of summer heat, and suggest (surprise, surprise) a fall climb. Winter snow converts the Guadalupes into a visual wonderland, but it can make hiking dangerous. If storms do not intrude, a winter hike can be very rewarding; game animals are easier to spot, and your endurance won't be sapped by desert heat. A call ahead is advised.

Southeast of park headquarters at Pine Springs, you can see a pitiful few of the rock walls of the Butterfield Stage Station constructed in 1858; the first eastbound stage dusted the first westbound stage on the desert floor below in September of that year. The record does not show if some of the hardy passengers were there for the turn of the leaves. Tourism was tougher in those days; Apaches quickly forced the Butterfield route south to a safer route with better water availability. The Gold Rush had greatly increased traffic, and the Apaches decided that "Texas friendly" would not be spoken here. Just twenty years after Captain Marcy correctly guessed the water sources, Lieutenant H. B. Cushing raided two Apache strongholds in the mountains, the second at Manzanita Spring a few days after Christmas 1869.

Today, you can hike the eighty miles of testing trails and stand a good chance of seeing creatures you won't see elsewhere in Texas, such as a gray-footed chipmunk, red squirrel, or Mexican vole. The diminutive desert fox and only slightly larger gray fox stay well out of the way of cougars and bobcats, as do antelope, rock squirrels, porcupines, and ringtails.

I think my favorite Guadalupe conservation program is a U.S. Fish and Wildlife partnership with the National Park Service: their clandestine activities, hidden deep in the upper McKittrick Canyon, with the objective to "promote peregrine breeding activities." Just how the rangers go about this promotion is not explained, but they do admit to "carefully monitoring the critical courtship periods." Whatever these dedicated rangers are doing, I'm told it is succeeding and nesting pairs of Peregrines are on the increase in protected aeries beyond the tainting hand of humans.

GYPSUM DUNES PRESERVE

The Nature Conservancy purchased its 226-acre Gypsum Dunes Preserve in 1983, in the gypsum hills of Hudspeth County, a transition zone between the desert plains grassland to the north and the Chihuahuan

The autumn foliage of McKittrick Canyon maples and oaks is special indeed, but this well-shaded Guadalupe Mountains National Park trail is a delight the year round. About four miles up from the trailhead is the fern-bedecked Grotto, a lovely spring, and on up the trail is a relict forest.

Desert to the south. The preserve is east of Dell City, 3,650 feet up the western flanks of the Guadalupe Mountains. These dunes are the southernmost extremity of the dune field protected within White Sands National Monument in New Mexico and, along with the monument, are the only known habitat of the grayish white lesser earless lizard.

Twenty years ago Dr. David K. Northington, then of the biology department at Texas Tech University, reported evidence of dune buggies trespassing on what was to become the preserve area, much to the distress of local ranchers and those aware of the rare, endemic plantlife. (Northington is now executive director of the National Wildflower Research Center.) All-terrain vehicles still threaten the red dune ecosystems near El Paso, to the west of the Hueco Mountains. They rip through the sand, leaving crazy-quilt tracks and the litter of beer cans. The reddish brown dunes were formed during the Pleistocene and are from the Rio Grande's deposits of more than a million years ago.

Primitive hunters and gatherers camped in the Gypsum Dunes area and collected salt from nearby flats, as did Mescalero Apaches and Spanish explorers. Zoologist Steve West, who conducted research at the Gypsum Dunes Preserve, said, "The value of inner peace and growth that a person can gain from a place like Gypsum Dunes cannot be imagined"—inner peace, that is, if one has water in this arid, barren, bleached-bone white land. Shifting, intimidating, 100-foot-high dunes glitter under a pitiless Texas sun, an environment suitable only for the special.

Rare rains flood the flats and quickly evaporate, leaving behind salts leached from the Permian limestone. Weathering releases the grains of gypsum, and the prevailing southwesterly winds transport them up toward the towering Guadalupes. As the air currents sweep up the limestone cliffs of El Capitan, the grains fall, constantly renewing the dunes, which march sedately across the desert basin, much like the dunes of barrier islands.

Calcium sulfate, or gypsum, is the most common of the grains that collect, but plenty of good old sodium chloride, or table salt, is also deposited—an important factor to Indians and those who followed them into this arid, inhospitable land. If one were fortunate enough to snare a few desert cottontails, black-tailed jackrabbits, kangaroo rats, or pocket mice, the salt would preserve excess meat for transport. Those same rabbits, kangaroo rats, and pocket mice are prey to kit foxes, coyotes, bobcats, striped skunks, and western diamondback and prairie rattlers.

The unusual flora of the dunes results primarily from evolutionary adaptations to a land that moves out from under its inhabitants, the dry climate, and high salinity. Annual plant species outwit the implacable movement of the dunes by broadcasting their seeds into the trade winds, scattering seeds ahead. About forty species occur in association with the dune fields, twenty-five endemic, eight very rare. Sand bluestem, broom pea, rosemary mint, soaptree yucca, and gyp grama are among the most important. New species are constantly being discovered (two in recent years, a species of *Lepidospartum,* a small shrub, and one of *Ericameria,* a member of the sunflower family).

Although not a birder's hotspot, the dunes have an unexpected diversity of birds. Say's Phoebes are common, as are Western Kingbirds, Loggerhead Shrikes, and Crissal Thrashers.

Even in the blistering summers, the dunes chill down at night, and in the winter the average night-time temperature is only 28 degrees Fahrenheit. There is an eeriness to the dunes on a moonlit, cold winter's night, a primeval quality that seems the stuff of science fiction and other planets.

MONAHANS SANDHILLS STATE PARK

Naturalist Roy Bedichek was one of those who campaigned to save these gleaming dunes. The tiny oak trees of the dunes feature relatively large acorns, prompting Dr. Bedichek to observe, in *Adventures with a Texas Naturalist* (1947), "I venture the statement, without research, that in no other forested section, the Amazon Valley not excepted, is there to be found a higher proportion of fruit to wood than in this Lilliputian jungle in the northern portion of Ward County." Who would think of fruits and jungles in this Arabian Nights desert setting? The dunes roll on for another 200 miles to the west into New Mexico. Anyone who has struggled to extricate a vehicle from deep sand will know that this landscape presents a formidable barrier. The dunes, bare of vegetation, as white as an Arab's burnoose, are constantly shifting and drifting. Some twelve thousand years ago, Indians found water beneath the dunes, and despite its forbidding appearance, this was a hospitable environment until the 1880s, when the railroad came through.

Where fresh water occurs within the dune field it sometimes forms shallow ponds. These are good places to look for wildlife and their signs. You're apt to see tracks of a larger animal stalking a smaller one, then a mishmash of signs where the larger dined upon the smaller. Mule deer and coyote forage in the Havard shin oak, the deer for the giant acorns dropped by the dwarf tree, the coyote for the smaller mammals that take cover in the sparse shade.

FRANKLIN MOUNTAINS STATE PARK

Where else in the United States can you step from the city into a biologically rich desert wilderness with peaks reaching to 7,200 feet? The grays of the upper mountains are memorials to the ancient sea bed, and the reds mark the flows of volcanoes. The TPWD purchased the 24,000 acres of Chihuahuan Desert mountains from the city and county of El Paso and from private individuals to protect these beautiful mountains, the canyons, and many hidden springs, fragile places where humans should always tread lightly, leaving no trace of their coming. Franklin Mountains State Park extends north about fifteen miles from the heart of the city to the Texas–New Mexico state line. Eastward from its peaks spreads a view of the desert landscape, of the Hueco Bolson flowing toward the Cerro Alto, which in turn shadow Hueco Tanks. Hueco Tanks water traps (*huecos*) have succored humans for twelve thousand years, as testified to by thousands of petroglyphs and pictographs, which can be viewed at Hueco Tanks State Park. To the south, the Gran Chichmeca of the Chihuahuan Desert stretches to the Paquime at Casas Grandes, ancestral home of the largest tribe of North American Indians who still preserve a native way of life, the Tarahumara, people of the mother mountains, Sierra Madre Occidental.

Carolina Ramos, park superintendent at Franklin Mountains State Park, reminds us that this park, the largest urban park in the world within city limits, is the reality of the "dream of farsighted El Paso residents to provide lasting protection for the outstanding scenic, ecological, and historic features of the Franklin Mountains," yet another example of a partnership approach to conservation. The Nature Conservancy recognizes this borderlands area as a place where two states and two nations must work together to achieve common conservation goals.

The North American Free Trade Agreement, while overall a major plus for conservation, will undoubtedly put new pressures on these fragile mountains and the El Paso–Las Cruces corridor. By 2010, it is estimated, more than 3.5 million people will live in the area, the majority in Juárez. This population explosion will put tremendous additional stresses on the mountains, already pressed into a U-shaped vise by the city of El Paso. When I hiked the mountains in mid-1994, a park employee, proud of the work he was doing to conserve the mountains, complained of the damage done by intruders, including people who stripped park picnic tables of their roofs for, he presumed, firewood.

This is one of the best places in Texas to find the handsome Gambel's Quail, its black teardrop plume bouncing forward as it scampers along, always close to a water source. The mountains provide habitat to many Chihuahuan Desert plants, such as sotol, lechuguilla and New Mexico agave, ocotillo, banana, Torrey and soaptree yucca, catclaw mimosa, longleaf teabush (so-called Mormon tea, used by pioneers to make tea), littleleaf desert sumac, desert willow, and Texas rainbow, prickly pear, strawberry pitaya, Devil's head, and other cacti. There are also limited relict oak and juniper woodlands and some riparian woodlands in spring-fed canyons. The Franklins have several endemic species, including the southwest barrel cactus, a target of cacti rustlers. Floral species of southwestern and northern Mexican distribution occur at the extreme eastern edge of their range here, usually Pleistocene remnants of more widespread plant communities.

Few improvements have been made to the park, and most of it is open just for day-use picnicking, hiking, and camping. Wherever you find water you will find a remarkable diversity of wildlife, from birds and amphibians to mammals such as mule deer and coyote. Bebopping Rock and Canyon wrens enliven the trails, and spring-fed canyons feature snakes, lizards, gray foxes, rabbits, squirrels, porcupines, and a variety of other birds, including Scaled Quail, Blue Grosbeak, Red-tailed Hawk, flycatchers, Common Raven, White-throated Swift, Violet-green Swallow, and in migratory months neotropicals such as warblers.

MEXICO
EPILOGUE

CHAPTER 10

A conservation ethic is now emerging in Mexico after eras of exploitation of this beautiful, convoluted, naturally rich land, the fourth most biologically diverse country on earth. Scientists estimate that as much as 16 percent of the flora and fauna found here is unique to Mexico.

Mexico's bountiful biological diversity is due, in part, to its rugged terrain as well as its size and the span of both temperate and tropical climates. Along the international boundary, 1,248 miles of which is formed by the Rio Grande's run, the United States and Mexico share exceptional terrestrial and marine ecosystems, economically important water resources, and significant numbers of migratory birds.

In 1994, as a result of the International Program Planning Project, The Nature Conservancy as a whole increased its commitment to protect Latin American ecosystems, including Mexico and the Caribbean. The plan projected a budget of nearly $100 million for the years 1995–1999. The plan projects that TNC activities will help direct an added $300 million of multilateral and bilateral funding to biodiversity protection that will flow directly to programs and partners, not through TNC accounts.

This expectation was heightened in June 1994 when the World Bank approved $918 million in loans for environmental projects in Mexico, to be matched with $1 billion from the Mexican government. More than $360 million of the World Bank funds was targeted for the borderlands. The bank loans also would help Mexico establish new national preserves across from U.S. national parks, including Big Bend and Padre Island in Texas. About $15 million of the loan programs would help Mexico manage these new preserves.

Initial TNC investments were to be used to strengthen the capacity of our Mexican partners to provide technical assistance to other Mexican conservation partners. In addition, those investments will enhance

OPPOSITE PAGE
The Sierra del Carmen across the Rio Grande from Big Bend National Park may one day be part of a 4,000-square-mile international park area.

TNC's ability to manage multilateral projects, focus on key learning initiatives, and help implement integrated conservation programs on a national and regional scale. The program will first build expertise in community-based conservation, to improve skills in working with communities, especially indigenous communities.

The economic and environmental health of all of North America is directly linked to this common natural heritage. Our biological wealth cannot be protected without cooperative efforts that span the international border.

Mexico has what may be the most outstanding and biologically diverse national park system in the western hemisphere—on paper. President Lázaro Cárdenas created thirty-nine national parks in 1935, 80 percent of the current national park system. These parks include a broad spectrum of ecosystems: the tropical rain forests of El Ocote Ecological Reserve with high biological diversity; the cloud forest of El Triunfo Biosphere Reserve with its relict populations of quetzal and Horned Guan; coastal mangrove swamps and lagoons such as those at Sian Ka'an Biosphere Reserve, Ría Celestún and Ría Lagartos wildlife refuges, and La Encrucijada Coastal Wetland Reserve. The latter comprise some of the most important migratory waterfowl habitats in North America, and many of the migration routes are through Texas.

Other park areas include broad expanses of lowland tropical forest and swamps, like Calakmul Biosphere Reserve, and the northern deserts, such as El Pinacate Biosphere Reserve with its endemic plants and animals. The Nature Conservancy scientific staff reports that these areas and others are being whittled away at an accelerating rate by agricultural development, logging, mining, grazing, and poaching.

The Nature Conservancy works closely with Secretaria de Desarrollo Social (Sedesol), the ministry responsible for the national system of protected areas and natural resource management, and has assisted Pronatura-Yucatán with reserves at Ría Celestún and Ría Lagartos. (Pronatura-Yucatán is a chapter of a private nonprofit organization, Pronatura-Mexico, established to protect the biological diversity of all Mexico.) These reserves jointly cover more than a quarter of a million acres of estuary, mangrove, and tropical deciduous forest on the northern Yucatán coast. They are 140 miles apart and are the bookends of another of The Nature Conservancy's bioreserve projects, like the Texas Hill Country and Pineywoods, a last great place filled with rich avian fauna, barrier beaches with critical nesting habitat for the endangered hawksbill turtle, and lagoons that are spawning areas for much of Campeche Bay's bountiful shrimp and seafood harvest. The surrounding tropical deciduous forest is home to the endangered, endemic Ocellated Turkey, given special status by the ancient Maya, probably because of the red-pebbled skin patch atop his shiny blue pate.

Negotiations for the North American Free Trade Agreement brought Mexico's environmental challenges and conservation efforts into sharp focus. The country's substandard environmental protection record, unfortunately showcased by the poor pollution control practices of many of the maquiladores (border factories), gave activist environmental groups in both countries (such as the Sierra Club, Earth First, and Mexico's Group of One Hundred) a lot of bad news with which to confront the treaty makers. Of course, many of the environmental problems in Mexico began long before any discussions of a trade agreement. For example, land has been cleared along the Gulf Coast since 1980 for citrus export, and the maquiladores have been puffing and polluting for years.

It is obvious that Mexico is at a turning point in the management of its natural resources. State governors have a greater interest in conservation and sustainable development than ever before, and they realize that economic planning and conservation planning must go hand in hand.

The Nature Conservancy's work in Mexico must rely more on partnerships and scientific help than on money alone. The Texas chapter has been assigned a major role in developing these partnerships, working with TNC's international staff. The Texas team will be focused on the adjoining Mexican states—Chihuahua, Coahuila, Nuevo León, and Tamaulipas—and their ecosystems, even when these ecosystems cross state borders.

The key to effective conservation in Mexico, as in the United States, is education on the importance of the environment, strong leadership, and the capacity to maintain stewardship of protected areas over the long term. This leadership must be developed within each Mexican state, and it must be built around local institutions that can influence planners and decision makers in the local society.

If you have followed the course of this book through the ecological areas of Texas, you know that TNC has a strong track record in building long-lasting, positive relationships with partners, private and public. This is accomplished through an unwavering commitment to the conservation goals of those partners. The same approach is being taken in Mexico, helping key partners develop innovative programs in protected-area management and in community programs focused on the compatible use of natural resources.

Working with partners such as Pronatura-Mexico, TNC is helping to protect six million acres of the most important, biologically diverse sites in the country. These include the Maya forest areas of Ría Celestún and Ría Lagartos, coastal wetlands in the Yucatán; the tropical forest Calakmul in Campeche; the Sian Ka'an coastal wetland and forest in Quintana Roo; El Triunfo cloud forest, El Ocote rain forest, and La Encrucijada coastal wetland in Chiapas. TNC is also involved in protecting the Pinacate area in Sonora.

Entomologist Edward O. Wilson, a member of TNC's National Board of Governors, calculates in his book *The Diversity of Life* (1992) that reduction in the area of tropical rain forest at the current rate "can be expected to extinguish or doom to extinction about half a percent of the species in the forest *each year*" (emphasis added). He estimates that the total extinction of species this will cause by 2022 will be between 10 and 22 percent, or at least 10 percent of all species on earth in rain forests alone.

CHIHUAHUA AND THE BARRANCAS

Flying over the vastness of the Mexican portion of the Chihuahuan Desert recently, I was reminded of how remote, how seemingly inhospitable it is. It takes a leap of faith in the skills of archeologists to believe that Indians lived here for at least twelve thousand years, longer than the modern desert itself has existed. This area, the Sierra de Tarahumara, was named for the Amerindian tribes that inhabit the 6,000-foot-deep, wild, majestic *barrancas,* canyons torn into the heart of the Sierra Madre. Five of these canyons are deeper and larger than Arizona's Grand Canyon.

COAHUILA

Coahuila's Rio Grande border sweeps from the Big Bend eastward almost to Nuevo Laredo, making Coahuila an important conservation neighbor to Texas. Perhaps the single most important issue is the possibility of a sister park or international park in the Sierra del Carmen and Maderas del Carmen opposite Big Bend National Park, which would incorporate the Sierra Rica across the Rio Grande from the Big Bend Ranch State Natural Area, in the state of Chihuahua.

As a member of the Governor's Task Force for Nature Tourism, I attended in March 1994 what was to be the signing of a two-nation agreement by Texas governor Ann Richards, Chihuahua governor Francisco Javier Barrio Terrazas, and Coahuila governor Rogelio Montemayor Seguy. This would enable the three states to work together on various conservation projects, including seeking protected status for the Santa Elena–Sierra del Carmen region in Mexico. The signing was postponed but was expected ultimately to take place. It would be another step toward a bioreserve on the south side of the Rio Grande, protected through the United Nations Educational Scientific and Cultural Organization's Man and the Biosphere Program. This program designates qualifying parks and preserves as international biosphere reserves. Of course, Big Bend National Park has been qualified as an international biosphere reserve for nearly twenty years. The National Park Service and the TPWD want to add the Big Bend Ranch State Natural Area and

Black Gap Wildlife Management Area to the biosphere protection, and TNC would welcome the program at its Brushy Canyon preserve.

One of the major benefits would be a framework for a continuing dialogue regarding management of cougar, black bear, and desert bighorn sheep, mining, timbering, air and water pollution issues, even drug smuggling and illegal immigration. On the Mexican side, President Carlos Salinas de Gortari endorsed a plan designated El Proyecto Reserva de la Biosfra Santa Elena–Sierra del Carmen, which is under the sponsorship of the Chihuahuan Department of Urban Development and Ecology. This plan would cover 1.5 million acres, split roughly between the states of Coahuila and Chihuahua, extending along the Rio Grande–Río Bravo from near Redford to La Linda. It would include the little-known Sierra Rica, mountains in northeastern Chihuahua that remind me of the Davis Mountains' "islands in a desert sea" ecosystem. When those are added to the protected areas on the U.S. side, almost four thousand square miles would be under biosphere reserve designation.

Of great interest to The Nature Conservancy is the central desert of Coahuila, an area of gypsum dunes where a river appears and disappears within the space of a few miles. Ichthyologist Clark Hubbs calls this area, known as Cuatro Ciénagas, one of "the two or three most unique biological habitats on the continent."

NUEVO LEÓN AND TAMAULIPAS

Nuevo León shares only a smidgin of border with the United States, a few miles of the Rio Grande before the state of Tamaulipas takes jurisdiction just above Laredo. But on the important floodplain of the border of both states, not much conservation is being practiced. Agricultural practices on both sides of the border have nearly wiped out any biodiversity, and almost twenty years of tax incentives to the maquiladores have obliterated nature about as thoroughly as possible. In 1993, however, Sedesol obtained funding to plant trees along the Rio Grande. There is a plan to develop a sister wildlife corridor to the one in the Texas Valley established by the USFWS. Twenty million trees were forecast to be planted in this area, which is 95 percent deforested today.

To the south, the cities of Monterrey and Saltillo are densely populated, with heavy manufacturing and its attendant pollution. Much of the surrounding landscape has been deforested, and there is much erosion in the floodplains of Nuevo León. Despite this, there are still major ecosystems that link with the borderlands that can be conserved.

An area of great interest to The Nature Conservancy's Texas chapter is El Cielo, the northernmost extension of cloud forest, located in the Sierra de Tamaulipas. Many Texas birders have utilized Rancho del Cielo as base camp for their outings in the cloud forest. Rancho del Cielo, a privately owned field station within El Cielo Biosphere Reserve, is managed by the Gorgas Science Foundation, which works in collaboration with American and Mexican universities. Bird watchers participate in projects at Rancho del Cielo as part of the continuing education classes at Texas Southmost College.

Of obvious conservation focus in Tamaulipas are the coastal wetlands so vital to millions of wintering waterfowl from the United States and Canada. Ducks Unlimited has surveyed this area to assess the terrible impact of extending the Gulf Intracoastal Waterway south of the Rio Grande through the Mexican Laguna Madre. This survey might also serve as background for a joint TNC–Ducks Unlimited presentation to the North American Wetlands Council to conserve this critical habitat.

Unfortunately, the major riverine system supporting much of this habitat is the Río Sota la Marina, which is fed by the Río Corona and Río Purificación. The latter has been abused by human use, and despite its name, it is filthy, with little natural vegetation. The Río Corona is better off.

A REVERENCE FOR NATURE

The Aztecs believed monarch butterflies were the souls of warriors. For 40,000 years or more these lacy butterflies have migrated on the cue of the autumnal equinox, their 3,000-mile flight originating in Canada, millions of beating wings on a course 300 feet over Texas. Their unfailing destinations are 9,000-foot coniferous forest sanctuaries northwest of Mexico City, at El Rosario, Angangueo, and Ocampo, all close to the town of Zitácuaro in Michoacán, one of the rare places on earth where they can survive the winter and breed to migrate again. These sanctuaries are said to be in heavy magnetic fields. The butterflies employ a technology unfathomable to humans, a chronometer device, a magnetic compass, some sort of radar, and a system that enables them to navigate by the sun. When the golden monarchs reach sanctuary, they blanket the pine trees, with dainty wings folded parallel to the grain of the bark, underside out. The underside wing design consists of gray stripes against an off-white background, blending perfectly into the tree trunk or limb, an illusion worthy of Mandrake the Magician. Attracted by aphrodisiac pheromones, the monarchs mate in March, millions dancing through the pines in a nuptial ceremony. Then the long flight north, to find the milkweed plants of the United States where they deposit their eggs, and metamorphosis begins anew. A few weeks later, the new monarch begins its singular nine months of life as our only migrating insect. If one had to guess, however, the monarchs probably won't make it another 40,000 years, because their Mexican sanctuaries are threatened by the tramp of loggers and by pollution from the megapolis to the south, and their milkweed sustenance is threatened by farming practices in the United States.

The Aztecs and the Maya actually cultivated the rain forest by collecting fronds for roofs, fruits, vegetables, healing herbs, and also by harvesting the edible wildlife. A score of food and fiber crops were cultivated within each small milpa, with trees left intact to control erosion. The birds and small mammals of the forest such as turkeys were perhaps trapped and kept for food, or hunted as necessary. In this fashion, the forest could be a sustainable resource forever. There is a Maya adage, "Who cuts the trees as he pleases cuts short his own life." The belief is that the ancients nurtured the rain forest, spreading useful vegetation such as fruit trees. They were practicing ethnobotany long before it had a scientific name; their names for tree sap and for blood are the same word. We at TNC believe that ethnobotany plays a critical part in conservation, especially in the biodiversity of the rain forest, where perhaps 1,200 species of plants, including medicinal raw materials, can be harvested for profit without destroying that biodiversity.

There is a cave in the desolate Tehuacán Valley unmarked and unknown except to a few botanists. The cereal grain that most believe had its origins in a grass that grew here seven thousand or more years ago could now feed one billion people. It currently keeps 200 million in less-developed nations from starving. Scientific records reveal that the oldest corn grew here, a tiny ear the ancients took a leisurely millennium to domesticate into one of the world's most important crops.

THE NEXT STEPS

In June 1993 I spoke at the United Nations on business and the environment, following the wrap-up of the first United Nations Commission on Sustainable Development since the 1992 Earth Summit at Rio de Janeiro. The good news from this meeting was that Timothy Wirth, head of the U.S. delegation, announced that our nation was committed to "easing the differences in geographic perspective and to join as a world partnership." One of the main thrusts of this meeting was how we could effect the transfer of sophisticated techniques of environmental protection to developing nations. An obvious starting point would be to transfer our technologies for improving environmental quality to less-developed nations, including Mexico. This infusion of technology would be a major step toward achieving other conservation goals, and I firmly believe a lot of progress will be made quickly.

I don't believe the developed world will give up its individual property and political rights or its wealth in some sort of socialistic transfer. But we can and will address environmental issues in less-developed nations in an economically prudent manner.

Dr. Paul Cox, professor of biology and range science at Brigham Young University and an ethnobotanist, has lived with many indigenous people throughout the world. At a meeting in 1993 he told me, "Indigenous people do not see the environmental crisis that surrounds them as an economic or political dilemma. They see it as a religious dilemma. They see their natural environment as something sacred. The spiritual side of the environment has somehow fallen by the wayside in Western cultures."

Dr. Cox continued,

What the word "savage" means in Latin is "of the woods." In our culture, when we want to commune with the sacred, we leave the woods and go into an object that is manmade called a church. But the indigenous people I work with, like the Navajos, are surrounded continually by what they consider sacred. They don't have to go into a cathedral. They simply walk into the forest and look up and see there the face of God. From their view, then, our environmental crisis is really a spiritual crisis. It's a question of how we relate to each other, how we relate to our dead ancestors. What if our discussions about what we do with the ancient forest and what we do with the wetlands were held not merely with developers, not merely with people who are concerned about economic potential, but what if we actually felt that the room was packed with the spirits of our ancestors, the ghosts of people who came before us from whom we inherited this land, and also our unborn children, grandchildren, and great grandchildren, and they were watching our deliberations? What a different context that would be. You were right as a child when you saw the butterfly or bird, and you wanted to save it, not kill it. Those impulses were correct, not wrong; they were not nostalgic, but they matched the sentiments we see in indigenous people everywhere. If we realize what is happening to the environment is a spiritual crisis, we can go a long way toward solving it.

Developing a conservation ethic is all about solving a spiritual crisis within ourselves and society, of coming to a value system that has great reverence for nature and people regardless of ethnicity or other otherness. It means leaving the world a better place than you found it in your allotted time here. When you think about it, that's how you cultivate your soul.

INDEX

Page numbers in italics refer to photographs and photograph captions.

C

D

E

F

G

H

Q

R

S

T

U

This book is set in Galliard,
with display type set in Lithos.

Printed on 128 gsm Japanese
NPI Matt Art paper and bound
by Regent Publishing Services,
Hong Kong.

Designed and composed by
Ellen McKie on a Macintosh
in Pagemaker 5.0 for the
University of Texas Press.